Science-Based Bioethics

By John D. Loike, Ph.D. and

Ruth L. Fischbach, M.P.E., Ph.D.

Center for Bioethics, Columbia University

New York, NY

Published 2014

FLIP

WITHDRAWN

TABLE OF CONTENTS

Chapter One

Introduction-What is science-based bioethics

The twentieth century has seen overwhelming advances in biomedical research as scientists throughout the world have engaged in innovative scientific discoveries. In the 21st century, the global scientific community now stands on the cusp of untold new frontiers. Advances in the fields of biotechnology including molecular genetics, synthetic biology, nuclear transfer technologies, stem cell research, and reproductive medicine will enable scientists to genetically modify a wide variety of organisms from viruses and bacteria to plants, animals, and human beings. These technologies also hold the promise of creating and designing new forms of therapies to diagnose, treat, cure, and prevent common as well as rare diseases that affect humankind.

Two of the potentially promising biotechnologies to emerge in the past decade are human cloning and stem cell science. These two technologies share common scientific knowledge and are poised to continue to develop rapidly. The success in these biotechnologies has evolved from four previous scientific breakthroughs. The first, reported in 1997 (Wilmut et al., 1997), was a method to utilize nuclear transfer technology to produce a mammal, a sheep called Dolly, cloned from an adult cell obtained from the mammary gland. The second breakthrough, reported in 1998, (Thomson, Itskovitz-Eldor et al. 1998) was a procedure for isolating human embryonic stem cells from discarded embryos and maintaining them indefinitely in culture. The third is induced pluripotent cell (iPS) technologies that allow the transformation of adult fibroblasts into embryonic stem cells (Takahashi et al. 2007). The fourth breakthrough, reported in 2013, was a method to generate human blastocysts using similar nuclear transfer technology used to clone Dolly in 1998. Together with the mapping of the human genome, these technological discoveries have ushered in a new era of human therapeutic or research cloning. They have brought us closer towards the creation of a society of human beings capable of controlling their own biological destiny.

Every new scientific advance and discovery generates a plethora of ethical questions and dilemmas. Human embryonic stem cell research and human cloning are just two examples that have spawned bioethical concerns. The global bioethical debates that encompass these biotechnologies set the stage for complex and challenging analysis of how bioethics and biotechnological development interact.

Aims of this Textbook

This book has multiple aims. It presents advancing perspectives on how scientific discoveries uncover or elicit bioethical concerns and challenges to all students interested in the future of scientific progress. Readers interested in enhancing or pursuing careers in sciences and allied fields will be pushing the boundaries of scientific discovery, and will need to deliberate bioethical issues that often arise from their scientific experiments. As their professional careers in science and medicine develop, their innovative research and ability to communicate science to the public will stimulate bioethical debate. In addition, good ethics begins with a factual understanding of the underlying science. This book provides the essential scientific background and bioethical information that should allow basic scientists, healthcare professionals, clinical researcher, and indeed the students, to better comprehend, appreciate, and address the complex bioethical dilemmas our society confronts.

In analyzing the interaction of science and ethics, it is important to predict what bioethical issues will emerge from new biotechnologies. Only then can there be an analysis of how to resolve, manage, or defuse the bioethical dilemmas. Identifying bioethical dilemmas within a sound scientific framework will aid in developing practical strategies to respond to bioethical conundrums. Rather than simply presenting hypothetical resolutions to bioethical dilemmas, this book outlines several different approaches and allows students to formulate their own practical strategies for identifying and resolving emerging dilemmas. While it is often impossible to resolve bioethical challenges, solutions may be proposed to either defuse or manage these dilemmas.

Four Specific Objectives of this Book

To promote these aims, this book has four specific objectives: (1) to present the scientific basis for new biotechnologies and discuss how these technologies trigger bioethical dilemmas. This objective is based on the premise that ethics begins with acquiring the most up-to-date facts about the case and science; (2) to explain how bioethical concerns in research differ from classical concerns of medical ethics; (3) to demonstrate how an historical analysis of ethical controversies arising from earlier biotechnological advances can, at times, provide insight into resolving current bioethical debates; and (4) to present appropriate scientific strategies that can be implemented to resolve, defuse, or manage bioethical disputes.

The first objective assumes that an appropriate mindset for bioethical reasoning requires an intimate understanding of scientific research and a clear understanding of how a technology may elicit bioethical dilemmas. Understanding both the potential and the limitations of a new technology is critical to discerning relevant bioethical questions. Bioethical dilemmas can sometimes arise from factual misinformation. Misconceptions about the underlying science may lead to misunderstandings of the emerging ethical issues that ultimately can generate bioethical shockwaves which reverberate through government, media and society, distracting from the more salient and factual issues. Thus, it is critical to grasp the valid underlying facts related to the bioethical dilemmas to ensure that discussions are not tainted by imprecise knowledge or scientific bias. In other words, the ability to address bioethical challenges begins with obtaining the most accurate information. Individuals are entitled to their own opinions, but they are not entitled to their own facts.

There are many misconceptions concerning the sovereignty of genetics in shaping human personality and abilities. Equally important, many students are unfamiliar with the emerging insights that can be obtained from epigenetics. In natural twinning, as one example, each twin experiences his/her individual environment simultaneously. In contrast, if someone is cloned using donor cells from a professional athlete such as Lebron James, there is a preconceived notion of how the clone's genetic endowment may influence his life's development. Will the cloned Lebron James also develop into a professional basketball superstar? What impact will the woman's uterine and hormonal environment have on the clone during fetal development? How much self-motivation and what environmental contributions will be required to develop this cloned child into a skilled athlete? These questions raise broader bioethical questions such as: will reproductive cloning challenge human individuality or autonomy? Would it be ethical to subject this cloned child to the psychological, physical, or financial pressures arising from knowledge of the successes and failures of his genetic donor, the original Lebron James? Moreover, what pressures could shape his environment in order to nurture his presumed athletic ability or future as a superstar basketball player?

The general public tends to underestimate the complexity of the interaction of nature and nurture in determining one's biological destiny. Epigenetic research addresses these issues in understanding how "software" in programming gene regulation is influenced by chemical modifications of DNA base pairs and their associated proteins without altering the base sequences of the genome. Through epigenetic research we are unraveling how environmental and genetic factors do not necessarily work in opposition; rather, a synergistic and continuous interaction of these factors orchestrates human behavior or human disease (Goldman, 2012; Marx, 2012). In particular, it is now increasingly evident that DNA is both inherited and environmentally interactive (Robinson 2004). Even the onset of a genetic disease, such as Huntington's disease, that was classically considered not to be influenced by environmental factors, is now understood to be influenced by a myriad of environmental factors. The combination of exercise and other environmental stimulation may help slow the onset of this genetic disease, which has no cure and is always fatal (van Dellen et al. 2008).

There are many examples of identical twins who, although genetically the same in all respects, display disparate accomplishments and skills. The baseball player Jose Canseco, for example, played in the major leagues for 16 years, hit 462 home runs and drove in over 1400 runs. He was the first player ever to hit 40 home runs and steal 40 bases in one single season. His identical twin brother, Ozzie, played in the major leagues for only three years, hit no home runs and drove in only four runs during his entire major league career. While both brothers were "talented" athletes and famous for their distinct running style - the "Canseco stride" - Ozzie never achieved the professional baseball success of his brother. An unknown but presumably different combination of genetic and environmental factors contributed to their contrasting successes; some reporters even proposed that possible steroid use by Jose enhanced his success.[1] Yet their common genetic background must not be neglected as a factor enabling both to emerge as major league baseball players.

Despite the stated goal of this book's first objective - to present the scientific basis for new biotechnologies and discuss how these technologies trigger bioethical dilemmas - there is the realization that scientific discoveries are developing and changing at such a rapid rate that it is impossible to write a book that will remain up to date with given emergent observations and discoveries. Chapter Six, for example, presents current evidence that embryonic stem cells may have more therapeutic potential in the treatment of Parkinson's disease than adult-derived stem cells, an observation that may change as research scientists throughout the world continue to compare the properties of adult and embryonic stem cells.

The second objective of this book is to focus on differences between research bioethics and medical ethics. Bioethics is generally perceived as an all-encompassing discipline that includes under its umbrella medical ethics,

---

[1] http://www.signonsandiego.com/sports/baseball/20040906-9999-lz1s6majmo.html

neuroethics, genethics, environmental ethics, and research ethics. Today, there is a need to formulate a clear conceptual understanding of an emerging new discipline, research ethics, and to apply appropriate guidelines that in the past focused on classical medical ethics. We define research bioethics as the study of ethical practice and the dilemmas that arise with the acquisition of scientific knowledge and the development of new biotechnologies as they influence life forms and the environment. In contrast, medical ethics focuses on those issues, such as physician-assisted suicide, abortion, and the definition of death, that directly impact the patient or the patient-healthcare professional relationship. Another difference is that situations in medical ethics often require immediate attention whereas in research bioethics the debates surrounding human embryonic stem cell research have been taking place for more than a decade. These conceptual differences lead to the formulation of unique guidelines for each discipline.

The concepts of this book are often rooted in research-oriented bioethics and these concepts elicit questions and issues that extend far beyond the research laboratory. Stem cell research is a good example that raises broader questions pertaining to the definition of human life, such as identifying the stage of embryological development at which human status is said to be attained. Another example is appropriate here. Research in synthetic biology (including gene transfer, gene therapy, and human artificial chromosomes) proposes the introduction of new genes or chromosomes into human beings for both research and therapeutic purposes. Also, introducing human embryonic stem cells into laboratory animals creating chimeras enables scientists to better investigate how cells differentiate to become specialized cells. These technologies raise the broader bioethical issues related to trans-species cloning and whether genomics (the analysis of unique DNA sequences) is sufficient to confer species identity. Will it be possible to introduce human genes or human stem cells into a chimp zygote or pre-implanted embryo to make these embryos "human-like"? Interestingly, the presence of the Y chromosome in the human male genome leads to a greater degree of DNA sequence similarity of a man's genome to the male chimpanzee genome than to a woman's genome (Culotta 2005).

As we progress and map out the genome of a Neanderthal human ancestor, should we use new tools in molecular biology that could lead to the generation of a human- derived stem cell line with the estimated 10 million base pair changes to match it to the Neanderthal genome (Noonan 2010)? If such a stem cell line were created, we could theoretically use it to clone a Neanderthal-like human with the aid of a human volunteer surrogate. Thus, recombinant DNA technology provokes profound new questions concerning taxonomic borders that raise several broad bioethical issues. Another example can be found in the 2005 report by the National Academy of Sciences which issued recommendations concerning the ethics of generating human-animal chimeras (Council 2005). Technology is emerging that will allow the transplantation of human pre-neural stem cells into a mouse or a non-human primate in order to reconstitute the animal's brain with human neurons. Would it be ethical to transplant human stem cells into mouse or chimp embryo in an attempt to reconstitute a human brain into an animal?

The third objective of this book is to demonstrate how the historical analysis of ethical controversies arising from earlier biotechnological advances can, at times, provide insights useful for resolving current bioethical debates. As an example, bioethical concerns about when human personhood begins in fetal development were raised in 1978 after Louise Brown became the first of over three million "test tube" babies produced by in vitro fertilization (IVF). In contrast, the current bioethical concerns in defining human life in stem cell research often neglects IVF as a historical precedent.

One lesson that can be extrapolated from history is that once a technology (such as IVF) is shown to be effective in treating a medical condition (infertility), the public becomes less concerned about possible bioethical questions inherent in these technologies. If and when stem cell research develops effective therapies, as with progressive acceptance of IVF technology, ethical concerns surrounding this technology may not be as socially and politically charged as those faced currently. This historical example also illustrates that as the technology is enhanced, what the public deems unacceptable shifts over time. This is a subtle societal process which also may dull awareness of serious ethical pitfalls, particularly if the new technology confers high benefits and value to society.

In addition, there are times when history can offer insights into conflict resolution and management. We have seen that the original motivation for biotechnological development often differs from its eventual application. The history of cloning Dolly is an excellent example. A biotechnology company, PLL, in collaboration with the Roslin Institute, cloned Dolly for commercial purposes— to develop technology for the production of biological pharmaceuticals in animal milk at a cost significantly lower than conventional production methods. This required the development of a procedure in the laboratory to genetically modify mammary epithelial cells to encode the production of a specific drug. Once these cells were appropriately modified in the laboratory, a procedure had to be developed to generate an animal that expressed these genetically modified mammary epithelial cells. Nuclear transfer technology using adult cells offered a viable solution to generate these types of genetically modified animals, and is the primary reason why Dolly was cloned. It was no coincidence that the term cloning never was found in their original report that appeared in Nature (Wilmut et al, 1997). Nonetheless, this publication triggered an intense bioethical debate regarding the use of cloning for human reproduction and for embryonic stem cell research. Applying historical analysis to this example, one might conclude that animal cloning may be ethical for commercial use such as for the development of cheaper and more efficient drugs; applying this limited technology to today's human reproduction, however, remains unethical since reproductive cloning is currently not allowed in most societies today.

Historical analysis also reveals that the rapid pace of biomedical research has seriously challenged society's ability to make informed and reasoned choices about whether and how to proceed with its development and use (Frankel and Chapman 2001). Traditionally we have proceeded in a "catch-up" or "reactive" mode, scrambling to match our moral values and social and legal policies to scientific advances. Potential breakthrough technologies such as gene transfer take decades to develop, yet choices must be made immediately regarding research directions to take and treatments to investigate.

A final example regarding lessons learned from scientific history emerges from the development of anesthesia in the mid-1800s. When first introduced as a pain-relief medical procedure for women in childbirth, anesthesia was immediately condemned as ethically wrong because women were "supposed" to suffer through labor and it was "unnatural" if they did not. Over time, this belief was dramatically revised and analgesia or anesthesia has since become common and the standard of care. Today, it might be considered unethical to withhold anesthesia from a woman in need. This historical lesson demonstrates the evolution of values as a result of new technological advances. Sometimes, and maybe even often times, what science and technology make possible soon becomes permissible and, eventually, expected and ethical. Thus, history demonstrates the potential of technology to have an impact on our moral value systems or even confound the very concepts central to norms and values.

Any historical analysis should include the role of government policy in biomedical research. The United States government policy on bioethical issues is often shaped by the moral beliefs of both those in power and public perception. The belief that conception is the beginning of human life led to restrictions on the use of Federal funds to support human embryonic stem cell research, initiated by President William Clinton in 1995. While many criticized this federal policy, there may be a silver lining in how our government has attempted to deal with the contentious bioethical issues associated with human embryonic stem cell technology. Surprisingly and generally unappreciated is that president Bush's ban on the use of federal funds to support human embryonic stem cell research created a void that stimulated many non-federally funded research efforts that ultimately helped extend and deepen the partnership between the fields of bioethics and biomedical research. New funding streams were created with private and State funds leading to important advances (such as iPS and transdifferention technologies) that spawned new ethical debate. In 2009, President Obama instructed the National Institutes of Health to issue new guidelines for federally supported human embryonic stem cell research to better coincide with the public's belief that stem cell research has the promise to yield dramatic new therapies (Daley, 2012).

While biomedical scientists are primarily driven by the challenge to understand biological processes or the need to create new cures and treatments for major diseases, bioethical issues have begun to play a greater role in defining the landscape of biomedical research, especially in stem cell science. This is but one example that highlights the role of politics in shaping the direction of biomedical research.

The book's fourth objective is to introduce science-based strategies as a method for resolving, defusing, or managing bioethical concerns. Bioethical management is a three-step process. First, the facts must be determined, then the issues and the stakeholders must be identified, and finally proposed strategies for resolution must be created. Determining the facts implies understanding the relevant science and identifying the underlying religious, cultural, legal, or political concerns related to the dilemma. The stakeholders could be patients, companies, or governments. Finally, developing strategies to help manage or resolve bioethical dilemmas involves an integrated approach.

Classically, philosophical paradigms and traditional ethical approaches have been useful in many situations. Ethical values, however, may be relative, never absolute, and often evolving. Today, we are witnessing a paradigm shift in applied bioethics where science-based strategies have begun to offer new integrated approaches to augment the classical philosophically-based strategies. To illustrate this point, if someone believes that an embryo attains human status at conception, no amount of scientific, philosophical, or ethical discourse can sway that individual to favor embryonic stem cell research because stem cells are currently derived from a conceived embryo that must be destroyed in the process of deriving stem cells. However, as scientists develop novel methods to generate stem cells, such as reprogramming a normal adult-differentiated cell into a stem cell (Wilmut et al., 2007), research utilizing these stem cells should be less ethically charged than using the cells of donated embryos. This book will highlight several traditional ethical approaches to help resolve issues and will illuminate how new scientific research approaches offer technological alternatives that could alleviate ethical aporias.

Political and financial considerations are also important factors in managing or resolving bioethical concerns. If new biotechnologies are banned or restricted by the federal government, there is a risk that persons with medical needs may be deprived of the future medical discoveries that could emerge from the prohibited research attempts. On the other hand, there are the doomsday scenarios, be they real or imagined, which create pressures to restrict or block basic biomedical research. As a case in point, the technology for creating synthetic biological organisms has the possibility of creating safer vectors for gene transfer in therapeutic protocols, but with "dual use" could also be applied to generate new pathogens that might trigger massive epidemics or serve as blueprints for future weapons of bioterror (Hunter, 2012; Keim, 2012). Risk-benefit analysis, treatment alternatives, and financial resource management all therefore are important considerations when deciding to fund or pursue a new direction in biomedical research.

The public, as taxpayers funding the scientific research community, has a right, perhaps even an obligation, to help shape the course of scientific research and could be playing a larger role in deciding which research is funded. While some within the scientific community fear that engaging the public into research funding decisions could be ineffective, lay leaders are, nonetheless, taking a more empowered role in funding biomedical research. Many foundations in the research-charity sector engage lay leaders (trustees) who are non-scientists to help shape and direct the research funded by these charitable organizations without hindering scientific advancement.

It is critical that scientists, physicians, and the professional scientific research community take responsibility to ensure that the science behind any technology is accurately presented and that the ethical concerns are identified and mapped. With that in mind, this book is designed so that each topic or new technology will span two chapters. Each topic will begin with a comprehensive survey of the science underlying a new biotechnology to be followed by an examination of the ethical, religious, legal, and social challenges that precipitate out of the technology. Finally, various ethical approaches will be explored to try to resolve the resultant bioethical dilemmas. This integrated format is designed to help the readers of this book explore, express, and formulate their own ideas. Topics will often include case studies for students to think about creatively and allow them to formulate concrete and practical ways to resolve these controversial bioethical concerns.

This book will cover selected areas of contemporary science-based bioethics. Several important areas (such as animal experimentation, environmental concerns, evolution, and religion) will not be addressed in detail, as they are beyond the scope of this book. Other topics such as research freedom, research responsibility and accountability, conflicts of interest, and scarcity of financial resources will be incorporated, appropriately, into several of the chapter topics.

New areas of biotechnology such as human cloning, embryonic stem cell research, eugenics, gene therapy, and forensic medicine are based upon concepts of molecular and cellular biology and genetic modification of plants and animals. The science discussed in this book is oriented towards these disciplines that drive the bioethical agenda. This book assumes an understanding that biological research can result in acquisition of knowledge that can potentially benefit or even possibly harm society.

Conclusions

In summary, bioethics and science intersect at various levels. The potential to understand basic principles in biology as well as the clinical impact of many of these biotechnologies often remains to be established as the resultant bioethical issues are further identified and debated. The resolution of bioethical dilemmas is a complicated process for several reasons. First, simple solutions to bioethical issues may be difficult to obtain because critical facts are not always available at the time when there is a need for practical decisions. Second, decisions in both science and bioethics have to be acted upon immediately in order to forge ahead in a timely fashion even when the facts are incomplete. Third, sometimes issues arise that generate a clash of ethical principles such as beneficence and autonomy. Grappling which bioethical principles will take precedence will have to be addressed. These compounding factors related to bioethics may restrict one's capacity to resolve a dilemma but may allow one to develop ways to manage a bioethical conundrum.

This book proposes that both bioethics and science should exist in a mutually beneficial and symbiotic relationship motivated by a common goal to acquire knowledge purely for its own sake and for its potential for needed therapeutic applications. This is the new mission in bioethics: to provide an integrated, multidisciplinary analysis to enable our future scientists, health care providers, lawyers, and politicians to manage and resolve the many significant emerging bioethical issues.

References

Council, N. R., Guidelines for Human Embryonic Stem Cell Research, National Academy of Sciences, 2005.

Culotta, E., "Genomics. Chimp genome catalogs differences with humans." Science, 309(5740): 1468-1469, 2005.

Daley, G.Q., "The Promise and Perils of Stem Cell Therapeutics." Cell Stem Cell, 10:740-749, 2012.

Frankel, M. S., and Chapman A. R., "Genetic technologies. Facing inheritable genetic modifications." Science, 292(5520):1303, 2001.

Goldman, D., "Our genes, our choices : how genotype and gene interactions affect behavior," (Elsevier Academic Press, London ; Waltham, MA, 2012).

Hunter, P., "H5N1 infects the biosecurity debate." EMBO reports, 13(7):604-607, 2012.

Keim, P. S., "The NSABB recommendations: rationale, impact, and implications." mBio, 3:1-2, 2012.

Khan, D.H., Jahan, S. and Davie, J.R., "Pre-mRNA splicing: role of epigenetics and implications in disease." Adv Biol Regul, 52:377-388, 2012.

Krause, J., et al., "The complete mitochondrial DNA genome of an unknown hominin from southern Siberia." Nature, 464(7290):894-897, 2010.

Marx, V., "Epigenetics: Reading the second genomic code.", Nature, 491:143-147, 2012.

Noonan, J.P., "Neanderthal genomics and the evolution of modern humans.", Genome Res, 20:547-553, 2010.

Robinson, G.E., "Genomics. Beyond nature and nurture.", Science, 304: 397-399, 2004.

Takahashi, K., et al., "Induction of pluripotent stem cells from adult human fibroblasts by defined factors." Cell, 131:861-872, 2007.

Thomson, J.A., et al., "Embryonic stem cell lines derived from human blastocysts." Science, 282:1145-1147, 1998.

van Dellen, A., et al., "Wheel running from a juvenile age delays onset of specific motor deficits but does not alter protein aggregate density in a mouse model of Huntington's disease." BMC Neurosci, 9:34, 2008.

Wilmut, I., et al., "Viable offspring derived from fetal and adult mammalian cells." Nature, 385:810-813, 1997.

Chapter Two

Traditional Ethical Approaches to the Analysis of Bioethics

Introduction

The capacity to reason and think rationally about the good or even the irrational is one major force motivating humanity to establish a morally and ethically-based society.   The deep-seated emotional and spiritual desire to receive justice for oneself and ensure it for others, and to create and live in a society that places value on motivations and actions beyond the most basic and self-concerned are other driving forces to establish morality.   A moral society attempts to examine individual human character, and human actions and institutions, in order to shape a set of beliefs and values that will obtain the most good for the greatest number of persons. The guiding values of a moral society have been defined as both absolute, objective, and eternal, and as somewhat relative and context dependent (see below).   The term "moral" is derived from the Latin word *mos* or *moralis* meaning custom and the term "value" denotes good, benefit, or truth in cognition.

The word "ethics," often used interchangeably with morals, is derived from the Greek word *ethike*, meaning habit, action, or character. Ethics is conceptualized as the branch of philosophy that deals with moral aspects of human behavior and is the study of how decisions are made, what is right and wrong, or what is better or worse. Ethical theory is the process used to define and justify how specific ethical decisions are made. Ethical theory recognizes that terms like morality, ethics, and values are difficult to define objectively or scientifically because they represent subjective assessments and often reflect what individuals or society are willing to sacrifice in order to follow them.

Medical ethics refers to the application of general and fundamental ethical principles to clinical practice situations including biomedical research. As described in Chapter 3, arguments will be presented to differentiate research bioethics from medical ethics.   However, it is important to first briefly summarize some of the moral/ethical principles that have been applied to medical ethics. Those interested in a more comprehensive study of the principles of bioethics should read from the following books (Beauchamp and Walters, 1999; Bulger et al., 2002; McGee, 2003).

Classical Ethical Theories

Before describing modern theories of medical ethics, it is important to highlight one continuing controversy underlying many ethical theories. The classical Greek philosopher Plato was one of the earliest philosophers to argue that the validity of moral cognition is absolute and objective. Thus, according to Plato, ethical laws and principles should be universal and apply to all cultures at all times. Secular "rationalist" philosophers, from Socrates to Immanuel Kant, argued that people should rely on intellect when distinguishing right from wrong. "Sentimentalists", like David Hume, believed the opposite: emotions, such as empathy, should guide moral decisions. Scientists, such as Dr. Joshua Greene (Shenhav and Greene, 2010) combined brain-scanning technology with classic experiments from moral psychology to show that both rationality and emotion influence moral choices. He likens the moral brain to a camera that comes with manufactured presets, such as "portrait" or "landscape," along with a manual mode that requires photographers to make adjustments on their own. Emotional responses, which are influenced by humans' biological makeup and social experiences, are like the presets. The behavioral responses in this mode are fast and efficient, but also mindless and inflexible. Rationality, like manual mode, is adaptable to all kinds of unique scenarios, but is both time-consuming and cumbersome.

These approaches to ethical theory have permeated medical ethics as well. In their classic work, Beauchamp and Childless divided medical ethical theory into two major ethical schools: a deontological approach and a utilitarian approach. Deontology is rooted in the Latin word *deon* which means 'duty', and maintains that the concept of duty is independent of the concept of good, and that the correct actions are not necessarily determined by goodness. In this theory, one has to determine what is right or wrong by asking whether an act or sets of action would likely produce the greatest benefit to a society. Deontological theories of ethics state that an act is considered proper and good if it fulfills basic requirements of ethical values, without regard to the expected or anticipated consequences. Many religions are founded on this ethical principle. Immanuel Kant is credited for developing a secular modern approach to deontology. He emphasized that there are ethical values that dictate actions categorically without compromise. Kant asserted that ethical law is not determined by experience but is an imperative - objective, absolute, and unrestricted. The consequences of actions are generally not considered. Rather, emphasis is on moral rules of duty, autonomy, justice, and kind acts.

The utilitarian approach, in contrast, emphasizes that actions are morally correct when they lead to the greatest possible **balance** of good consequences. In other words, actions should promote maximum benefits with minimum harm. Utilitarian ethics has a specific goal and each action is designed to achieve that goal. The utilitarian approach has its origins in the writings of David Hume, Jeremy Bentham, and John Stuart Mill, who believed that consideration of the consequences of action are vital in any decision-making process. Mill emphasizes this in his two fundamental principles of utilitarianism. The first is the principle of utility. Actions are moral and right in proportion to their ability to promote happiness. It is necessary to determine the "goodness" and "badness" of a set of consequences. Specifically, Mill's theory advocates that morally right actions are determined by the non-moral value produced by their performance. Non-moral values are general characteristics of human striving and include pleasure, friendship, knowledge, and health.

Mill's second principle is a psychological one intrinsic to human nature. Mill believed that most people have a basic desire for unity and harmony with other people in order to produce the greatest possible balance of value over disvalue for all individuals. According to Mill and his proponents, actions are judged right or wrong solely by their consequences. Right actions are those that produce the greatest balance of happiness over unhappiness. Each person's happiness is equally important. Thus, a good action is one that brings the most beneficial results to the most people.

Kant's ethical deontological philosophy has been challenged on several levels by the development of utilitarianism. First, it is difficult to determine who decides on absolute values and how to implement them. Second, Kant's theory completely disregards the consequences of actions. Finally, the deontological theory does not provide a mechanism to decide between two or more universal values that are in conflict.

In response to these challenges, various neo-Kantian theories have been proposed. Some ethicists combine deontology with utilitarianism (see below) and emphasize the need to evaluate both absolute and universal values to structure values that moral cultures can follow. Other ethicists, such as John Rawls, author of "A Theory of Justice," (Rawls, 1999) emphasize the principles of honesty, equality, and social justice within a deontological framework. In this view, social justice is the highest ethical value and different characteristics of individual peoples are ignored. Rawls objected to the principle of utilitarianism by proposing that maximizing benefits can violate basic individual liberties and rights that should be guaranteed by social justice. According to Rawls, a practice is just if it is in accordance with a particular set of morally defensible principles of justice that the participants agree on for a specific situation. For Rawls a social contract is a hypothetical not an historical contract. He proposed that each individual in a society be permitted the maximum amount of equal basic liberty compatible with a similar liberty for others. Thus, once equal basic liberty is assured, selected inequalities in social benefits would be permitted only if they benefit everyone and only if everyone has an equal opportunity to receive those benefits.

The utilitarian approach to ethics has also been challenged. First, in many situations it is difficult to weigh the expected benefit if varying and conflicting actions are occurring simultaneously. Second, utilitarianism can lack ethical consistency in decision-making processes because it changes with different expected outcomes. Third, benefiting the majority may create serious harm to the remaining minority and lead to unjust social distributions of benefits. Finally, utilitarianism is based on the premise that ethical acts themselves have no intrinsic value and outcome and consequence are the prime determinants of action. Hence, some actions could be ethically wrong but still justified because their outcome produces the desired benefit.

Beauchamp and Childress summarize the differences in these two schools quite clearly. "The utilitarian holds that actions are determined to be right or wrong by only one of their features -- their consequences --; while the deontologist contends that even if this feature sometimes determines the rightness and wrongness of acts, it does not always do so" (Beauchamp and Childress, 1979).

In the last fifty years, other ethical theories have been developed in an attempt to create a school of ethics that actually works in the context of both bioethics and medical ethics (see Moore, 2012 for a review). For example:

1. ETHICAL RELATIVISM - No principles are universally valid. All moral principles are valid relative to cultural tastes. The rules of the society serve as a standard. The objective is to bring about tolerance of other cultures.
2. DIVINE COMMAND THEORY - Moral standards depend on a higher being such as an omniscient god. Any act that conforms to the law of this higher being is right; any act that breaks this law is wrong.
3. VIRTUE ETHICS - Morals are internal. The Virtue Ethic seeks to produce good people who act out of spontaneous goodness by emphasizing living well and achieving excellence.

Steps in Resolving Ethical Dilemmas

While there is no consensus among modern ethicists which of the above theories is best applied to resolve issues of bioethics or medical ethics, there are common views on identifying the steps in analysis. These steps include:

1. *Identifying and recognizing the ethical issues.* With respect to stem cell research, for example, this would include the issue of when or if an

embryo or zygote attains human status or personhood.

2. *Identifying the key facts, important definitions, and what remains to be discovered.* Most scientists believe, based on their limited experimental and clinical evidence that stem cell research will lead to new therapeutic applications in humans. It remains unclear, however, whether adult or embryonic-derived stem cells will offer the best therapeutic approach.

3. Usually you need to identify the stakeholders – who are involved – in this case, patients with disorders or injuries that could be treated or cured with regenerative therapies.

4. *Identifying those ethical principles that best apply to the case.* Many of the basic guidelines in medical ethics may apply in general but do not lead to resolution in specific cases. As a case in point, applying a utilitarian approach to the issue of personhood and obtaining embryonic stem cells might not favor its continued pursuit, because the technology involves destroying an embryo or potential life. In contrast, a deontological perspective would favor embryonic stem cell research because there is a moral imperative to do what will create an effective therapy, despite having to destroy an embryo before the 14th day.

5. *Evaluating how this course of action will impact these specific issues and attempting to speculate about their subsequent outcome and their impact on other related social or biomedical issues.* Randomized controlled trials using both adult and embryonic stem cells will be necessary to determine the safety and efficacy of each approach of stem cell research. Once stem cell research is shown to be effective and safe, public opinion will accept and welcome the new advance.

Fundamental Guidelines in Bioethics and Medical Ethics

Ethics and science differ in several aspects. First, specific conclusions and future directions in science are based on objective observations through the process of experimentation. In contrast, bioethical or medical ethical questions are generally not subject to controlled experimentation. Since no single set of ethical considerations will prove consistently reliable as a means of ending disagreements and controversy, many ethical theories have been proposed to deal constructively with moral disagreements. Second, the primary objective of scientific research is to arrive at a conclusion based on the scientific method, whereas bioethical resolutions provide recommendations or decisions that could be influenced by historical, philosophical, socio-cultural, or religious attitudes.

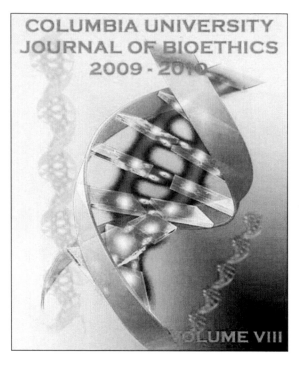

In classical medical ethics, there are four basic guidelines considered in evaluating ethical dilemmas (Bulger et al., 2002):

• *Autonomy, Respect for Persons, or Self-determination* is the right of the individual to determine his/her own destiny. Respect for persons implies that every person has intrinsic value and incorporates two ethical convictions. The first is that all individuals have a right to personal liberty, i.e., they are autonomous, and should be properly informed to promote self-determination. The granting of autonomy implies that society recognizes and accepts the free choice of each person even if that choice seems inappropriate or even life-endangering. The second is that those individuals who do not have the resources, education, or capacity for self-determination should be protected. There are several important features included in the principle of autonomy and respect. The first is that the individual's right to act should be mediated by reason and not desire. The second is based on Mill's arguments that social and political control over individual action is only legitimate if it requires the prevention of harm to other individuals affected by those actions.

For autonomy to be realized a patient must have the capacity for understanding the situation with its risks, benefits, and alternatives and of reasoning through to a decision that appreciates the consequences. It is a tremendous responsibility for caregivers to educate patients adequately. How much information is material and sufficient? While autonomy is highly valued in the United States, it is often difficult to be confident that the physician has provided all the information necessary for the patient to make complex medical decisions. Even the most educated patient may not have sufficient understanding of all medical issues and concerns to weigh all risks and benefits correctly. In addition, autonomy has to be modified when dealing with mentally challenged individuals, children, comatose patients, or even those who are highly traumatized who are temporarily or permanently not competent to make decisions for themselves and hence do not have autonomy.

- *Beneficence* is the capacity to do good or what is best for the patient. Therapeutic privilege also comes under beneficence: the physician's subjective determination of what seems to be in the best interests of the patient is a critical component of beneficence which may preclude providing fully informed consent to avoid causing anxiety or depression.

- *Non-maleficence*. While incorporated in the concept of Beneficence, this is often considered as a separate guideline. Non-maleficence operationalizes the Hippocratic doctrine to strive to "do no harm," and has three sub-themes: not to inflict evil or harm; to prevent evil or harm; and to remove evil or harmful forces or conditions in society.

- *Justice* demands fairness in distribution and what is deserved. In research, the benefits and the burdens (risks) are to be shared equally. Justice requires the division of rights and assets in an equitable and appropriate manner. Equally important is striving to fairly distribute duties and burdens. Injustice occurs when some benefit is denied or some burden is imposed without reason or acceptable justification.

Rawls's Theory of Justice (1999) revolves around the adaptation of two fundamental principles of justice which would, in turn, guarantee a just and morally acceptable society. The first principle guarantees the right of each person to have the most extensive basic liberty compatible with the liberty of others. The second principle states that social and economic positions are to be (a) to everyone's advantage and (b) open to all.

What is a disease?

Any discussion of bioethics in the 21st century has to focus on defining what a human disease means in scientific and social terms. A basic assumption within modern medicine is that health is the absence of disease (Scadding, 1988), and illness is the patient's personal experience of disease. The World Health Organization (WHO) defines health as a state of complete physical, mental, and social well-being, not merely the absence of disease or infirmity. Yet, these definitions are clearly neither precise nor scientific. One problem is that it is unclear if health, illness, and disease are purely biological issues. In fact, purely biological approaches to chronic illness often do not produce the anticipated benefits. It is now well accepted that psychosocial factors play a major part not only in the experience of illness, but also in the development of disease (Engel, 1977). This has led other scholars to propose a 'reverse view' concept of disease, that the process doesn't start with dysfunction as abnormal function, but with the patient's experience of illness as 'action failure' (Fulford, 1999). Immune/health status is now a form of *habitus* or personal "capital" that increasingly is used in society to establish a general kind of fitness or even moral virtue.

The categorization of disease can dramatically change in society. The World Health Organization (WHO), for example, previously viewed osteoporosis as an unavoidable part of normal ageing. But in 1994, WHO finally recognized osteoporosis as an official disease process since osteoporosis is an impairment to health. A reverse example is homosexuality. In the first half of the 20th century, many physicians viewed homosexuality as an endocrine disturbance requiring hormonal treatments or as a psychiatric disorder that could be treated using conditioning or psychotherapeutic methodologies. At this time it was classified as psychological pathology or abnormality. Yet in 1974, homosexuality was officially de-pathologized by the American Psychiatric Association when they removed it from their list of disease states.

Today, our definition of disease still remains imprecise but nonetheless important. Defining a condition as a disease is associated with decisions concerning whether or not it is important to allocate research and medical funds to correct or treat this condition. Defining a disease also has an impact on the system of health insurance. Medical insurance coverage requires that a code specifying a medical condition, symptom, or procedure be entered. Without a code, there would be no reimbursement.

Many conditions that heretofore have been considered within normal human variation, such as baldness or short stature, have now become medical conditions. In 2004, Medicare discarded its declaration that obesity is not a disease. This policy change allowed millions of overweight Americans to make medical claims for treatments such as bariatric (stomach) surgery and prescription diet regimens. Likewise, baldness and short stature are classified as medical conditions because medical treatments for them now exist that healthcare professional administer and which are highly profitable.

Finally, defining a disease state is vital for major pharmaceutical companies in their analysis of whether developing treatments for a particular disease would be marketable and economically sound. Successful examples would include treatment for infertility or sexual problems (e.g., Viagra for erectile dysfunction). Pharmaceutical companies also look for new marketing opportunities to prescribe already tested and approved drugs for new untested and "off-label" uses. Many are concerned about the influence of the Internet as well as direct to consumer advertising on medical decision-making. The examples above illustrate how medical-information seeking and decision making has expanded well beyond the doctor patient relationship and the domain of traditional medical ethics. What should be the role of medical ethics?

Ethical and definitional quandaries abound. For example, how do we define a person who is either a carrier for a genetic disease or has a genetic predisposition to a disease? As one example, everyone agrees that government funds should be allocated to enhance breast cancer diagnosis and treatment. But is a 16-year old teenage girl with a genetic predisposition to a breast cancer already considered ill or having a pre-existing condition? Should the government fund her to begin preventive care (such as a mastectomy) at her age?

The awareness of such a diagnosis may have traumatic psychological implications on this 16 year old. Similarly, is a carrier of a genetic disease state such as Tay Sachs disease, considered ill even though carriers appear to have no medical adversities? However, if two carriers marry, then 25% of their children will be born with this fatal condition. These issues intersect with bioethical concerns with respect to eugenics or designer babies. For example, many ethicists believe it is moral to undergo pre-implantation genetic diagnosis (PGD) to eliminate those in vitro fertilized eggs that carry two genes for Tay Sachs disease. Is it ethical to also destroy those fertilized eggs that only carry one gene for Tay Sachs and who will not be born with this condition? As another example, can parents who are hearing impaired use PGD to select a child who is also hearing impaired, the better to fit into their world?

What are Appropriate Medical Applications for Gene Therapy Research?

How should ethicists deal with pre-natal testing for diseases that have late-in-life onset, such as Alzheimer's disease, breast cancer, or Huntington's disease? Would a Woodie Guthrie, one of the most celebrated and influential folk singer-songwriters of the twentieth century, be born today? Would his parents, who carried the Huntington's disease gene, bear a child with the known risk that can be established by genetic screening? Many have argued that certain individuals born with genetic or congenital conditions that constrain their lives in challenging ways are driven to be more productive in society, considerably as a result of their disabilities.

CASE STUDY- In early 2002, a lesbian couple who both had a congenital hearing impairment wanted to have a child with the same genetic impairment. They obtained sperm for artificial insemination from a donor with a heritable form of deafness to increase their chances and so far have two children with hearing impairment. In contrast, another hearing impaired coupled utilized PGD have a child who exhibited normal hearing function. Did just one of these couples engage in ethical behavior?

Conclusions

There are many diverse theories regarding medical ethics that have been applied to bioethical dilemmas. In this book, we propose that resolving these dilemmas requires a multidisciplinary approach that ideally should integrate philosophy-based theories with the understanding of the underlying science. In addition, any attempt to resolve bioethical issues should consider an historical review to assess whether there are important lessons that can be learned from previous bioethical dilemmas that we, as a society have faced.

References

Beauchamp, T. L. and Childress, J. F., Principles of biomedical ethics. New York, Oxford University Press, 1979.

Beauchamp, T. L. and Walters, L., Contemporary issues in bioethics. Belmont, CA, Wadsworth Pub, 1999.

Bulger, R. E., et al., The ethical dimensions of the biological and health sciences. Cambridge, U.K. ; New York, Cambridge University Press, 2002.

Engel, G. L., "The need for a new medical model: a challenge for biomedicine." Science, 196(4286):129-36, 1977.

Fulford, K. W., "Nine variations and a coda on the theme of an evolutionary definition of dysfunction." J Abnorm Psychol, 108(3):412-20, 1999.

McGee, G., Pragmatic bioethics. Cambridge, Mass., MIT Press, 2003.

Moore, W., Application of Modern Moral Theories in Medical Ethics, 2012.

Rawls, J., A theory of justice, Harvard University Press, 1999.

Scadding, J. G., "Health and disease: what can medicine do for philosophy?" J Med Ethics, 14(3):118-24, 1988.

Shenhav, A., and Greene, J.D., "Moral judgments recruit domain-general valuation mechanisms to integrate representations of probability and magnitude." Neuron, 67:667-77, 2010.

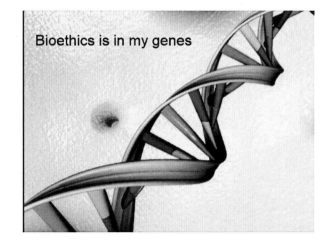

Chapter Three

Redefining Research Bioethics

Introduction

Medical ethics has traditionally been the principle ethical discipline in health care and science. Over the past forty years, ethics in medicine and science has branched out in numerous directions. Today, these branches include: genetic ethics, neuroethics, animal ethics, research ethics, legal bioethics, environmental ethics, and life science ethics. While the general term "bioethics" is used to include all these areas, current trends and analyses reveal that each of these areas of study can be viewed as intrinsically different in nature, scope, and application. The first part of this chapter focuses on the need to define research bioethics and how it should be distinguished from medical ethics. The second part of this chapter outlines specific ethical guidelines that address some of the unique characteristics of research bioethics. The re-conceptualization of research bioethics is designed to link various avenues of science-based research into one ethical discipline that emerges from biotechnology and life-science discoveries. Furthermore, it aims to distinguish this area of study from classical medical ethics.

Bioethics Within a Medical Ethical Context

From the time of Hippocrates until the present day, discussions relating to medical ethics have generally focused on clinically related issues such as health care professional-patient relationships. Thus, scientific discoveries that directly have an impact on the rights of the patient, the rights and obligations of the physician, and the operations of health care facilities, naturally fall within the domain of medical ethics. Such patient-related issues in medical ethics include abortion, contraception, *in vitro* fertilization, other assisted reproductive technologies, end of life issues, advanced directives, euthanasia, informed consent, and organ transplantation. In addition, over the last half a century, ethical guidelines have been formulated in order to protect the rights of human volunteers participating in clinical or research studies that apply new technologies or therapies into an approved clinical framework.

As discussed in Chapter Two, medical ethicists have developed three (or four) general principles or guidelines to provide a framework for discussions and/or resolution of medical ethical dilemmas. They are: 1) *autonomy/respect for persons*- a person's right to choose and control his/her own life and destiny and the acceptance of individual responsibility for his/her medical choices; 2a) *beneficence*- the moral and contractual calling to benefit a person who seeks help; 2b) *non maleficence* – avoiding intentionally created, needless harm or injury to a person, either through acts of commission or omission; and 3) *justice*-allocating medical resources fairly.   Resolving medical ethics dilemmas often requires balancing conflicting guidelines such as the rights and autonomy of the individual versus the rights of society, the potential benefit versus the risk to the individual, the short-term suffering and pain versus the long term benefits, and the moral versus medical obligations to the patients.

A significant reformulation in medical ethics came in the early 1970s as new scientific technologies such as genetic engineering were beginning to emerge.   Dr. Van Rensselaer Potter was one of the first to define bioethics as "biology combined with diverse humanistic knowledge forging a science that sets a system of medical and environmental priorities for acceptable survival." (Rawls 1999) In this reformulation, the term "bioethics" was coined to incorporate ethical issues that arose from biomedical research breakthroughs. In this vein, the *Encyclopedia of Bioethics* (1970) defined bioethics as, "the interdisciplinary examination of the moral and ethical dimensions of human conduct in the areas of life sciences and health care.   The discipline encompasses the study of medical, legal, scientific, religious, philosophical, moral and ethical issues of life sciences."(Post, 2004).

The National Research Act was passed in 1974 in light of the revelations from the egregious Tuskegee Syphilis Study. In this forty-year natural history investigation, supported by the United States Public Health Service, it was uncovered that over 400 participants (predominantly African American males) were denied anti-syphilis treatments.   This legislation created the National Commission for the Protection of Human Subjects of Biomedical and Behavioral Research, which was charged to identify the basic ethical principles that should underlie the conduct of biomedical and behavioral research involving human subjects. Furthermore it hoped to develop guidelines that should be followed to assure that such research is conducted in accordance with those principles. In 1978, Casper Weinberger, President Gerald Ford's Secretary of Health, Education, and Welfare, drafted the Belmont Report.   This crucial *document outlines guidelines for protecting human subjects in both clinical and research environments. It incorporated biomedical research into a larger medical ethics framework based on the three principle guidelines cited above* [respect for all people, beneficence, and justice].

The Belmont Report provided concrete and useful suggestions to protect participants involved in life science research studies. Considerable debate has recently emerged, however, regarding whether the principles proposed in the Belmont Report adequately addressed the broader ethical issues related to biomedical research. A number of prominent bioethicists such as Dr. Daniel Callahan, cofounder of The Hastings Center in 1969; Dr. Albert Jonsen, author of the classic work "Birth of Bioethics"; and Gilbert Meilaender, a Christian medical ethicist at Valparaiso University and current member of the President's Council on Bioethics; all questioned whether these medical ethical principles that often clash, could be applied to "real life" bioresearch ethical issues. Even Dr. Thomas Beauchamp, one of the pioneers in bioethical education, questioned the role of classical ethical theories in resolving modern issues of research bioethics (Beauchamp, 2007). Thus, the "principlist" approach may not be useful in grappling with bioethical dilemmas where technology confronts ethics.

The Need to Redefine Biomedical Research Ethics

Since the 1970s, new biotechnologies in the areas of molecular biology, genomics, and reproductive biology, have been developed, affecting life-science research. These new technologies have challenged the basic definitions of human life such as when human life begins and how we define ourselves as an individual species. Embryonic stem cell research and human cloning are important contemporary examples of evolving biotechnologies that require informed discussions about the scientific implications of this research and the bioethical issues that inevitably arise. Recent biotechnological discoveries, such as..., necessitate the development of a discipline with rules, strategies, and definitions that address the real and never-before-seen bioethical dilemmas that scientists as well as society must confront. The genetic engineering of plants, for example, may not be a relevant problem for the patient-doctor guidelines of medical ethics, but it certainly raises the ethical issue of changing the "natural environmental order." Obviously, a different method of analysis is required to address genetically modified organisms than that of classical medical ethics.

The first step in differentiating research bioethics from medical ethics is developing an operational definition of bioethics. In 1970, Dr. Van Rensselaer Potter coined the term bioethics and defined it as "the science of survival to overcome the extinction of the environment of the earth and to protect the extinction of human beings" (Potter, 1972). Today, a broader definition that better fits contemporary biotechnological innovation is necessary. Bioethics is defined in this book as a broad field of study that examines the ethical issues emerging from biotechnologies that affect human beings, the animal world, the plant kingdom, and the environment. We coin the term *research bioethics* as **the study of ethical dilemmas arising from the acquisition of scientific knowledge and its impact on life forms and the environment.** This definition helps to establish an ethical approach to the acquisition of scientific knowledge as it positively and negatively influences and interacts with human society and the environment at large.

The new definition of research bioethics distinguishes it fundamentally from medical ethics in one critical area. Research bioethics focuses on scientific discoveries that affect human society, animals, plants, and the environment as a whole. In contrast, medical ethics is more circumscribed, and generally focuses on any condition that involves an individual or volunteer participating in medical experimentation or that creates a care provider-patient relationship.

If one accepts this definition of research bioethics, then a reformulation of the basic guidelines for research bioethics is required to deal with the specific and unique ethical concerns relating to science, society, and the environment. Historically, scientists who have attempted to apply bioethical-medical ethical principles (as defined by the Belmont Report) (Beauchamp, 2008) to research settings have discovered that the principles may not provide a useful framework for addressing many relevant ethical **research** concerns. In fact, the three principles discussed in the Belmont report—respect, beneficence, and justice— can introduce conflicts and contradictions when applied to research bioethical issues.

For example, the first Belmont principle, respect for persons (or autonomy), can have a utilitarian, rather than a moral goal. The Belmont Report incorporates John Stuart Mill's utilitarian views of personal autonomy that, "only fully conscious, rational adults capable of acting autonomously are considered moral agents with moral responsibilities" (Callahan, 1994). However, those incapable of acting autonomously (such as infants, comatose patients, or Alzheimer's disease patients), were defined under the Belmont bioethical principles as non-moral agents and are thus "non-persons" who lack any rights of self-determination. In addition, there are many situations in medical ethics that focus on how the individual infringes on the general welfare of society. Confidentiality of the individual right to privacy in the diagnosis of HIV infection, for example, may compromise public health needs to survey the infected in order to protect the uninfected.

The second principle, beneficence, incorporates a Hippocratic understanding of beneficence as doing good for the patient. However, the Belmont Report also included a second definition of beneficence that is utilitarian and involves, "one doing good for society at large" (Callahan, 1994).   The Belmont Report further declares that "citizens have a strong moral obligation to take part in experimental research for the greater good of society." This contradicts the Hippocratic interpretation of beneficence and violates time-honored international medical ethical guidelines such as the Nuremberg Code and the Helsinki Declaration, which oppose physicians experimenting on volunteer subjects unless the subjects **directly** benefit from the procedure. Research done in South Korea by Dr. Huang, for example, recruited over 2000 women to donate their oocytes for stem cell research even though these volunteers did not directly benefit from the procedure.

The third Belmont principle, justice, is also defined in terms of a "fairness" that allocates the benefits and burdens of scientific research equitably across the different social and economic populations. This principle varies a great deal from the classic Aristotelian definition of justice used in medical ethics that emphasizes the fair and just treatment of every human being. Applying fairness in biomedical research is often difficult to ensure. How are decisions made to allocate research funds for Huntington's disease, which affects fewer than a million people around the world, when millions of people are dying of AIDS or malaria? Heart transplants provide another challenge associate with the principle of justice. In the USA about 3000 heart transplants are performed at a cost of close to 1 billion dollars. Would this money be better allocated to develop new drugs that could benefit the 500,000 people who develop heart problems each year?

Differentiating research bioethics and medical ethics can also manifest into practical ramifications. First, these two disciplines can target two distinctly different participants. The classical audience for medical ethics has been health care providers, clinical researchers, insurance companies, and health care institutions that require guidelines to make complicated decisions regarding the value of human life and patient care. In contrast, biomedical and life science researchers both in academia and corporate America need ethical guidelines appropriate and relevant for the testing and application of new biotechnologies that are being developed across the globe.

A second ramification of the differentiation between research bioethics and medical ethics relates to education via case studies. Medical ethics case studies are generally obtained from real-life situations. Seeing the patient in the health care facility is essential to resolving and/or managing medical ethical issues. In contrast, real-life situations in bioethics are less opportune when the technology is still under development. Society and government are hesitant to allow research with novel biotechnologies to progress without discussing end results. Consequently, bioethical dilemmas are often hypothetical with regards to patient applications. For example, no accessible facilities are currently engaged in human cloning to provide a real situation where bioethicists can study a cloned human and its impact on society. Furthermore, new biotechnologies are often introduced in a corporate setting where governmental access is also limited. For example, introducing genetically modified organisms (GMOs) that have been developed in the corporate sector presents new challenges of how to appropriately evaluate the impact of GMOs on the environment.

The third ramification relates to the different compositional structures of regulatory committees and commissions dealing with medical ethics versus bioethics. Medical ethics committees are typically composed of individuals involved in health care including practicing physicians, nurses, other health care professionals, hospital administrators, medical ethicists, insurance experts, theologians, and lawyers. Medical ethics committees often focus on the influence of managed care with respect to the patient's best interest or deal with issues that may interfere with the daily operations of health care or medical institutions. In contrast, it appears appropriate for research bioethics committees to be composed of basic research scientists, physician-scientists, bioethicists, political analysts, environmentalists, sociologists, theologians, and lawyers. Government officials could also serve on research bioethics committees because of relevant legislation being considered for regulating these technologies. An example of this type of committee is the President's Council on Bioethics that focused on human cloning and stem cell research. While the recommendations of the council have been controversial and may never be implemented as originally designed, the Commission was thorough in dissecting the ethical issues and arguments relevant to these technologies.[1]

The final distinction between medical ethics and research bioethics includes the time frame that is necessary to propose practical ways to resolve the ethical dilemmas. In cases involving patient- health care medical ethics, there is a more immediate need for resolution. The classical case-study whether a neurologically brain dead patient should be removed from a respirator or whether a terminal cancer patient should be denied the option of euthanasia requires an immediate response. In contrast, many bioethical dilemmas related to embryonic stem cell research, reproductive cloning, or genetically modified organisms have been debated over the last decade, often without the need for immediate resolution.

---

[1] http://bioethics.georgetown.edu/pcbe/reports/cloningreport/ and http://bioethics.georgetown.edu/pcbe/reports/stemcell/.

One possible way to tackle this issue would be to expand existing Institutional Review Boards (IRBs) established in universities, and allowing them to focus on bioethical issues emerging from new biotechnologies. However, if the existing IRBs are overworked and overwhelmed, separate research bioethical committees may have to be organized to work with the IRBs.

Four Additional Principles for Reformulating Guidelines for Research Bioethics

The following four additional research bioethical guidelines are proposed to regulate the pursuit of scientific knowledge and inquiry: 1) respecting the value of human life and personhood and balancing the needs of the society versus the needs of the individual; 2) respecting the bio-environment and the biological order; 3) using scientific research to alleviate specific bioethical concerns, rather than causing harm; and 4) applying practical lessons gleaned from past bioethical conflicts.

Human Dignity: At times, respecting human dignity or the value of human life and personhood, and balancing the needs of society versus the needs of the individual has been invoked in contemporary bioethics regarding human genetic enhancement as well as generating human-nonhuman chimeras (de Melo-Martin 2008; Loike and Tendler 2008). Regarding this guideline there are two controversial parameters that must be delineated. The first is to define human dignity and the second is to identify cases when it is appropriate to apply this principle.

Human dignity can be viewed either within a secular or religious perspective. Immanuel Kant proposed a secular definition that human dignity is associated with the capacity to think for oneself and direct one's actions. Using a Kantian moral framework of human dignity, human beings possess an unconditional and incomparable worth that is independent of metaphysical or religious precepts (Paton 1971; Macklin 2003; Karpowicz, Cohen et al. 2005). According to Kant, human beings have dignity because of their reasoning faculties, which give them the freedom and ability to distinguish moral from immoral actions. Using this Kantian definition, however, some scholars have argued that not all human beings have dignity. Patients in a permanent vegetative state, for example, have irreversibly lost their autonomy and may no longer have dignity (Loike and Tendler 2011).

In contrast to this secular definition of human dignity, a religious-based definition formulates or characterizes human dignity as an inviolable right invested by God in all human beings including fetuses, comatose patients, and patients in a permanent vegetative state (Kass 2006; Loike and Tendler 2011). In its simplest religious formulation, human dignity can be equated with the sanctity or infinite worth of human life and assumes that there is something uniquely valuable about human life. From a religious Judeo-Christian view, human dignity emanates from the first chapter of Genesis that records how human beings were uniquely fashioned and divinely created (Soloveitchik 1983). Several Biblical scholars comment that the Bible describes that God created Human beings using two different processes (Soloveitchik 1983). The first process was biological/genetic as indicated by the fact that human beings were created on the same day as other animals. The second process was metaphysical as God infused into human beings a spiritual entity that differentiates human beings from all other creatures. This metaphysical, and almost divine quality of human beings, confers a sanctity that exists within each human being from the beginning of life as an embryo until natural death.

One outcome of respecting human dignity is reflected in their moral virtues. Moral virtues that people often consider as being good are being courageous, compassionate, and altruistic. Without such moral virtues and human cooperation of its members, a society cannot survive.

If one accepts the principle and outcomes of human dignity, then it is appropriate to examine the role human dignity may play in bioethics. On the one hand, bioethicists, such as Ruth Macklin, points out that respecting human dignity is a vague restatement of other bioethical guideline, beneficence or autonomy, and brings no significant value or greater understanding to bioethical dilemmas (Macklin 2003). Ruth Macklin states,

> "[Human] dignity is a useless concept…. It means no more than respect for persons or their autonomy…A close inspection of leading examples shows that appeals to dignity are either vague restatements of other, more precise, notions or mere slogans that add nothing to an understanding of the topic."

In addition, Dr. Macklin presents other philosophical arguments that weaken the validity of the principle of respecting human dignity (Macklin 2003).

Other scholars and bioethicists (Kass 2006; Loike and Tendler 2011) argue from a secular and religious perspective against Ruth Macklin and advocate the paramount importance of applying the principle of respecting human dignity in bioethical matters. Mahmudur Rahman Bhuiyan summarizes the views of the bioethicist, Francis Fukuyama (Fukuyama 2002) who uniquely blends a secular approach of human dignity with the unique nature of the human species.

> "Fukuyama fears that human nature is the most valuable thing that may be affected by recent advances in human biotechnology. He defines human nature as "species-typical traits" of human beings (such as language and cognition, which provide the grounds for feelings such as pride, anger, shame, and sympathy), arising from genetic factors. According to Fukuyama, these species-specific traits of humans differentiate us from all other nonhuman species, and this differentiation constitutes the basis of human dignity. The reduction of shared traits among humans will result, according to Fukuyama, in the degradation of human dignity … thus makes human nature uncertain (Bhuiyan 2009)."

Under what situations should respect for human dignity be applied? Research programs, for example, designed to examine whether cows can serve as surrogate incubators for human embryos should not receive priority over programs engaged in examining artificial incubators for premature babies because it raises the issue of respecting human dignity. In another situation publicized in April 2008, British researchers claim to have created human embryos using human cells and the egg cells of cows. They said they had hollowed out the egg cells obtained from cattle and inserted human DNA to create a growing embryo in order to later isolate human embryonic stem cells (http://www.sciam.com/article.cfm?id=scientists-make-human-cow).

There is also an intimate connection between respecting human dignity and infringing individual rights. For example, obtaining the genetic fingerprint of every individual in a population for the purpose of crime control or prevention of terrorist attacks infringes on the individual's right to privacy and confidentiality, but may be a practical method to solve crimes. Genetic profiles and fingerprints of potential criminals or terrorists have been shown to help manage crime control and potential terrorist attacks and may serve to improve the safety of society in general (Barber and Foran, 2006; Berger, 2006). Another example involves the genetic testing of newborns or adults. Currently, New York State screens every newborn for cystic fibrosis and several other genetic disorders. This appears to reduce the number of children born with these diseases. However, additional genetic screening for certain types of cancers or neurological diseases is more controversial, especially when these tests may not medically benefit the individual research subject. Sometimes, such results could harm research subjects who are not properly educated or prepared to handle the implications of the results of the screening. Genetic tests done in a research laboratory as part of a research study and not in conjunction with an appropriate clinical laboratory may not be reliable or meaningful and the results should not be shared with the volunteer subjects. Identifying the gene for Familial dysautonomia (Anderson et al., 2001) was clearly accelerated by using a DNA database established exclusively to screen for Tay Sachs disease. Those individuals who originally provided samples for the Tay Sachs database were never informed that their DNA samples would be used for other research purposes. Were the scientists justified in using this database? What protective measures of confidentiality or informed consent were implemented for this study? Is it justified to screen for new disease markers utilizing genetic data banks that were obtained from other studies without obtaining permission (informed consent) from the donors. The underlying justification for such screening is the belief that the more genetic information obtained regarding a disease process, the greater that possibility that scientists will be able to design more effective future therapies. Moving forward, it is clear that it is important to obtain permission from donors to extend the use of their genetic material any other genetic research studies that examine disease markers.

A final example relates to the ongoing debate over how to handle the publication of scientific research findings that could threaten national security (see Chapter 13). 'Publish or perish' has always been a guiding characteristic of the academic life of investigators in the sciences. However, since the Anthrax mail attacks of 2001, there have been debates regarding which results of biological research should be published. Similarly, there is concern that research in synthetic biology in which scientists are attempting to build all-new life forms from artificial DNA may pave the way to create new powerful bioterrorist weapons. There is a fear that publishing the underlying methods behind these types of scientific project could fall into the hands of terrorists, possibly jeopardizing national security.

Policies should be established enabling the scientific community to publish research without revealing details that could endanger the safety of the nation. Who should oversee exactly what information is published: governmental agencies, authors, research institutions, journals, or some combination? Policy guidelines should establish strategies for preventing the misuse of biotechnology while preserving scientific inquiry and the dissemination of appropriate scientific data.

In summary, this first additional guideline assumes that all human beings have infinite or immeasurable value and that saving lives is a significant long-term objective of current scientific research activity. Thus, a primary objective of research must be to utilize and develop new life-science technologies to improve health care, disease treatment, and disease prevention. In fact, the recent roadmap proposed by the National Institutes of Health [http://bioethics.georgetown.edu/pcbe/bookshelf/] reflects these objectives. Biological research with unclear societal applications should not receive equal priority as research with clear societal applications.

Respect for the bio-environment and biological order: Respecting the environment is a critical concern for bioethics, but is not typically relevant in discussions of medical ethics. The use of biotechnology to improve the color, taste, nutrition, and production of food began in ancient times, when farmers first cross-bred different plant strains and realized that they could produce varieties with the optimal characteristics of both of the original plants. Today about 2-4% of farmlands are planted with genetically modified (GM) crops and most of these GM crops are planted on US soil.[2] Agricultural researchers have designed a wide variety of genetically modified plants with traits deemed beneficial to those who grow, market, and consume them. In addition, these plants can serve as a source for manufacturing recombinant proteins to be used for therapeutic purposes. Plant- based production of therapeutic proteins is predicted to cost 4-5 times less than production by classical cell culture techniques. However, the general concern over any genetically modified plant or organism is that transgenes will spread through the environment and ultimately affect non-targeted organisms. In addition, there is a fear that introducing genetically modified organisms could disturb the ecological balance of other plants and animals. Scientists have only begun broadly examining the effects of genetically modified plants on the environment as recently as the 1990s.

This guideline (respect for the bio-environment and biological order) would ensure that research into GMOs incorporates safety measures in addition to studying the possibilities of how a genetically modified organism could affect factors of the bio-environment such as the consumer, other plant life or insect habitats. In 2003 and 2008 The Food and Drug Administration in the US concluded that meat from **cloned** animals is as safe as conventionally bred animals. Clones are genetic copies of donor animals; unlike genetically modified animals, their DNA is not changed, but used to introduce desirable traits into herds. In contrast, Australia's current policy is that cloning is restricted to breeding stock cattle and sheep which are not entering the food supply. It is unclear why such a statement was issued without the appropriate scientific studies justifying such a conclusion. Just as new drug investigations require

---

[2] http://www.newscientist.com/channel/life/gm-food

safety controls, research involving GMOs should include appropriate safety tests. Such safety controls should be instituted whether (or not) the GMO is developed by industry or academic institutions. The fact that most European countries are considering a ban of GMOs or have already banned GMOs highlights the difficulty in scientifically assessing their environmental impact. A 2007 study reported that rats fed on a globally available version of genetically modified maize developed liver and kidney toxicity, and concluded that the particular strain of GM corn, MON863, is not safe for consumption (Seralini et al., 2007).

The second guideline proposes that the development of genetically modified organisms should include a comprehensive survey of potential environmental impacts. One could envision that routine test phases could be implemented, similar to the test phases implemented with the development of new therapies. Phase I development would examine the effects of GMOs within a test field that examines other plants, whereas phase II development would include the effects of GMOs on larger farms and fields and a study of their impact on insects, animals, and other plants.

Another component of this guideline, which is generally adhered to by all research institutions, is to provide health care and ethical treatment of animals used for scientific research. This issue is becoming more difficult, owing to the fact that as we learn more about animal behavior, science recognizes that many animals exhibit social skills and characteristics that resemble human behavior. On December of 2011, the NIH adopted strict new limits on using chimpanzees in medical research, saying most studies do not require the use of these non-human primates and that science has advanced using other animal models or in vitro models that chimps seldom would be needed to help develop new medicines. Chimps' similarity to people "demands special consideration and respect," is what the director of the NIH, Dr. Collins is quoted as saying. As the complexities of animal behavior are revealed, the classical distinctions that differentiate human beings from animals become blurred. Therefore, there is a greater need today for scientists to: a) evaluate whether their research can only be accomplished using animal models rather than cell models, and b) consider the degree of animal suffering and sacrifice within each experimental design.

Respecting biological order also falls within the second guideline and is rooted in the diverse religious and cultural backgrounds of human beings. A variety of religious groups and cultures believe that while the pursuit of scientific knowledge is valuable, there may be areas where humans should not "play God" by engaging in activities that do not reflect the natural order of life. Examples of inappropriate or low priority scientific investigations may include: research into male pregnancy, the creation of two-headed animals, or creating chimeras where human embryonic stem cells are transplanted into mice or chimps to reconstitute part of a human brain in these animals (see Chapter 8), and using germ line gene therapy when research into somatic gene therapy has not been fully developed.

Many cultures believe that some higher power is responsible for creation of the world and that there is a valid reason behind biological order. Other cultures believe that natural evolution has ultimately resulted in a functional biological order that operates efficiently in this world. Therefore, technologies that alter this biological order are viewed with great skepticism; the fear is that these technologies will destroy humanity or the environment. For example, there is currently a heated debate over whether it is ethical for scientists to create artificial organisms using commercially available DNA. A group led by J. Craig Venter has reportedly created an artificial virus with the identical genetic code of a simple virus already known to infect and kill bacterial cells.[3] The researchers hope that this type of technology will help create genetically-based solutions for treating diseases or dealing with environmental challenges.

There are also significant concerns that scientists do not know enough about the effects of synthetic organisms on biodiversity, the environment, or society. Moreover, there is a fear that this technology could be used to create bioterrorist organisms that are even more destructive than anthrax or smallpox. Developing such technologies should take into consideration that sometimes the unknown may lead to undesired paths.

A major question facing scientists related to this guideline is whether there should there be limits to scientific research. For example, transplanting human embryonic stem cells that contain specific genetic predispositions for disease into mouse embryos enables scientists to effectively investigate how such diseases develop within a whole animal, providing an animal model to test new therapies. However, examining whether transplanting human brain cells into mice to study human behavior or mental capacity raises issues of animal welfare concerns and whether such a mouse would have human-like consciousness. Clearly, there are many factors that must be considered. Is creating such human-mouse chimeras the only way to examine neuro-biological questions (see Chapter 8)? Does this type of research show disrespect for biological order?

Use of scientific research to alleviate bioethical concerns. The third guideline reflects a current trend in research bioethics. There are times when bioethical concerns appear to be irresolvable. The contentious debate over when a pre-

---

[3] http://www.economist.com/science/displayStory.cfm?story_id=2224008).

embryo or embryo attains human status or personhood has been ongoing for many decades, restraining the progression of embryonic stem cell research, which is influenced by how one views the beginning of human life (see Chapter 7). The scientific community has responded to this apparently irresolvable issue by trying to utilize creative science to circumvent or defuse the bioethical concerns. For example, research on de-differentiating an adult cell to a pluripotent stem cell or obtaining embryonic stem cells from a morula without destroying the pre-implanted embryo is not as ethically troubling as conventional therapeutic cloning using embryonic stem cells.

The Asilomar Conferences of 1973 and 1974 highlight a unique situation in which life science research was restricted. The first conference was organized in response to the research program of Dr. Paul Berg to determine if the simian virus 40 (SV40) could be used to transfer a foreign gene into a common bacteria found in the human intestine. In 1971, Dr. Robert Pollack contacted Dr. Berg to discuss the safety issues related to Dr. Berg's proposal. One safety issue was the fear that transfecting a common bacteria with SV40 might potentially expose millions of people to this virus, resulting in an increase in the incidence of cancer. Thus, the overall bioethical issue discussed at the first conference was determining the risks of joining DNA from animal viruses with DNA from bacteria. In 1974, a second conference was called when it became possible to safely splice and recombine different DNAs and join DNA from animal viruses with DNA from bacteria.

The Asilomar Conferences proposed a set of scientific guidelines for recombinant DNA research that incorporated safeguards into this technology. The most important guideline proposed was to establish biological and physical safeguards to restrict the viability of these new recombinant organisms within a laboratory environment. The biological barriers mandated the use of bacterial hosts that could not survive outside the laboratory and that physical barriers such as gloves, hoods and filters were required to ensure that recombinant organisms never left the laboratory. The third safety net prohibited the use of highly pathogenic organisms until more knowledge was gained. The Asilomar Conferences challenged the autonomy of biological science and showed that scientists and the public must share the responsibility of preventing the negative effects of scientific research on society in general. Moreover, the proposed guidelines worked as so far, no pathological organism has ever been released from such research.

New biotechnologies are being developed that raise similar safety issues, yet we lack a consensus regarding how this research should be regulated. Manipulating the genetics of organisms using cross-breeding techniques has long been a part of human tradition. In 2010 Craig Venter succeeded in creating the first synthetic life form made entirely with pieces of lab-assembled DNA (Moore, 2012). This may lead to the synthesis of proteins with novel biological, chemical, and physical properties, posing significant consequences for biotechnology and medicine. The move from creating new proteins to creating new life seems only a small step away from a long-standing dream, or nightmare, of creating artificial life.

History can serve as a master teacher about research bioethics. The fourth and final guideline proposes that historical analyses can provide lessons in resolving research bioethical issues associated with contemporary biotechnologies. As discussed in Chapter Seven, both the development of in vitro fertilization (IVF) and embryonic stem cell research raise similar bioethical issues regarding the initiation of human life. As IVF became a more accepted treatment for infertile couples, these ethical concerns declined in importance for the American public. One might extrapolate this observation and predict that if embryonic stem cell research develops into an accepted therapy, the bioethical issue of whether or not a pre-implanted embryo is considered a human being will be less concern to society in general.

Unfortunately, historical lessons cannot always provide insight into the resolution of bioethical issues. The court of law may not be an effective forum for resolving bioethical issues. Consider the 1973 Supreme Court's *Roe v. Wade* decision regarding a woman's right to abortion. An interpretation of the Court's ruling in *Roe v. Wade* would indicate there should be no law banning or restricting embryonic stem cell research. Similarly, various interpreters of the U.S. Constitution believe that the ability to reproduce is a fundamental human right. Within this context, infertile couples should be allowed to engage in reproductive cloning as long as the medical risks are minimal. Nonetheless, reproductive cloning is not as yet considered acceptable by either the research community or the public.

Conclusions

The acquisition of scientific knowledge is a fundamental characteristic of human society and can generate a variety of ethical issues that differ in principle from medical ethics. Thus, the call to conceptually differentiate these two disciplines is the focus of this chapter. The reformulated definition for research bioethics serves as the fulcrum for developing the four principles of bioethics described here. As in any moral and ethical system, there may be clashes between the four principles proposed for research bioethics. Nonetheless, these guidelines are designed to ensure the ethical pursuit of scientific inquiry and to establish a structural framework in research bioethics in order to develop appropriate applications of scientific technologies to society.

The aforementioned guidelines are valid only if they enable ethicists and scientists to respond to bioethical issues related to new biotechnologies in a more effective way than prior medical ethics or bioethical conceptualizations. In this period of economic uncertainty, society can no longer fund biological research simply for the pure acquisition of scientific knowledge. Thus, another objective in describing research bioethical guidelines is establishing priorities regarding which research activities should be pursued by evaluating how the research will benefit the public or the environment.

In the final analysis, research bioethics is inclusive enough to incorporate genetics ethics, environmental ethics, and neuroethics, among other fields. Bioethics in general would then be the overall subject covering both research bioethics and medical ethics. Despite the differences in philosophical focus between the two, there is a common thread underscoring both life-science research and clinical research that can best be summarized by a famous Hippocratic aphorism: "Life is short, the art long, experience fleeting, experiment perilous, judgment uncertain."[4] Applying appropriate ethical guidelines to science and clinical research can promote our ability to extend the frontiers of scientific and clinical knowledge.

References

Anderson, S. L., et al., "Familial dysautonomia is caused by mutations of the IKAP gene." Am J Hum Genet, 68(3):753-758, 2001.

Barber, A. L. and Foran D. R., "The utility of whole genome amplification for typing compromised forensic samples." J Forensic Sci, 51(6):1344-1349, 2006.

Berger, M. A., "The impact of DNA exonerations on the criminal justice system." J Law Med Ethics, 34(2):320-327, 2006.

Bhuiyan, M. "Imagining the Consequences of Human Biotechnology." Journal of Health Politics, Policy and Law 34: 829-839, 2009.

Callahan, D., "Bioethics: private choice and common good.", Hastings Center Report, 24: 28-31, 1994.

de Melo-Martin, I. "Chimeras and human dignity." Kennedy Inst Ethics J 18(4): 331-346, 2008.

---

[4] Hippocrates. Aphorisms. Available at:
http://classics.mit.edu/Hippocrates/aphorisms.html

Fukuyama, F. (Our posthuman future : consequences of the biotechnology revolution. New York, Farrar, Straus and Giroux, 2002.

Karpowicz, P., C. B. Cohen, et al. "Developing human-nonhuman chimeras in human stem cell research: ethical issues and boundaries." Kennedy Inst Ethics J 15(2): 107-134, 2005.

Kass, L. R. Life, Liberty, and the Defense of Dignity: The Challenge for Bioethics. San Francisco, Encounter Books, 2006.

Loike, J. D. and Tendler, M. D. "Halachic Bioethics Guidelines." Journal of Halacha in Contemporary Society 16: 92-118, 2011.

Macklin, R. "Dignity is a useless concept." BMJ 327(7429): 1419-1420, 2003.

Moore, W., "Application of Modern Moral Theories in Medical Ethics." in Proceedings of the XXII World Congress of Philosophy, 3:69-74, 2012.

Paton, H. J. Caterorical Imperative: A study in Kant's moral philosophy. Philadelphia, University of Pennsulvania Press, 1971.

Post, S., Encyclopedia of Bioethics. New York, Macmillan Press, 2004.

Potter, V. R., "Bioethics for whom?" Ann N Y Acad Sci, 196(4):200-205, 1972.

Rawls, J., A theory of justice., Harvard University Press, 1999.

Soloveitchik, J. B. Halakhic man. Philadelphia, Jewish Publication Society of America. 1983

Seralini, G. E., et al., "New analysis of a rat feeding study with a genetically modified maize reveals signs of hepatorenal toxicity." Arch Environ Contam Toxicol,52(4): 596-602, 2007.

Chapter Four

The Science of Reproductive Cloning

Introduction and History

Cloning can be defined in broad terms as the identical reproduction of fragments of DNA, genes, cells, or whole organisms from a single ancestor. All cells that divide via mitosis engage in a form of cellular cloning. While most plants and animals reproduce via sexual reproduction, some plants and lower animals engage in asexual reproduction, also a form of cloning. In addition, invertebrates, such as earthworms and starfish, can be cloned or regenerate into two complete organisms if cut into two pieces. This unusual property of complete regeneration disappears as one climbs the phylogenetic scale, but some higher vertebrates, such as some lizards, sometimes can regenerate a severed tail or limb.

The history of vertebrate cloning spans over 100 years (McKinnell, 1985). In 1902, Hans Spemann used a strand of hair as a noose to successfully split apart the cells of a two-celled salamander embryo and observed that a normal salamander developed from each individual cell. This was the first recorded instance where scientists could mimic the natural "cloning" that generates identical twins and triplets.

Interestingly, the word "clone" was coined by H. J. Webber (Webber, 1903) a year later to describe a colony of organisms derived asexually from a single progenitor. The term clone stems from the ancient Greek "klon" which is a twig and probably refers to the fact that a twig can give rise to another tree identical to its parent tree. Looking for a word to describe small sections of a plant that can be cut off and transplanted, Webber chose the word "clon" for its uniqueness and easy pronunciation.

The next milestone in vertebrate cloning technology occurred 25 years later when Spemann transferred a nucleus obtained from a cell isolated from a sixteen-cell salamander embryo to another single salamander embryo cell whose nucleus was removed. The enucleated embryo cell fused with the transferred nucleus and developed into a normal salamander. Based on his research, Spemann proposed, what he called, "the fantastic experiment," that involved cloning by nuclear transfer of adult somatic cells. Unfortunately, he was never able to successfully demonstrate nuclear transfer using adult salamander cells.

In the late 1950s, Robert Briggs and Thomas King (Briggs, 1952) used the term clone to describe their efforts to produce a frog species, Rana pipiens that was genetically identical to a parent frog. They used the phrase "nuclear clones" to describe their experiments of transplanting the nucleus from one frog cell to another enucleated cell. However, it wasn't until the 1960s and 70s that John Gurdon (Gurdon, 1962) successfully transplanted the nucleus of frog embryos into enucleated oocytes and stimulated these cells to grow to adulthood. Fifteen years later, Steen Willadsen and Neal First used nuclear transfer to clone

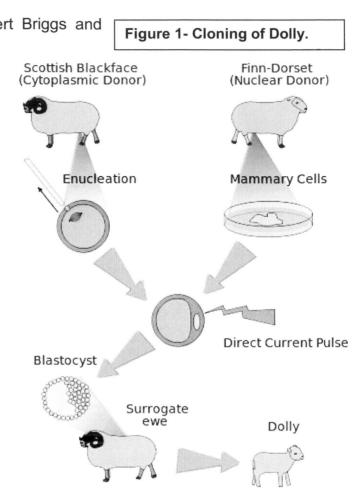

Figure 1- Cloning of Dolly.

sheep and cows from embryonic cells [see (Di Berardino et al., 2003) for a review]. Finally, in 1997, scientists from Roslin Institute in Scotland used nuclear transfer to generate Dolly, the first mammal cloned from a cell obtained from an adult animal (Wilmut et al., 1997). Currently, many different animal species, including dogs, cats, mice, horses, and cows have been cloned using nuclear transfer technology. In 2012, John Gurdon received the Nobel Prize for his work.

In 1970, the ethical and social impacts of cloning were changed dramatically, in part by an influential book by Alvin Toffler called Future Shock. In this book, Toffler predicted "...man will be able to make biological carbon copies of himself." Clones, formerly viewed as the simple progeny of asexual reproduction, were now seen as sophisticated products of biological engineering capable of being used by scientists to control nature for their own agendas. This new perception of cloning became more popular as a result of the publication of a book and movie entitled The Boys from Brazil that depicts the cloning of many copies of Adolph Hitler. The idea that human beings could be cloned set the stage, in part, to foster many debates regarding bioethical issues related to human cloning.

Mechanisms of Asexual Reproduction

Currently, nuclear transfer technology is considered the primary method of human cloning. With this technology the cloned child's nuclear genes come from a cell of a single individual or parent. However, there is another form of asexual reproduction, called parthenogenesis, where all the genetic information is derived from a single individual or parent. Parthenogenesis comes from the Greek word for virgin birth. In biology it describes a form of reproduction in which the ovum develops into a new individual without any fertilization or genetic contribution from a male.

A variety of insects and lower animals can reproduce via parthenogenesis. For example, the queen honeybee mates once and retains the sperm for the rest of her reproductive life. When the queen lays her eggs, she deposits them in different sized receptacles within the wax matrix. Each sized receptacle codes for a different resulting offspring. The smaller cells, about 5 mm in diameter, contain fertilized eggs that are destined to become sterile female workers. The larger cells, about 7 mm in diameter, contain future male drones. These eggs are not fertilized, and reproduce via parthenogenesis, in which the polar body generated during oocyte meiosis fuses with the egg restoring a complete set of chromosomes (diploid).

Usually, at the time of fertilization, and in particular human fertilization, the egg is in the middle of meiosis (Text Box 1) and only completes the second round meiotic division with release of the second polar body after fertilization. In parthenogenesis, this second polar body can act like a sperm and re-enter or fuse with the egg. Essentially, the egg fertilizes itself! The second polar body is produced by normal division of an already haploid cell and therefore contains genetic material identical to the egg. Thus, the outcome of parthenogenesis is a resulting diploid cell with the same or similar genetic makeup, i.e., a clone, as the female parent. Genetic differences between the parent and offspring may arise due to imprinting processes (Zhang and Meaney, 2010).

Dolly, the First Mammal Cloned From Adult Cells

In science, credit often goes to the man who convinces the world, not the man to whom the idea first occurs (Darwin, 1914). As stated above, nuclear transfer experiments began in the beginning of the 1900s. Yet, it wasn't until the birth of Dolly was announced in 1997 by Dr. Ian Wilmut, Schnieke, and colleagues, (Wilmut et al., 1997) that government and religious leaders throughout the world began raising ethical concerns about human cloning. Dr. Wilmut at Roslin

Textbox 1- Meiosis

Meiosis is a process by which germ cells (eggs and sperm) are produced. In normal cell division, or mitosis, every chromosome is first duplicated, and then one copy of every chromosome is drawn to each end of the cell. When the cell divides, each daughter cell contains exactly the same genetic complement as the parent cell. Meiosis, on the other hand, is a two-stage process, which ultimately produces four cells. In the first division the chromosomes are not duplicated; rather, the homologous chromosomes line up together and one from each pair is drawn to opposite ends of the cell. The resulting daughter cells now contain only half the genetic material of the parent and are called haploid cells. The second stage of meiosis proceeds similarly to normal cell division where each chromosome is duplicated before division occurs. Thus, meiosis produces four haploid cells, two of them containing one half of the parent's original DNA and the other two the remaining half. In the female, three of these four cells contain predominantly the genetic material. The majority of the cytoplasm is retained by the fourth cell, which becomes the egg. The other three cells, called polar bodies, are generally reabsorbed into the female's body. In humans the dissociation of the second polar body from the egg only occurs after fertilization. Thus, the human oocyte is never technically haploid whereas human sperm is.

Institute in Scotland who headed the team to clone Dolly stated that their research was focused solely on animal cloning and not human cloning. The primary objective of Dr. Wilmut and his team was to develop a new technology called "pharming" where expensive drugs (like insulin or tissue plasminogen activator) could be produced, inexpensively, in the milk of sheep (see Textbox 2).

Dolly was cloned from the frozen mammary epithelial cells of a white ewe that had died six years earlier. The oocytes used in these experiments were obtained from a black sheep. Dr. Wilmut, it is said, named Dolly after his favorite country music singer Dolly Parton. This landmark paper triggered scientists all over the world to attempt to use nuclear transfer to clone a variety of animals.

While the journal Nature published the cloning of Dolly, the scientists and the editors at Nature recognized the bioethical issues that this technology would elicit and allegedly omitted the term cloning from the title of this landmark publication. They called cloning in their paper somatic cell nuclear transfer (SCNT). Nonetheless, newspapers all over the world reported this discovery within the framework of cloning.

Textbox 2: Advantages of pharming

Pharming is the production of human pharmaceuticals in farm animals. Some proteins can only be produced in large mammals (Melo, et al., 2007). Their chemical structure is so complex that it is not possible to produce them in cell culture or in bacteria. For example, *Factor IX*, an enzyme important in clotting and needed by hemophiliacs, normally is obtained from human blood plasma. Supplies are limited and expensive. The current strategy to achieve these objectives in pharming, is to transfer a modified gene that encodes for the protein that contains a DNA sequence that directs the production of this protein to the mammary gland. In this way the mammary gland of these animals will synthesize and secrete the protein only in the milk. Since the mammary gland and milk are essentially "outside" the main life support systems of the animal, there is virtually no danger that the protein will leak into the blood system of the cow or generate an immune reaction. There two major advantages of using large mammals to produce proteins in their milk. First, it will be economically cheaper than using cell culture technology and second, this system reduces the risk of transmitting infectious agents to the patients which is a major concern in those cases where the proteins are obtained from donated human blood. Sheep producing Factor IX in large quantities have now been born. Pharmed animals produce large quantities of proteins in their milk. In fact, *Bio Sidus*, an Argentinean company, claimed to produce transgenic cows that could produce enough insulin in their milk to supply over 1 million diabetics (http://presszoom.com/story_130779.html). Milk is not the only product for pharming. Currently, studies are utilizing chicken eggs as another source to produce proteins. The advantage of chickens is that their gestational period is in weeks rather than in months, and they are cheaper to maintain and breed than cows.

Currently, some of the proteins being testing for commercialization in pharming include tissue plasminogen activator (used in treating heart attacks), Factors XIII and IX (treatment for hemophiliacs), and Human Protein C (an anticoagulant).

Why was Dolly a Scientific Breakthrough?

For developmental biologists, Dolly's existence challenged several fundamental tenets of their field. Before Dolly, conventional scientific wisdom dictated that differentiation, the gradual process of specialization that allows the fertilized egg to develop into the hundreds of cell types that make up the entire animal, was an irreversible process. It was believed that once a cell differentiates into a specific liver or nerve cell it remains committed to that cell type for the life span of the organism. In differentiated cells, DNA methylation[1] is one of several post-synthetic modifications (epigenetics) that generally results in gene silencing and, in turn, serves as a critical factor in gene regulation. The production of a live lamb from a differentiated mammary cell demonstrated that differentiated cells are not immutably committed to one cell type. In other words, the genes essential for embryonic development that were silent or methylated in the mammary cells could be turned on again to initiate embryological development. Wilmut's remarkable scientific breakthrough demonstrated that the oocyte has the capacity to reprogram adult cell DNA or to reactivate these silent genes, and proved that differentiation was a reversible process. In this manner, Wilmut's study disproved a "dogma" in the area of cellular dedifferentiation.

The second scientific breakthrough that emerged from cloning Dolly was that her telomeres were significantly longer than telomeres obtained from the six year old sheep. Telomeres, a Greek word for "the part at the end," are specialized regions at the tip of chromosomes that serve both as a molecular bookend and a cellular clock. They are made from DNA replications patched and folded with specific proteins. Functional telomeres protect the ends of chromosomes from being recognized as DNA double-strand breaks that could otherwise trigger damage responses such as cell-cycle arrest or apoptosis. Telomeres shorten during each cycle of cell division, providing a counting mechanism to limit the number of times a cell can divide. Once telomeres reach specific shorter lengths, they trigger apoptosis or programmed cell death. In certain aggressive tumors the telomeres grow longer after each cell division, providing a possibly mechanism for how these cells continue to proliferate in an unregulated manner.

Theoretically, one would expect the length of telomeres of the cloned animal to be equal to that of the telomeres found in the donor cell using in nuclear transfer. However, research with cloned calves showed that telomere rebuilding occurs during embryonic development and is critical for successful nuclear transfer. Thus, Dolly and other cloned mammals expressed rebuilt telomeres during the process of nuclear transfer. In certain cloned animals, telomere length was not only restored but extended beyond that of the donor cell (Wakayama et al., 2000).

---

[1] DNA methylation is a type of chemical modification of DNA that can be either inherited or subsequently removed without changing the original DNA sequence.

Figure 2. Telomere location on chromosomes (from NIH.gov image library)

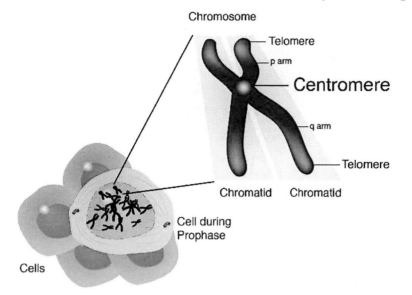

A final aspect of cloning relates to the origins of DNA replication. In embryonic cells, there are many more sites for replication than are found in somatic cells. The huge size of the nucleus of early embryonic cells is thought to provide a platform or scaffolding necessary to support more places where DNA replications can begin, thereby allowing the DNA to replicate quickly. It is unclear how the oocyte can reprogram and rapidly replicate DNA from adult cells used in nuclear transfer technology.

What were the Technological Innovations in Cloning Dolly?

Dr. Wilmut's innovation in cloning Dolly was to synchronize the cell cycles of the donor and recipient material through serum deprivation. Serum deprivation restricts the flow of nutrients to the donor cells and slows the normally active DNA replication process, thereby allowing the oocyte more time to reprogram the DNA. Without nutrient deprivation, cell division in the donor cell would occur too rapidly and the recipient oocyte would not have sufficient time to reprogram the DNA without making fatal mistakes in cell division. These DNA mistakes would, in turn, generate nonviable embryos.

Therefore, extreme care must be employed when handling the oocyte and nucleus for cloning experiments. The recipient oocyte is prepared by drawing out its DNA containing nucleus via micropipettes. The donor cell is prepared by retrieving the nucleus in a sterile pipette and discarding the rest of the cell. The next step is transferring the nucleus in between the outer region of the egg known as the zona pellucida and the plasma membrane and then subjecting this cell mixture to gentle bursts of alternating current. This treatment perforates the nuclear membrane of the donor and the inner membrane of the egg. Finally, direct current electrical pulses are administered to simultaneously fuse the nucleus and oocyte together.

The origin of Dolly's mitochondrial DNA was one critical piece of information omitted from in the original paper. While Dr. Wilmut's group clearly proved that the nuclear genome of Dolly was identical to the nuclear genome of the adult donor mammary cell, there was no information regarding the cellular source of Dolly's mitochondrial DNA.

In normal embryos, only about 0.1% of the total genetic material comes from the mitochondria found in the cytoplasm of the egg. Yet, the genetic information encoded in mitochondria is critical. Spontaneous or acquired mutations in mitochondrial DNA are believed to play an important role in the aging process and neurological pathways. In normal fertilization, the mitochondrial genes are maternally transmitted and the sperm mitochondria are destroyed. In 1999, Drs. Eric Schon and John Loike (Evans et al., 1999) compared the genetic sequences of Dolly's mitochondria with both her donor cells and recipient oocyte and showed that Dolly was not a true genetic clone since her mitochondrial DNA came from the oocyte and not the donor cell.

The success of cloning mice using nuclear transfer technology was initially extremely low. In the Wilmut experiment, 277 nuclear fusions were attempted and 12% of the zygotes achieved blastocyst stage. Of these, only 3% achieved the fetus stage, 2% (five) became live lambs, and only one survived—Dolly. The overall rate of success was about 0.4%.

Dr. Teruhiko Wakayama's group in 1999 (Wakayama et al., 1999) refined Wilmut's technique and improved the success rate in mice by separating the fusion and activation processes. First, the donor nucleus was placed inside the yolk sac of the recipient. Then, 1-6 hrs later, activation was achieved by putting the cell in a chemical bath that mimicked the acrosomal milieu of fertilization. Their method improved the success rate five-fold to an overall rate of 2% versus the original 0.4% for Dolly's research team. In 2006 the success rate for nuclear transfer in mice only reached 5% (Kishigami et al., 2006). The low frequency of successful cloning is not surprising since over 70% of all human conceptions either fail to implant or result in spontaneous miscarriages due to chromosomal abnormality. Although SCNT is more efficient in cattle than in any other species tested so far, a 2007 paper reported that over a 5-year period, only 9% of the

SCNT embryos transferred to recipients resulted in the birth of a live calf (Panarace et al. 2007).

The low success rate in cloning is thought to be related to reprogramming the DNA (Bowles et al., 2007; Fulka and Fulka, 2007). In order for the fertilized egg to begin normal embryological development, the DNA and histones (specific proteins associated with DNA) of the fertilized egg must be reprogrammed to remove epigenetic modifications (chemical changes in the phenotype without changing the genotype). Acetylation and methylation of histones and DNA cytosine residues are part of the complex epigenetic regulatory process that must be erased.

In normal fertilization, the oocyte is designed to reprogram the sperm's genome. Only a few hours after fertilization, the DNA in the sperm-derived pronucleus of the mouse, human, pig, and often in cows, rapidly demethylates. In the mouse, in the next few cleavage divisions, cytosine methylation that remains on maternally inherited DNA is almost completely abolished. The low efficiency of animal cloning and the increased birth defects observed in cloned animals (see below) are thought to be related to the oocyte's difficulty in reprogramming adult donor DNA during somatic cell nuclear transfer. Some scientists speculate the low success rate is due to the fact that we are forcing a somatic cell to turn into a gamete in a manner of hours while normally this process takes months (Jaenisch and Wilmut, 2001). Other scientists report that cellular dedifferentiation leads to genetic variation, genome instability and consequently to cell death (Grafi, 2009).

New techniques are being tested to improve the efficiency of SCNT and reduce birth defects in the cloned animals. For example, the reproductive cloning efficiency using embryonic stem cells is five to ten times higher than using somatic adult cells as donors. In addition, gene-expression profiles characteristic of early embryonic development are seen more often in chromatin transfer versus nuclear transfer. In chromatin transfer technology, donor cells are treated with streptolysin, a protein that makes membranes more permeable, which in turn makes the chromatin more accessible to mitotic factors from the oocyte (Sullivan et al., 2004). However, a direct comparison between nuclear transfer and chromatin transfer will be required to fully assess the merit of each technique.

Reproductive Versus Therapeutic Cloning

Since Wilmut's report on cloning Dolly, cloning has been subdivided into two types, reproductive cloning and research cloning. In reproductive cloning an embryo is implanted into a pseudo-pregnant animal[2] and is used to generate an animal that has the same nuclear DNA as another currently or previously existing animal. The second process, called research or therapeutic cloning, is used to generate embryonic stem cells, without ever implanting the embryo into a female host. The SCNT generated zygote is incubated for several days to the blastocyst stage and then stem cells are isolated and allowed to proliferate. To achieve identical genetic backgrounds (from both nuclear and mitochondrial DNA) in human research cloning, the oocyte must be obtained from the same person or mother or grandmother of the donor cell. Achieving an identical genetic background (excluding imprinting or epigenetics) is a critical milestone to achieve since its application in medicine requires the patient receiving the stem cells not to immunologically reject the donor stem cells.

The goal of research cloning is not to create cloned human beings, but rather to harvest stem cells that can be used to study human development and to treat disease. This is not the only method to generate patient specific stem cells. Adult stem cells and iPS technology (see chapter 6) can also be employed for therapeutic cloning. The use of non-embryonic cells for cloning is a vital bioethical issue that will be discussed in Chapters 6 and 7.

Human Reproductive Cloning

Rhesus monkeys have been reported to be cloned via nuclear transfer using embryonic cells and have shown no developmental or physiological abnormalities. Until 2006, nuclear transfer using adult cells to generate primates had not been accomplished. The difficulty in using adult cells for nuclear transfer in primates was thought to be a difference in mitotic spindle organization between primates and other mammals. In primate cells, spindle-forming proteins, which act as molecular motors, attach to chromatin and are not readily available to participate in cell division. In non - primate cells the spindle proteins remain detached and effectively participate in cell division. Thus, cell division in a cloned primate cell is associated with a random mix of chromosomes, rather than the ordered separation of chromosomes.

In 2004 and 2005, a group of South Korean scientists announced the first successful nuclear transfer of adult human cells with an enucleated human oocyte (Hwang et al., 2004; Hwang et al., 2005). Their goal was not to develop protocols for human reproductive cloning. Rather, they wanted to apply nuclear transfer technology to generate human embryonic stem cells for use in research cloning. Unfortunately, their research was fraudulent. One may speculate that a

---

[2] An animal that has been injected with hormones to allow her to accept a fertilized egg.

complete investigation of their research activities might one day uncover meaningful data that would benefit future attempts in applying nuclear transfer to human oocytes. Still, achieving human stem cells via nuclear transfer technology using adult cells is quite difficult. In 2008, scientists first reported that SCNT can produce human blastocyst-stage embryos using nuclei obtained from differentiated adult cells (French et al., 2008). In May 2013, Shoukhrat Mitalipov and his colleagues at the Oregon Health and Science University published a milestone article describing the use of IVF technology to transfer genetic material from any non-sperm cell into a human egg (_Tachibana, Amato et al. 2013_). Dr. Shoukhrat Mitalipov and his colleagues successfully fused the nucleus obtained from a baby's skin cell and applied SCNT technology to generate human blastocyst from which they could isolate and maintain human embryonic stem cells. The technical modifications presented in this paper are noteworthy for several reasons. First, previous attempts in applying SNCT to human oocytes failed because premature completion of meiosis occurred during the process resulting in the subsequent loss of the capacity of the oocyte to reprogram somatic cells to a pluripotent state. In their procedure the authors, added caffeine to the culture medium to slow meiotic completion and facilitate the differentiation of the oocytes into blastocysts. Second, the authors discovered that using fetal cells as the source for donor nuclei improved the success of SCNT. Finally, the authors reported that oocytes obtained from women who produced fewer mature oocytes in response to hormonal stimulation were better suited for SCNT than oocytes obtained from women who generated many mature oocytes.The scientific motivation by Dr. Shoukhrat Mitalipov to apply SCNT to human beings was not to clone a human being. Rather, it was to obtain patient-derived embryonic stem cell lines that can be used to study and potentially treat various human diseases. In fact, their group chose to generate stem cells from a patient with a genetic defect called Leigh syndrome.[3] These embryonic stem cells derived from the baby with Leigh syndrome will be used to considering various types of therapeutic stem cell repair without the fear of transplant rejection because they will be obtained from the patient. This type of stem cell application to specific patients could lead to important future treatments for neurodegenerative diseases such as Parkinson's, Huntington's, ALS and Alzheimer's as well as heart and liver diseases.

---

[3] Leigh syndrome is a severe genetic neurological disorder that typically arises in the first year of life. This condition is characterized by progressive loss of movement and mental functions and results in death within a couple of years.

Health Risks Associated with Reproductive Cloning

Since there has been no reported generation of a human clone using nuclear transfer, it has been difficult to assess the medical risks the technology would pose in humans (Lane, 2006). The only available data come from animal studies. For example, cloning experiments on mice show damage to immune systems, increased risk of death from pneumonia, increased development of tumors, liver failure, spontaneous abortions, and abnormal births. Notably, out of 12 cloned mice born- apparently healthy at birth, only two lived out a normal life span of 800 days. In cattle, cloning is associated with a high rate of abortion and stillborn births. Even Dolly developed arthritis prematurely as well as a type of lung disease prevalent in older sheep. In summary, cloned animals exhibit a wide variety of medical abnormalities and defects that depends, in part, on the species being cloned.

Unfortunately, the medical problems observed in cloned animals may be difficult to apply to humans for several reasons. First, there may be differences in embryological development between humans and animals. For example, small blebs (protrusions) of plasma membrane-enclosed cytoplasm are associated with early human embryo cleavages. This process is called fragmentation and is not as common in mouse embryos. Second, scientists have more experience culturing human embryos than culturing animal embryos. In vitro fertilization technology is over 25 years old and has provided tremendous experience in maintaining human embryos in culture. Third, IVF specialists have developed more rigorous screening criteria in selection of the human embryos versus animal embryos for implantation.

Benefits of Reproductive Cloning Research

While research in reproductive cloning may yield medical benefits, most countries around the world have banned this procedure. For example, reproductive cloning may present a viable treatment for infertility by allowing certain infertile couples to have children. A heterosexual couple in which the husband was completely sterile because he could not produce sperm could use adult nuclear cloning to produce a genetically related child. An ovum from the wife of this couple would be fused with a skin cell from the husband, enabling both partners to contribute genetic information to the child. The wife would provide genetic information from her donated mitochondria and the husband would provide genetic information from his donated nucleus. This process is likely to be more satisfactory for the couple than using sperm from another man. The process would also allow female lesbian couples to elect to have a child by

SCNT rather than by artificial insemination by a man's sperm. Each of the women would then contribute to the fertilized ovum: one would donate the ovum, and the other the nuclear genetic material. Both would have the satisfaction of knowing a part of each woman was involved in the conception. There are other social or medical reasons that support reproductive cloning:

1. Parents who want to have a child who is a perfect bone marrow match for another family member suffering from cancer.
2. Parents who want to "replace" a dying child or loved one. Interestingly, the first cloned cat, named "Copy Cat", and Dolly were cloned using cells that were frozen after the donor animals had died. This suggests that it may be possible to obtain cells right after death to use immediately or to freeze cells for future use.
3. A woman who prefers to have one set of identical twins, rather than undergo two separate pregnancies in order to have two children. She might prefer this to minimize disruption to her career or to make a normal vaginal delivery possible because twin fetuses are usually smaller than a single fetus.
4. A woman who prefers to have twin children so that one could contribute an organ, such as a kidney, to the other if ever necessary.

Commercial Applications of Cloning

SCNT technology has applications in the preservation of specific animal species. For example, Genetic Savings & Clone was a leader of the emerging pet cloning field and offered gene banking for cats and dogs as well as wild and/or endangered relatives of cats and dogs. Cloning a cat or dog for tens of thousands of dollars may not sound commercially or socially viable, and one could argue that the millions of strays euthanized in the United States each year need homes more. Interestingly, this company closed its doors in 2006. As of 2009, Viagen appears to be the principle company that is cloning pets and livestock commercially. As of 2009, Viagen Inc. and Trans Ova Genetics already have produced more than 600 cloned animals for U.S. breeders, including copies of prize-winning cows and rodeo bulls. The commercial incentives from this technology may be dramatic since some of these animals are worth hundreds of thousands of dollars.

There are other possible commercial benefits associated with animal cloning. Creating transgenic animals is also a major technology used in both academic and commercial science. A transgenic animal is one that carries a foreign gene that has been deliberately inserted into its genome. The foreign gene is constructed using recombinant DNA methodology. There are two classical methods to generate transgenic animals. The first involves transfecting (i.e., introducing sequences of DNA into cells by non-viral methods) embryonic stem cells with the desired gene construct, and then injecting those stem cells into the inner mass of a blastocyst and lastly, implanting it into the uterus of a mouse. Foster mice are then tested for the presence of the gene and heterozygous offspring are mated to produce homozygous transgenic strains.

The second method is to inject the DNA construct into a pronucleus of the fertilized egg and then implant that into the uterus and test the offspring for the presence of the gene. Nuclear transfer technology cell culture techniques may be a more efficient method for inserting the DNA construct into a cell line and fusing it with an enucleated oocyte.

Sometimes it is easier to work with adult cells than with embryonic stem cells. As discussed above, transgenic farm animals generated by nuclear transfer technology are used in pharming—they are engineered to produce specific therapeutic proteins in their milk (Bauman et al., 2006). There are over 10 drug products being produced and evaluated using pharming. In early 2009, the FDA approved an anticoagulant protein, human anti-thrombin, that is produced in goat's milk to treat a hereditary disorder and marked the culmination of a meandering 15-year journey for GTC Bio therapeutics, a spin-off of the biotech giant Genzyme. Other research centers and companies, such as Roslin Institute, are trying to use SCNT to direct the production of therapeutic proteins in chicken eggs. Using transgenic chickens may offer certain advantages over sheep or cows. First, it takes less than a year to generate a transgenic chicken that produces the desired protein such as insulin in its eggs. Second, the egg white is contained in the sterile environment of the eggshell; thus, the therapeutic protein is maintained in a sterile state until the shell is broken as it enters the purification process. Finally, it is relatively easy and inexpensive to develop chicken farms for commercial production.

Transgenic animals also can serve as important animal models for diseases. For example, normal mice cannot be infected with the polio virus. They lack the cell-surface molecule that, in humans, serves as the receptor for the virus. Transgenic mice, however, expressing the human gene for the polio virus receptor, can serve as an animal model to study the effects of polio virus and as a screen to test for new therapeutics.   Nuclear transfer also can be used to produce transgenic pigs for xenotransplantation, (the use of organs from other animals). Although organ transplants have helped thousands of people, there is still a scarcity of organ donors and the need to develop methods to prevent tissue rejection.   A number of attempts at xenotransplantation have been made to use hearts, livers, and kidneys from primates such as chimpanzees and baboons but with limited success rates. One reason is that xenotransplants are usually attacked immediately by antibodies of the host resulting in hyper-acute rejection. Transgenic pigs represent an interesting source for organ donation because their organs are about the right size for use in humans. Transgenic technology could be used to remove the genes responsible for the production of those cell surface proteins that trigger immune rejection. However, pigs contain retroviruses (called PERV = porcine endogenous retrovirus) and there are fears that these might infect the human recipient in much the same way that a primate retrovirus seems to have made the jump to humans in the form of human immunodeficiency virus. Only a few transplants of pig tissue into humans have been done to date: skin grafts, heart valves, and grafts of pancreatic islets. Most of these recipients have been monitored for signs of infection by PERV and — even though PERV can infect human cells growing in culture — there is no evidence that any of the patients exposed to pig tissue have become infected (See chapter 8).

Applications of Cloning to Genetic Anthropology

Cloning Technology is improving at a rapid pace. In 2009-2010, scientific breakthroughs in genomics, presented a unique opportunity to examine the origins of the human species. The Neanderthal Genome Project, initiated in 2005, aspired to sequence the Neanderthal genome from fossilized Neanderthal bones that are tens of thousands of years old (Noonan et al., 2006; Noonan, 2010). Using new technologies, such as metagenomic approaches, it will be possible to recover significant amounts of Neanderthal genomic DNA with high-throughput sequencing to comprehensively characterize all sequences present in a sample and the origins of each sequence by comparison to known genomes (Tringe and Rubin, 2005). Another technology, multiplex automated genome engineering (MAGE), is being developed to change millions of base pairs of the human genome in order to create a cell line containing a Neanderthal genome (Wang et al., 2009; Winters et al., 2011). It would be theoretically possible to then create stem cells composed of the Neanderthal genome and use these cells to generate gamete-like cells to produce a Neanderthal zygote for implantation into a human surrogate.

Generating a Neanderthal like primate could be extremely useful in enhancing our evolutionary roots and how Homo sapiens differ, neurologically, from our anthropological ancestors. This type of technology could be applied to any ancestorial species where its genome can be sequence and would open a new vista in evolutionary biology. Yet, the ethical ramifications of such a project are highly controversial (Marcus, 2012).

Generating Human Embryos From Multiple Parents

As mentioned above (pg 58) Dr. Mitalipov published a milestone paper

regarding the use of SCNT to generate human embryonic stem cells. While Dr. Mitalipov and his colleagues claim that their SCNT technology is not designed to clone human beings, their technology does in fact have the potential to be used human blastocyst into a woman to create a human embryo. What is significant is that a variety of cell sources aside from sperm and eggs can be theoretically fused with an egg obtained from a woman to create a human embryo. One of many potential outcomes of this research is the ability to create a human embryo without any male genetic contribution—by transferring the nucleus from one woman into an enucleated egg of another woman—or to create an embryo from even more than three genetic parents—by merging multiple embryos into a single chimeric infant, as has already been achieved in rhesus monkeys (Tachibana, et al., 2012). The ethical ramifications of this technology will be discussed in Chapter 12.

Conclusions

Nuclear transfer technology can be used to generate a genetic copy of an animal, a person or for therapeutic cloning. As of 2012, nuclear transfer technology has been performed in over 20 different species. This chapter focused on the underlying science of reproductive cloning. Chapters 6 and 7 will focus more on stem cells and therapeutic cloning. Nuclear transfer technology is rapidly developing to be applied in both animals and people. While the South Korean scientists did not actually successfully apply nuclear transfer to human oocytes, their fraud will probably stimulate the race to achieve therapeutic cloning in humans. The ethical concerns of this potential technology will be presented in the next chapter.

Creative Bioethics challenges

What experiments would you design to examine why nuclear transfer technology is so difficult to perform using human cells?

Can you suggest other methods to generate human clones besides the classical nuclear transfer technology?

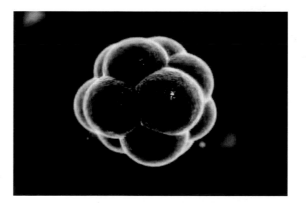

Figure 3: Morula

References

Bauman, D. E., et al., "Major advances associated with the biosynthesis of milk." J Dairy Sci, 89(4):1235-43, 2006.

Bowles, E. J., et al., "Nuclear transfer: preservation of a nuclear genome at the expense of its associated mtDNA genome(s)." Curr Top Dev Biol, 77:251-90, 2007.

Briggs, R., and King., T.J. "Transplantation of Living Nuclei from Blastula cells into Enucleated Frog' eggs." Proc Natl Acad Sci, U S A 38:455-463, 1952.

Darwin, S. F., Eugenics Review, April 1914, 1014.

Di Berardino, M. A., et al., "The golden anniversary of cloning: a celebratory essay." Differentiation, 71(7):398-401, 2003.

Evans, M. J., et al., "Mitochondrial DNA genotypes in nuclear transfer-derived cloned sheep." Nat Genet, 23(1):90-3, 1999.

French, A. J., et al., "Development of human cloned blastocysts following somatic cell nuclear transfer with adult fibroblasts." Stem Cells, 26(2):485-93, 2008.

Fulka, J., Jr. and Fulka, H., "Somatic cell nuclear transfer (SCNT) in mammals: the cytoplast and its reprogramming activities." Adv Exp Med Biol, 591:93-102, 2007.

Grafi, G., "The complexity of cellular dedifferentiation: implications for regenerative medicine." Trends Biotechnol, 27:329-332, 2009.

Gurdon, J. B., The developmental capacity of nuclei taken from intestinal epithelium cells of feeding tadpoles." J. Embryol. Exp. Morphol, 34:93-112, 1962.

Hwang, W. S., et al., "Patient-specific embryonic stem cells derived from human SCNT blastocysts." Science, 308(5729):1777-83, 2005.

Hwang, W. S., et al., "Evidence of a pluripotent human embryonic stem cell line derived from a cloned blastocyst." Science, 303(5664):1669-74, 2004.

Jaenisch, R. and Wilmut, I., "Developmental biology. Don't clone humans!" Science, 291(5513):2552, 2001.

Kishigami, S., et al., "Production of cloned mice by somatic cell nuclear transfer." Nat Protoc, 1(1):125-38, 2006.

Lane, R., "Safety, identity and consent: a limited defense of reproductive human cloning." Bioethics, 20(3):125-35, 2006.

Marcus, A., The ethics of human cloning in narrative fiction. comparative literature studies, 49 : 405-433, 2012.

McKinnell, R. G., Cloning: Of frogs, mice and other animals. University of Minnesota Press, Minneapolis, USA, 1985.

Melo, E. O., et al., "Animal transgenesis: state of the art and applications." J Appl Genet, 48(1):47-61, 2007.

Noonan, J. P., "Neanderthal genomics and the evolution of modern humans." Genome Res, 20(5):547-53, 2010.

Noonan, J. P., et al., "Sequencing and analysis of Neanderthal genomic DNA." Science, 314(5802):1113-8, 2006.

Panarace, M., et al., "How healthy are clones and their progeny: 5 years of field experience." Theriogenology, 67(1):142-51, 2007.

Sullivan, E. J., et al., "Cloned calves from chromatin remodeled in vitro." Biol Reprod 70(1):146-53, 2004.

Tachibana M, et al. "Generation of chimeric rhesus monkeys". Cell 148(1-2):285-95, 2012.

Tachibana, M., et al., "Human Embryonic Stem Cells Derived by Somatic Cell Nuclear Transfer" Cell, **153**:1228–1238, 2013.

Tringe, S. G. and Rubin, E. M., "Metagenomics: DNA sequencing of environmental samples." Nat Rev Genet, 6(11):805-14, 2005.

Wakayama, T., et al., "Mice cloned from embryonic stem cells." Proc Natl Acad Sci U S A, 96(26):14984-9, 1999.

Wakayama, T., et al., "Cloning of mice to six generations." Nature, 407(6802):318-9, 2000.

Wang, H. H., et al., "Programming cells by multiplex genome engineering and accelerated evolution." Nature, 460(7257):894-8, 2009.

Webber, H. J., "New horticultural and agricultural terms." Science 28:501-503, 1903.

Wilmut, I., et al., Viable offspring derived from fetal and adult mammalian cells. Nature, 385:810-813, 1997.

Winters, M., et al., "To clone or not to clone: method analysis for retrieving consensus sequences in ancient DNA samples.", PloS One, 6, e21247, 2011.

Zhang, T.Y. & Meaney, M.J., "Epigenetics and the environmental regulation of the genome and its function.", Annu Rev Psychol, 61:439-466, C431-433, 2010.

Chapter Five

Bioethics of Reproductive Cloning:
Patenting a Designer Human Being

Introduction

Somatic cell nuclear transfer technology (SCNT) can be used for either reproductive or therapeutic/research cloning. As discussed in the previous chapter, reproductive cloning is generating an exact genetic copy using a donor cell and the enucleated oocyte obtained from the same individual, (oocytes may also be obtained from the donor's mother, sister, or grandmother). Since mitochondrial DNA comes from the oocyte, obtaining an enucleated oocyte for nuclear transfer from any donor other than a maternal relative will result in progeny that is not an exact genetic clone because the individual would possess nuclear DNA identical to the donor cell and mitochondrial DNA identical to the oocyte. Although mitochondrial DNA represents less than 1% of the total DNA of a cell, it contains critical information regarding the energetics of a cell. Another problem with generating an exact genetic clone using SCNT is gene expression variation related to epigenetic instability.[1] This is why identical twins may have the same genetic information but are not precisely identical in behavior, health, and even physical traits.

There are various situations that elicit profound ethical debates related directly to reproductive cloning. The most obvious is cloning a human being. In addition, to employing SCNT to generate embryos from multiple parental donors, this procedure can be used in other potentially ethically challenging ways. In a recent cloning experiment, Dr. Inoue and colleagues obtained a female mouse from an immature (male) Sertoli cell.[2] This 'male-derived female' clone grew into a normal adult and produced offspring by natural mating (Inoue K, et al., 2009). Although this was an accidental phenomenon arising from a sex chromosomal error, the result unequivocally suggests the possibility of producing females from male donor animals if the techniques of sex chromosome manipulation are sufficiently well developed. The ethical outcome of these debates is highly

---

[1] epigenetics effects refers to changes in gene expression that are not determined primarily by the underlying DNA sequence.
[2] A Sertoli cell is a 'nurse' cell obtained from the testes that is part of a seminiferous tubule.

significant since it will determine how various governments either support or ban its cloning research and clinical applications.

Academic Arguments Against Human Reproductive Cloning

Current research in animals indicates that the success rate of reproductive cloning is quite low; therefore, many fertilized zygotes or embryos will be destroyed or discarded during any attempts in human beings. While chapter four provided some scientific reasons to support research in reproductive cloning, there are at least two cultural or morality-based arguments and three science-based arguments against it.

Cultural and Moral Arguments

The first morality-based argument against reproductive cloning is the belief that life begins at conception and that all human beings possess intrinsic and unique value from the moment of conception. Those individuals advancing this argument oppose human cloning on the grounds that human zygotes and embryos, whether generated by cloning technology or in vitro fertilization, deserve "full moral respect." They support the view that, as in "natural fertilization," a cloned embryo produces a new and complete human organism whose development into a child follows a genetic-based cellular protocol. These human embryos possess a unique genome and the epigenetic primordial for self-directed growth into adulthood. Since SCNT involves the destruction of many pre-implanted embryos in order to generate one viable organism, opponents of reproductive cloning believe there should be a ban on reproductive and therapeutic cloning research to prevent these necessary losses of pre-implanted and implanted embryos that are considered as viable or potential human beings.

The second morality-based argument for banning reproductive cloning is that this technology is artificial, unnatural, and beyond the ethical boundaries of human experimentation. Thus, reproductive cloning is immoral because human beings should not "play God" or tamper with nature in an inappropriate manner.

Scientific Arguments Against Human Cloning

From a scientific or medical perspective, reproductive cloning is associated with a high medical risk and potential dangers inherent in the SCNT process. Opponents of reproductive cloning cite the many animal studies that associate reproductive cloning with many harmful side-effects, such as a dramatic increase in spontaneous miscarriages during various stages of fetal development, as well as birth defects in the new born animals. Cloning experiments in animals also document increased damage to the immune system, risk of death from pneumonia, development of tumors, and risk of liver failure. Almost half of all cloned animals suffer from a condition known as *Large Offspring Syndrome* (LOS) which can cause terminal problems including enlarged placentas, fatty livers, and underdeveloped vital organs. In addition, some cloned animals (especially mice) may appear healthy at birth, but in fact have a reduced life expectancy as compared to animals generated by natural reproductive processes. While there is no clear data on the potential medical risks of reproductive cloning in human beings, many opponents of reproductive cloning believe that the high risks in animals are a valid indicator for similar high risks in humans.

There are also reported risks to animals carrying cloned fetuses. For example, animal welfare organizations point to the fact that even the Food and Drug Administration's report in 2007, just prior to their approval of using cloned farm animals for food, have found that "weak or non-existent uterine contractions, poor mammary development and failure to lactate" in animals carrying cloned fetuses.[3]

The second science-based argument presented by opponents to human reproductive cloning is psychological in nature. Opponents argue that cloning is a threat to human individuality. Normal human reproduction is designed to combine genetic elements from two parents to form a single progeny. In contrast, reproductive cloning can generate an identical or a nearly identical DNA- copy of one parent, which could create a great psychic burden on the cloned child. Opponents of reproductive cloning believe that children should be valued for how they develop as individuals, not according to how closely they meet their parents' genetic expectations. In other words, each child has a right to naturally obtain a unique set of genetic information. A child born as a genetic copy of another may endure undue pressure to become either like or unlike his or her progenitor. Reproductive cloning technology has the potential to engage in designing babies based on gender preference, appearance, athletic potential, or behavioral characteristic, rather than health.

Designing babies for purposes of vanity could affect the nature of the family unit and parent-child relationships and in turn the psychological pressures of the cloned child. Anti-reproductive cloning bioethicists supporting this argument cite studies showing that natural identical twins may exhibit increased psychological problems related to their inability to define their unique individuality (Sutcliffe and Derom, 2006).

---

[3] http://www.fda.gov/AnimalVeterinary/SafetyHealth/AnimalCloning/ucm124840.htm.

The third science-based issue is that reproductive cloning presents a moral hazard detrimental to the diversity of the human population as a whole. Leon Kass, a leading detractor of many new forms of reproductive technology, proposed that reproductive cloning is "the first step toward a eugenic world in which children become objects of manipulation and products of will."[4] Moreover, he believes that cloning will destroy the idea of the humanness of our human life (what makes each human being an individual) and the meaning of our embodiment, our sexual being, and our relations to ancestors and descendants. Cloning experiments will breach a natural barrier, which is moral in character, and take humans into a realm of self-engineering that vastly exceeds any prior experiments with new reproductive technology. This fear of eugenics and loss of fundamental humanistic values all cultures ascribe to human individuality permeates in many arguments opposing human reproductive cloning.

Arguments that Promote Reproductive Cloning Research

One of the main objectives in developing reproductive cloning technology is based on the belief that the current proscription against reproductive cloning may not be immutable if advances in the technology yield a process superior to traditional assisted reproductive techniques in treating infertility. In addition, those who favor research in reproductive cloning believe that the science-based arguments against reproductive cloning are weak but more importantly, as this technology improves, it will provide new insights into human embryological development.

Bioethicists who favor reproductive cloning research first and foremost believe that a fertilized zygote or pre-implanted embryo does not constitute a human being. They believe that SCNT resembles tissue culture technology. Any replicating cell contains the genetic information to develop into a potential fetus but this information is suppressed. Unless implanted into a uterus, the zygote, or pre-embryo cannot develop into a human being and, therefore, does not have human status. Thus, the destruction of many pre-implanted zygotes and pre-implanted embryos, required for human reproductive cloning, do not present an ethical problem for these bioethicists. Indeed, most eggs fertilized in vivo fail to generate a viable child and are subsequently discharged from the woman. Thus, sperm and oocytes are functionally and morally identified as any other cellular components of the male or female body. In fact, one could envision a situation where fibroblasts could be de-differentiated into oocytes or pluripotent stem cells capable of developing into fetus if implanted into a uterus.

---

[4] http://www.bioethics.gov/transcripts/feb02/feb13session4.html

Those scientists who support reproductive cloning research also believe there is nothing immoral in man "playing God', especially when there may be medical benefits to be gained from this research. Moreover, reproductive cloning is not an unnatural event in biology and occurs in several species. For example, the little fire ant, *Wasmannia auropunctata*, can clonally reproduce (Schwander and Keller, 2012).

Most scientists or bioethicists who support reproductive cloning recognize the unwarranted risk of fetal defects and spontaneous miscarriages associated with the procedure in animals. However, they believe that this technology is early in development and further experimentation will greatly reduce these medical risks. In fact, several recent studies have shown that calves and pigs cloned using SCNT are born healthy, and do not express many of the afore mentioned medical problems seen in other animals (Archer et al., 2003; Lanza et al., 2003). Scientists who support reproductive human cloning has also suggested that many of the defects observed in animal cloning are, de facto, due to poor culture conditions, and that culture conditions have been improving and becoming more optimized for human embryos and cells over the 23 years of IVF and other assisted reproductive technologies (Zavos, 2003). Additionally, scientists have also noted that LOS appears to be correlated to incorrect imprinting of the *IGF2R* gene (Young et al., 1998) and that this gene is not imprinted in humans or other primates (Killian et al., 2001), suggesting that these species may be safer to clone.

Despite the differing opinions, almost all proponents for reproductive cloning believe that human experimentation should not begin until animal models demonstrate minimum danger or risk. The argument that cloning challenges definitions of individuality or may influence the psychology of the cloned individual does not present a real problem to proponents of human cloning. They claim that this argument ignores the normality of naturally born identical twins. Nurture is of equal, if not greater, importance to nature in the development of human personality. Moreover, using SCNT technology for human cloning will generate offspring that have significant differences in their mitochondrial DNA from the person providing the donor cells, unless the oocyte is obtained from the same person as the donor cell or a female blood relative of the cell donor. Even an exact genetic clone would not necessarily develop the same personality as the parent. Epigenetic events during embryonic stages, and environmental factors during development and growth of the child, are major forces in shaping personality and behavior. However, confusion about the effects of genetics on people's lives could produce fears about an individual's sense of self. Professor Dan W. Brock from Harvard University wrote, "Our valuable uniqueness is not just genetic, but is the full array of qualitative traits ... that define an individual's sense of identity".[5] He continued, "much of what defines our unique individuality concerns our history, the particular relationships with specific others that we have formed, our particular projects and achievements or accomplishments, how we are treated by others, and the times we have lived through" (Brock, 2002). In some cases, cloning may undermine our genetic diversity, but never our full individuality. Finally, proponents for reproductive cloning claim that the normalcy of naturally born identical twins argues against the possibility that a cloned child will experience psychological harm emanating from a diminished sense of individuality and personal autonomy.

Historical Insights into the Debate Related to Reproductive Cloning

A historical review of the medical risks associated with in vitro fertilization (IVF) is relevant to the debates surrounding reproductive cloning. One historical lesson from IVF is that it takes decades to assess the medical risks associated with reproductive technologies. Almost four million IVF generated babies have been born worldwide and over one half million in the USA since its inception in 1978. Yet, only in the last several years have studies examined prenatal complications associated with the procedure. In general there are no significant medical risks to babies born via IVF technology (Schimmel et al., 2006; Florjanski et al., 2010). However, some of the reported risks to the mother are thought to result from the hormones taken to induce ovulation and maintain the pregnancy, rather than the actual IVF procedure. Other risks to the mother include infections, and a risk of hemorrhaging- but these are easily managed. If there is a medical need to engage in reproductive cloning, then care will be taken to begin human trials only when animal studies show its safety.

Another question is whether reproductive cloning will lead us down the slippery- slope road to eugenics. If IVF serves as a valid historical model, then reproductive cloning will not lead to designing babies or eugenics. The universal use of IVF technology has not created legions of less-than human children, or contributed to a disintegration of the nuclear family. Originally, IVF was viewed as a technology that would continue to spawn more sophisticated and possibly objectionable forms of reproductive technology. However, clearly this vision has not been realized and the potential domino effect of IVF to nuclear transfer technology is less likely to occur. Nonetheless, whether or not these historical lessons of IVF can be applied to human cloning still remains controversial.

---

[5] http://www.brown.edu/Administration/News_Bureau/2001-02/01-116.html

Reproductive cloning is fundamentally different from IVF in one respect. The goal of IVF is to produce a genetically unique human being that carries genetic information from two parents. In contrast, nuclear transfer technology produces offspring that may only differ in their mitochondrial DNA and possible epigenetic variation while remaining essentially genetically identical to their donor cell. Attempting to ascribe a percent difference between the donor and genetic clone can be uninformative since human beings and chimpanzees differ in their DNA by about 1-2%. DNA homology from a human male, however, more closely resembles the DNA of a male chimpanzee, than the DNA from a human female because of the Y chromosome. In clones where there are just mitochondrial differences, genomic differences could account for up to a 1% difference between donor and clone.

Assessment of any reproductive technology will require decades of observations on human development from infancy into old age to determine the medical and psychological risks of such a procedure to the individuals involved and to society. It is interesting that on a theoretical level one would have expected the FDA to engage in these long-term studies before approving IVF procedures to ensure that there are no effects on the mother or child. Nonetheless, one could speculate that political pressure from the 10% of couples in the United States who are infertile have influenced FDA decisions, even though there is already an array of alternate methods for treating infertile couples.

Religious Beliefs Regarding Human Cloning

Different religious beliefs concerning when human life begins, and whether human beings should engage in "unnatural biological processes for conception", deter consensus on controversial issues such as cloning and stem-cell research (Frazzetto 2004). Ironically, and tellingly, both the Old and New Testament offer sanctified and hallowed examples of cloning: Eve was cloned from Adam, and Jesus was cloned from Mary and the Holy Spirit. According to the Bible, both of these "cloned individuals" were technically created from a single genetic human being, thus creating human beings from a single parent is of great significance in both Judaism and Christianity.   Yet, current human reproductive cloning technologies may challenge the boundaries of parenthood and social responsibility as were described in the Bible. For example, who is the cloned child's genetic mother or father? As we understand those terms from a biblical perspective, if a woman cloned herself, would the child be that woman's daughter or her twin sister? Will the cloned child be "fatherless?"

Not surprisingly, organized religion, such as the Catholic Church, has taken a strong interest in the cloning debate. Many priests, bishops, pastors, and preachers, have issued strong words of caution, or outright condemnation, of any research that creates, uses or destroys human embryos. The impact of their campaign against cloning can affect public opinion and has indeed influenced scientific policy; many Western countries with primarily Catholic populations have banned human cloning and or the creation of human embryonic stem-cell lines, or at the bare minimum, have at least issued strict regulations for such research. Aside from the issue of when an embryo attain human status, many of the major theistic religions strongly reject reproductive cloning because it is unnatural, and life is to be considered as a "gift"' from God.

Nevertheless, religious leaders rarely speak with a unified voice. Although some faiths hold irrevocable positions against cloning, other religions have found room in their beliefs and traditions to accommodate the potentially beneficial aspects of this technology. In essence, different attitudes towards human cloning center on a few fundamental questions. Does an embryo hold the status of a person? Is its destruction during research a murder? Does cloning corrupt family relationships? And, ultimately, does cloning mean tampering with God's creation, and millennia of human ethical, social and sexual arrangements?

Varying Religious Views on Reproductive Cloning

In order to prepare for the bioethical dialogue concerning cloning, one must be able to address a significant population that has a stake in the debate – the followers of various religions. Although polls have already shown that a great majority of Americans oppose cloning, opposition is nonetheless the most represented among religious people. An ABC poll carried out in 2001 asked a random national sample of American adults whether human cloning should be legal (Bainbridge, 2003). 95 percent of evangelical Protestants wanted it to be illegal, compared with 91 percent of Catholics, 83 percent of non-evangelical Protestants, and 77 percent of non-religious respondents.

As stated above, the Catholic Church has become the leading voice against any form of human cloning, and even against the creation of human embryonic stem-cell lines from "excess" in vitro fertilization (IVF) embryos. Their prohibitive stance is based on a 1987 document entitled, "Instruction on Respect for Human Life in its Origin and on the Dignity of Procreation (Donum Vitae)," published by the Congregation for the Doctrine of Faith. Roman Catholics are taught that cloning is categorically considered contrary to the moral law, since it is in opposition to the dignity both of human procreation and of the conjugal union. Any attempts at cloning are therefore a violation of the dignity of the human embryo that in Catholicism, is granted the status of a person from the point of fertilization of the oocyte.

The above Catholic doctrine provides a relatively recent definition of personhood in the Christian tradition. The medieval church, in line with Aristotelian doctrine, believed that an embryo acquired a soul only when it took recognizable human form. Consequently, abortion was only considered to be a minor sin in the Middle Ages, not a deadly sin comparable to murder. A drastic change took place in 1869 when Pope Pius IX, who was probably influenced by advances in embryological research, declared that an embryo bore full human status from the time of fertilization (Lachmann, 2001). Since then, the Catholic Church has upheld the position that the destruction of an embryo after conception is murder. No distinction is made between embryos conceived naturally and those created through IVF or cloning, although many Catholic leaders strongly oppose unnatural methods of reproduction, as well as reproductive cloning.

Buddhism,[6] by contrast, does not have the same fundamental opposition to cloning as the Catholic Church. "Many of these theological objections disappear when cloning is viewed from a Buddhist perspective," said Damien Keown, a Reader in Buddhism in the Department of History at Goldsmiths College, University of London, UK, and an authoritative voice on Buddhist responses to cloning and other biomedical issues. The Buddhist view of the world, and mankind's place in it, differs from that of monotheistic religions. In Buddhism, there is no supreme or divine creator whose plan might be distorted by human tinkering with nature. In addition, Buddhists believe that the creation of life is not a fixed or unequivocal process. "Buddhism teaches that life may come into being in a variety of ways, of which sexual reproduction is but one, so sexual reproduction has no divinely sanctioned priority over other modes of procreation," explained Keown. Life can, therefore, begin in many ways and, theologically, cloning would not be seen as a problematic technology. Furthermore, in contrast to other mainstream religions, Buddhists regard human individuality as an illusion or mirage. Cloning, therefore, would not threaten or devalue the personality or character of an individual (Falls et al., 1999; Simpson et al., 2005).

Similarly, Hindu views adopt a somewhat neutral position towards cloning. Hindu views are incredibly diverse internally within the religion. There have been

---

[6] Buddhism is divided into roughly three major branches: the Theravada, the Mahayana, and the Vajrayana. The Theravada claims to be the oldest school and has at its goal self-liberation. The Mahayana shares much with the Theravada but espouses the idea of saving other beings as the highest goal. The Vajrayana is an occult Buddhism that emphasizes esoteric rituals and practices taught by a master.

scriptural traditions that assert conception as the initiation of human existence, but there are also views focus predominantly on the compassion and "healing" of cloning research (Banchoff, 2008).

Islamic law remains concerned with reproductive cloning procedures, and particularly their impact on inter-human and familial relationships. "Islam regards interpersonal relationships as fundamental to human religious life," said Abdulaziz Sachedina, Professor of Islamic Studies at the University of Virginia (Charlottesville, VA, USA) and a leading scholar of Islamic views on cloning. The preservation of the parent–child lineage is of utmost importance to Muslims, as are the spousal relationships that encourage parental love and concern for their children. Thus, Islam is concerned with moral issues related to the genetic replication and embryonic manipulation associated with these technologies. Will these technologies lead to incidental relationships between a man and a woman without a spiritual and moral connection between them?

According to the Muslim sacred text, the Koran, moral personhood is a process and is not granted at the embryonic stage. Unlike the Catholic Church, most Sunni and Shiite jurists would "have little problem" endorsing ethically regulated research on embryonic stem (ES) cells, because the fetus is accorded the status of a legal person only at the later stages of its development (Hug, 2006). Muslims would therefore endorse reproductive cloning to help infertile couples, only if it was within marital bounds, and would reject it if it were to break familial relationships. However, Islam does not support surrogate parenting or adoption. Therefore, under Islamic law, excess embryos or embryos generated via IVF could not be used by anyone other than the couple who created them.

However, it is sometimes unclear if this view is sharing by all Muslims. According to a 2001 poll by the Council on American-Islamic Relations (CAIR), 81 percent of 1008 Muslim respondents said they were opposed to human cloning. Furthermore, in 1983, the Islamic Organization for Medical Sciences (IOMS) convened a seminar on the Islamic view of human reproduction, and ultimately determined that human cloning was not permissible.[7] The Islamic Fiqh Academy had a unique view on the topic. After a conference in Casablanca, the academicians concluded that although human cloning does not question Islamic belief and the Will of Allah, for "cloning is a cause and only through Allah's Will it can produce the effect", human cloning does bring forth "extremely complex and intractable social and moral problems".[8]

---

[7] http://www.islamset.com/healnews/cloning/index.html
[8] http://www.albalagh.net/qa/ifa.shtml

In Conservative and Orthodox Judaism, human status or personhood requires implantation of a fertilized egg into a woman and for the embryo to develop at least for 40 days. However, reproductive cloning may challenge deeply-held beliefs about creation and mankind's relationship with God. If God is seen as the only Creator with creation of the world being a completed act, then human beings have no right to tamper with it. Conversely, many Jewish thinkers regard God as the Power of Creation and view creation as a transformative process that requires human participation. Several Jewish scholars advocate the view that reproductive cloning represents a process that human beings should utilize to accomplish good. "The process or 'mechanical' aspects of human cloning present no major legal obstacles from a Jewish perspective," commented Reichman (Frazzetto, 2004). He further stated that the low efficacy and potential adverse outcomes of human cloning are legal concerns that would lead us to reject any human cloning at this time. Prospectively, creating people of legally ambiguous lineage, who may suffer profound social and psychological complications, may preclude any future acceptance of cloning despite perfection of the procedure from a medical perspective (Frazzetto, 2004). But unlike the Catholic Church, these Jewish thinkers do not believe that ensoulment occurs at conception.

Government Regulation of Human Cloning

Governments around the world have expressed a wide range of policies on human reproductive cloning – many countries complete prohibition of reproductive cloning while others have no policies on record. Over 30 countries, including France, Germany and the Russian Federation, have banned human cloning altogether. Fifteen countries, such as Japan, the UK and Israel, have banned human reproductive cloning, but permit therapeutic cloning. Many other countries, such as the US, have yet to pass any official legislation (Camporesi and Bortolotti, 2008). In the United States, various congressional bills are proposing a one-million dollar fine, plus a ten year prison sentence, for any individual who engages in reproductive cloning. However, there are only a limited number of laboratories in either academia or corporate environments that have reported using SCNT in animals. The restrictions of government funding in supporting research in reproductive cloning have opened the door for entrepreneurs to support the technology via private funding. There was even a company called *Genetics Savings and Clone* that would clone your cat for about $30,000. However, in October of 2007, this company had to close down because the market for cloned cats or dogs was too small and therefore not profitable.

Does society has the right to ban or limit scientific advancement or progress (UNESCO 2009)? There are many advocates of reproductive cloning who propose that procreative liberty and reproductive freedom are intrinsic rights within the American Constitution.[9] However, most advocates of human reproductive cloning believe that society should, at least for now, refrain from human experimentation until the medical risks seen in animals have been defined and eliminated.

The history of science supports the assertion that new technologies often lead to valuable benefits. Supporters of reproductive cloning believe that this technology will eventually provide both valuable basic research, and the possibility for spin-off technologies that will enhance our capacity to improve animal and human reproduction and development and help develop new therapies in the area of reproductive medicine and maybe other health care areas as well.

Dr. Glenn McGee, a leading bioethicist from Albany Medical College, argues that the government should treat cloning like adoption (McGee, 1999). Our society has reached consensus that, in the best interest of the child, adoptive parents must be screened in advance of the adoption. Potential adoptive parents have to talk with a judge about their motives, and demonstrate that they meet a certain minimum standard of adult competence to be responsible and nurturing parents. Why do we do this to adoptive parents when natural parents can do anything they please and may even engage in child abuse? Should a similar screening process that is currently in place for adoption be extended to cloning in an attempt to ensure the safety and freedom of children? These questions are still being debated.

Other Bioethical Issues of Human Cloning

From a biological perspective, cloning may challenge biological diversity or eliminate the need for the male species since the ova and donor cells could be obtained from two women or the same woman. Large-scale cloning could deplete genetic diversity making a species susceptible to specific diseases and many scientists believe it is diversity that drives evolution and adaptation. However, proponents of cloning would argue that the high cost of cloning would limit such a large-scale use as to threaten human biodiversity.

---

[9] http://writ.news.findlaw.com/grossman/20011120.html

Cloning Noah's Ark: -Trans-species Cloning.

Since 2000, several groups have successfully used SCNT technology to clone an endangered species using members of non-endangered species as surrogate mothers. For example, in 2000, a humble Iowa cow gave birth to a rare, endangered, ox-like Asian gaur. For this experiment, almost 700 enucleated oocytes were obtained from regular cows and allowed to fuse, via nuclear transfer technology, with fibroblasts obtained from the skin of a male gaur. Only about 80 zygotes grew into blastocyts, 40 of which were actually implanted. Eight cows became pregnant, but only one gaur was born. This was the first example of trans-species cloning. Incidentally, and perhaps humorously, the newborn gaur was named Noah. It was implied, then, that Trans-species cloning could help *reincarnate* some species that are already extinct.

Several other successes at cloning exotic or endangered species have been reported. Examples are the Gaur (*Bos gaurus*), Banteng (*Bos javanicus*) and Bucardo (*Capra pyrenaica pyrenaica*). In another experiment, an African wildcat was cloned using an ordinary house cat as the oocyte donor and surrogate mother. Other endangered animals cloned include the Indian desert cat, a bongo antelope, a Mouflon sheep, and a rare red deer. Efforts are currently underway to use nuclear transfer technology to clone giant pandas, the Siberian Tiger, white rhinoceros, and Arabian oryx as well.

The distinguishing feature of all these examples is that they employed trans-species cloning. In these instances, the oocyte cytoplasm being used to create embryos was derived from common domesticated species, while the cell nucleus was obtained from the endangered species of interest. Trans-species clones, inevitably, differ from both of the parental species in their nucleo-mitochondrial characteristics. At the very least, mitochondria inherited from the recipient oocyte would influence specific functions in the trans-species organism, such as muscle development. Yet, trans-species cloning offers a method for animal conservation in situations where other reproductive technologies, such as artificial insemination, have failed. In addition, animals resulting from these trans-specific cloning efforts are scientifically valuable for their insights into the functional relationships involved in nucleo-mitochondria dialogue.

The major ethical questions raised in trans-species cloning include: a) Does the creation of nuclear-mitochondrial hybrid animals interfere with natural species evolution? Is it appropriate to play God and create nuclear-mitochondrial hybrid animals? b) Will this technology inevitably lead to the use of large mammals such as cows as artificial incubators for human embryo development? c) How will these trans-species be valuable in species conservation?

With respect to the last issue, there are several problems with trans-species cloning. The clone would be born to a surrogate mother, most likely from a different species, and may have to be raised partially, or even entirely, by humans. More research must be done to examine the impact of one species nurturing another species.   Furthermore, for many species, successful reintroduction to the wild after human rearing is rarely achieved. Therefore, this technique would be of limited use in terms of replenishing a viable population of the endangered species. There are, nonetheless, scientific literature that suggest certain species, including some amphibians, may benefit from restoration efforts of reproductive cloning, due to their intrinsic biological systems having more favorable characteristics that increases the likelihood of success (Holt et al., 2004).

Cloning our Neanderthal Ancestors

Since the initial extraction of the Neanderthal DNA (See chapter 4), bioethical contentions, provoked by the pursuit of the Neanderthal genome, have appeared in the public. The use of SCNT and other genetic-based technologies to clone a Neanderthal being may create a situation that would be an affront to many religious and moral beliefs.

Firstly, the objections against human reproductive cloning, whether religious or moral, would very likely arise in the hypothetical situation of cloning a Neanderthal ancestor of human being, for, in many ways, a Neanderthal would be considered human. Much opposition comes in response to the uncertain behavior and abilities of the Neanderthal clone. From anthropological evidence and genetic analysis, such as mitochondrial DNA (mtDNA) sequencing, it is postulated that the early Neanderthals would have many similar rational capability as the modern Homo sapiens, hence calling into question about the

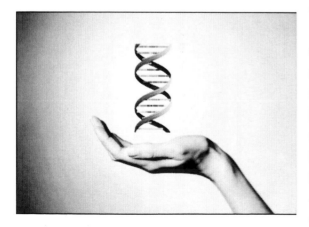

ethical responsibilities in cloning Neanderthals. Would they have the same rights as us? In fact from mtDNA sequence analysis, the number of differences between the human mtDNAs and the Neanderthal mtDNA varied from 201 to 234, which is less than the differences between human and its closest living species – the chimpanzee (Clark 2008). Given that Neanderthal might express human-like cognitive abilities, would it have the same rights as human beings? And does it demand us to reconsider bringing to life an individual that may very well express great ability of individualism, intelligence and autonomy? Would we be able to provide the clone with a suitable habitat, given the potential great offense may people take at its existence? Most likely, such a creature would live an existence as a research subject.

Secondly, objections may come forth concerning the method in which this would occur. It is possible to implant a Neanderthal embryo inside a human uterus. This would again question the bioethical principles of human dignity, as well as potentially violate other principles suc h as non-maleficence and justice. The use of technology to create human-like organisms that may not have the same cognitive potential as human beings violates human dignity. Biotechnologies should be used to enhance human beings, animals, and the environment. In research and medicine, biotechnological applications should be guided not by what you can do, but rather what you should do.

Conclusions

It is always difficult to predict which innovative biotechnology will be accepted. When IVF was first introduced in 1978 many scientists and bioethicists speculated that this technology is too dangerous and will result in too many babies born with birth defects. However, as this biotechnology gained wide-spread acceptance as a viable alternative for infertile couples to have children, the ethical concerns dissipated.

As of 2012, there are many health and psychological concerns regarding reproductive cloning. If this biotechnology were improved to demonstrate a low risk procedure and if the medical need for reproductive cloning became established, one could speculate that the ethical concerns related to this new technology may also become diminished.

Bioethical Challenges: Case Scenario

Case 1. An unmarried 35-year-old woman desperately wants a child. She has just read that bone-marrow or body fat- derived stem cells can be triggered to differentiate into either ova or a potential "sperm-like cell" capable of fertilizing her ova. She would serve as the surrogate mother, and in this way be able to give birth to her own child. What are the underlying bioethical issues that she should consider in making an informed decision about whether or not to differentiate her own stem cells to generate an embryo?

Case 2. In 2008, the FDA stated that milk and meat from cloned cattle was safe for human consumption. What are the bioethical issues that emerge from this FDA announcement?

References

Archer, G. S., et al., "Hierarchical phenotypic and epigenetic variation in cloned swine." Biol Reprod, 69(2):430-436, 2003.

Bainbridge, W. S., "Religious Opposition to Cloning." Journal of Evolution and Technology, 13, 2003. [http://www.jetpress.org/volume13/bainbridge.html]

Banchoff, T. F., Religious pluralism, globalization, and world politics. USA, Oxford University Press, 2008.

Brock, D. W., "Human cloning and our sense of self." Science, 296(5566):314-316, 2002.

Camporesi, S. and Bortolotti, L., "Reproductive cloning in humans and therapeutic cloning in primates: is the ethical debate catching up with the recent scientific advances?" J Med Ethics, 34(9):e15, 2008.

Falls, E., et al., "The koan of cloning: a Buddhist perspective on the ethics of human cloning technology." Second Opin, No. 1:44-56, 1999.

Florjanski, J. et al., "Complication rates in the second and third trimester of spontaneous twin pregnancies and twin pregnancies after in vitro fertilization." Neuro Endocrinol Lett, 31(3), 2010.

Frazzetto, G., "Embryos, cells and God." EMBO Rep, 5(6):553-555, 2004.

Holt, W. V., et al., "Wildlife conservation and reproductive cloning." Reproduction, 127(3):317-324, 2004.

Hug, K., "Therapeutic perspectives of human embryonic stem cell research versus the moral status of a human embryo--does one have to be compromised for the other?" Medicina (Kaunas), 42(2):107-114, 2006.

Inoue, K., et al., "Sex-reversed somatic cell cloning in the mouse." J. Reprod. Dev. 55, 566–569, 2009.

Killian, J. K., et al., "Divergent evolution in M6P/IGF2R imprinting from the Jurassic to the Quaternary." Hum Mol Genet, 10(17):1721-1728, 2001.

Lachmann, P., "Stem cell research--why is it regarded as a threat? An investigation of the economic and ethical arguments made against research with human embryonic stem cells." EMBO Rep, 2(3):165-168, 2000.

Lanza, R., et al., "Comment on "Molecular correlates of primate nuclear transfer failures"." Science 301(5639):1482; author reply 1482, 2003.

McGee, G., "Cloning, the family, and adoption." Sci Eng Ethics, 5(1):47-54, 1999.

Schimmel, M. S., et al., "Very low-birth-weight-infants conceived by in vitro fertilization are not at higher risk for mortality and morbidity: a population-based study." Fertil Steril, 85(4):907-912, 2006.

Schwander, T. and Keller, L. "Evolution: sociality as a driver of unorthodox reproduction.", Curr Biol, 22:R525-527, 2012.

Simpson, B., et al., "Contemplating choice: attitudes towards intervening in human reproduction in Sri Lanka." New Genet Soc, 24(1):99-117, 2005.

Sutcliffe, A. G. and C. Derom. "Follow-up of twins: health, behaviour, speech, language outcomes and implications for parents." Early Hum Dev, 82(6):379-386, 2006.

UNESCO The Right to Enjoy the Benefits of Scientific Progress and its Applications. France, UNESCO, 2009.

Young, L. E., et al., "Large offspring syndrome in cattle and sheep." Rev Reprod, **3**(3): 155-163, 1998.

Zavos, P. M., "Human reproductive cloning: the time is near." Reprod Biomed Online, **6**(4):397-398, 2003.

Chapter Six

Human Stem Cell Research-The Alchemists' Dream

Introduction

Conceptually, stem cell research can be viewed as a form of modern alchemy that transforms stem cells into specialized, differentiated cells that can be used to replace damaged cells or organs and may revolutionize medicine. There is great anticipation that the first application will use stem cells to correct organ failure, either by replacing destroyed cells of an organ, or as a source to grow new organs *in vitro* for organ transplantation.

The clinical applications of stem cell-based therapy are vast. The potential exists to treat some of the most disabling diseases plaguing human beings, including diabetes, Alzheimer's disease, spinal cord injuries, macular degeneration, multiple sclerosis, heart disease, neurological diseases, and cancer. According to the statistics published online (in 2013) from various organizations including the CDC (Center for Disease Control and Protection) there are over 200 million people in the United States suffering from chronic diseases (about 5 million Americans with Alzheimer's disease, 27 million with some form of cardiovascular disease, 26 million with diabetes, 79 million with a pre-diabetic condition, 11 million with macular degeneration, 1 million with Parkinson's disease, 13 million with cancer, and over 50 million with osteoporosis) that are potentially treatable with stem cell-derived therapies. Moreover, some bioethicists such as Glenn McGee predict that a billion individuals around the world may be treated with human embryonic stem cells before the decade comes to an end.[1]

Stem cell research will also lead to a better understanding of fundamental aspects of biology in the areas of cellular differentiation, trans-differentiation, epigenetics, and de-differentiation. In this light, stem cell research simultaneously represents a domain of fundamental discovery in human biology, and also a therapy with the potential to affect human health and quality of life.

However, embryonic stem cell research is also one of the most morally controversial scientific areas of the 21st century because, until recently, these

---

[1] http://www.springerlink.com/content/g3h427539krqp648/fulltext.pdf

stem cells could not be isolated without destroying the early embryo. While stem cells can also be isolated from adult tissues, the current view is that embryonic stem cells obtained either from non-implanted early embryos or from discarded embryos offers the best potential source for therapeutic application, for reasons that will be explained later. There are almost 500,000 frozen embryos stored in IVF clinics across the US that could be donated to stem cell research.

Rarely do democratic governments try to regulate new forms of medical research; however, governments around the world are trying to regulate and restrict basic embryonic stem cell research. Why? The prevailing cultural and religious views in many Western countries claim that once an ovum is fertilized by a sperm, even outside of the womb, the resulting zygote attains human status, making the destruction of such early embryos unethical, immoral, and possibly even a form of murder (see Chapter 5). To better appreciate the dilemmas associated with stem cell research, this chapter focuses on understanding and updating the basic biological principles of stem cell development and research. The bioethical dilemmas associated with stem cell research are examined in the following chapter.

Defining and Characterizing Stem Cells

In many organisms, life begins from a fertilized egg that divides, grows, and differentiates into all the various specialized cells—such as neurons, muscle cells, pancreatic cells and blood cells—that an animal needs to function. Cell differentiation begins with the fertilized zygote and is a process that regulates the functional and structural specialization of cells in all organ systems within a multicellular organism. Specifically, differentiation occurs via differential gene activity, in which each specialized cell type turns on or turns off selected genes unique to that cell type. Cell specialization for over 200 histologically different cell types characterized in the human body is thus determined by the activation and suppression of a specific subset of the 20,000-25,000 genes in the human genome.

As the egg divides and grows, new stem cells are generated to allow for the full embryological development of the organism. Stem cells are **self-renewing,** primitive cells that can develop into functional, **differentiated** cells. Stem cells are naturally occurring in all multi-cell complex organisms, and are found at every stage of development from fertilization until death. In adult tissue, stem cells are used to replenish the wear, damage, and disease that affect tissues during the lifespan of the organism (for more information visit our online course (**stemcellbioethics**.wikischolars.columbia.edu/).

All stem cells exhibit two fundamental properties: self-renewal and plasticity. Self-renewal is the ability of stem cells to divide indefinitely, producing a population of identical offspring. Plasticity describes the capacity of stem cells to undergo an asymmetric division, on cue, to produce two dissimilar daughter cells. One daughter cell is identical to the parent and continues to contribute to the original stem cell line (Fischbach and Fischbach, 2004), and the other can differentiate into specialized cell types. In general, stem cell proliferation is associated with only one, not both, of the daughter cells differentiating: the other retains its undifferentiated state to maintain the reservoir of stem cells.

Before describing the different types of stem cells, it is important to review some basic elements of early human embryology. After fertilization, the haploid nuclei of the egg and sperm in the zygote merge to form a single nucleus containing 46 human chromosomes. The zygote, derived from the French word *zygous* (joined), undergoes cellular proliferation to form a compact ball of cells called the morula, which has the appearance of a mulberry (the Latin term *morus* means mulberry). As the morula flows in the oviduct, the cells in the embryo continue to proliferate and the morula enlarges to form a hollow sphere called a blastocyst (or blastula). Within this hollow sphere, a few specialized cells form an inner cell mass within the cavity. This cellular cluster is a primary source of embryonic stem cells. The time from fertilization to implantation of the human embryo in the uterine wall is approximately 14 days.[2]

There are several types of stem cells:

1. Totipotent stem cells are cells that can differentiate into any one of the over 200 specialized cells in the human body. These cells are obtained only in early cell divisions of the zygote or fertilized egg. A stem cell is defined as totipotent if it has potential to develop into a complete fetus and a placenta. In general, cells derived from a fertilized egg retain **totipotency for about 3-5 cell divisions (about 3 days).** By the time the embryo implants into the uterus, totipotency is lost. As the embryo develops, however, germinal cells are formed. Germinal cells are specific cells in the fetus that give rise to egg and sperm, and they retain totipotency. In the fetus, these cells migrate into the primitive gonad, also called the genital ridge, and differentiate into either female or male germ cell precursors, depending on the sex of the fetus.

2. Pluripotent Stem Cells are cells that have the capacity to differentiate into any other cell type, but they cannot be implanted into a uterus to create a fetus. After fertilization, the zygote undergoes a series of cell divisions called cleavages. In

---

[2] http://writ.news.findlaw.com/grossman/20011120.html

the cleavage process, unlike normal cell division seen in somatic cells, the zygote decreases in size as it cleaves apart and gives rise to two smaller cells. As the number of cells approaches 32-64 (equivalent to a five to six day old embryo) a blastocyt is formed containing a cell-free center within the expanding cluster of cells. If a blastocyst is implanted in the uterus of a mammal, its outer cell layer, which contain cells called trophoplasts, differentiates into the cells responsible for the formation of the placenta and the inner cell mass. In turn, the inner cell mass, which contains cells called embryoblasts, will develop into a fetus. Since the inner cell mass cannot develop into a fetus without a placenta, these stem cells are not totipotent, but are *pluripotent*. After separating the inner cell mass from the blastocyt, the isolated stem cells can be adapted to grow in a Petri dish and can be maintained in culture either as stem cells or can be induced by biological substances or cellular environment to undergo differentiation into a wide variety of cell types.

3. <u>Multipotent Stem Cells</u> are generally found in adult tissue and are technically pluripotent. They were originally thought to be responsible for the regeneration of only a very restricted set of cell lineages. However, it is becoming increasingly evident that some multipotent stem cells show considerably plasticity, and can be triggered to differentiate into a wider variety of specialized cells. Still, they cannot differentiate into as many different kinds of specialized cells as pluripotent stem cells. For example, Hemopoietic stem cells are *multipotent* because they have the potential to develop into red blood cells, platelets, white blood cells, and even additional cell types such as myoblasts (Wang et al., 2008). The underlying biological mechanisms on why multipotent or pluripotent stem cells do not have the same capacity to differentiate as totipotent stem cells remains an intense area of ongoing investigation.

Figure 1. Stem cell differentiating into beta-insulin producing cells (left) and into neurons. (from NIH image gallery)

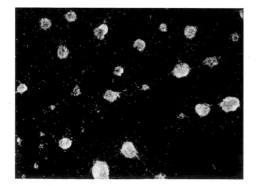 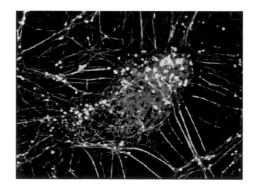

Embryonic stem cell research will provide better understanding of the underlying mechanisms of cellular differentiation. For example, a basic principle is that once stem cells differentiate into a specific cell lineage, they do not change to other cell lineage pathways. Stem cells that begin differentiating into white blood cells will not change course and become red blood cells. In contrast, many tumor cells can jump cell lineages or de-differentiate. Therefore, there is a great need to understand the complete biology of stem cells, to identify how physiological and non-physiological products and processes regulate gene expression and differentiation.

Stem Cell Replacement Therapy

A specific lure of stem cells in cell and organ replacement therapy is based, in part, on the fact that stem cells offer an unlimited supply of potential cells for transplantation. Cell replacement therapy involves transplanting stem cells into damaged tissue and stimulating stem cells to grow into new and healthy tissue. In addition, stem cells obtained from the patient offer a promising method of cell or organ replacement without the risk of tissue rejection. In contrast, conventional organ transplantation involves finding a donor whose HLA antigens express the greatest compatibility with the patient's own tissue. Since it is usually difficult to find appropriate tissue-compatible donors, recipients of transplants often must be placed on medications for at least a year, if not longer, to prevent their immune systems from rejecting the transplanted organs. These medications are associated with many side effects that can cause dangerous health risks, such as infections and renal failure (Griffith and Naughton, 2002). Although the technology to use stem cells to generate complete organs is in its infancy, cell replacement therapy in the future may offer a viable clinical alternative for classical organ transplantation.

One of the biggest historical breakthroughs in human stem cell research occurred in 1998 when researchers at the University of Wisconsin at Madison, led by James Thomson, isolated and grew stem cells derived from human embryos (Thomson et al., 1998). These human pluripotent embryonic stem cells were derived from fertilized embryos that were less than a week old. Five independent stem cell lines were developed that could either be perpetuated in culture for long periods of time or could be frozen and recovered at a later date. Using this technology, Dr. Thomson developed these stem cell lines from 14 blastocysts that were obtained from donated, surplus embryos produced by *in vitro* fertilization. This was the first time human embryonic stem cells had been successfully isolated and cultured in a laboratory. Amazingly, this discovery came just seven years after the first reports of isolating and culturing embryonic stem cells from mice (Evans and Kaufman, 1981).

At the same time that Thomson reported his results, researchers from Johns Hopkins University, led by John Gearhart, described a method to isolate and culture immature germ cells from 5 to 8 week-old fetuses that were donated anonymously by women undergoing therapeutic or spontaneous abortions (Shamblott et al., 1998). These scientists placed the stem cells, obtained from the germinal centers of the ovaries or testes, in plastic dishes and added factors that enabled the germ stem cells to continue to divide while remaining in a state of suspended development, preventing differentiation. These germ cell-derived stem cells can also be frozen, recovered, and maintained as stem cells in culture. Interestingly, Gearhart's initial purpose for his research was merely to develop a tool for studying Down's syndrome.

The success of both Thomson's and Gearhart's research was based on their ability to retain and maintain the two fundamental properties of stem cells: self-renewal and plasticity. Maintaining stem cells in a *self-renewable* state is generally achieved by sub-culturing undifferentiated stem cells onto feeder layers to form established cell lines that can be grown in the laboratory indefinitely. To maintain self-renewal of stem cells, clumps of dividing stem cells must be physically broken up, often using difficult and time-consuming procedures. Nonetheless, both research groups showed that these cells could be repeatedly frozen and thawed while still maintaining their characteristic undifferentiated stem cell properties.

Once techniques were developed to isolate and culture human embryonic stem cells, many scientists around the world began to generate other human stem cell lines. These stem cell lines have been used as cell models to understand the regulation of cell differentiation and as potential sources for stem cell replacement therapy. One major clinical objective in cell replacement therapy is to use differentiated cells, such as neurons, to replace cells injured due to trauma (spinal cord injury) or neurodegenerative diseases such as Alzheimer's disease or Parkinson's disease. There are currently many ongoing clinical trials attempting to use cell replacement therapy for a variety of diseases. However, one major obstacle in these trials is the potential immunological rejection of the transplanted cells by the recipient patient. Ideally, stem cell therapy would be best implemented using the patient's own stem cells. The quest for generating patient-specific stem cells has led to the search for a method to utilize somatic cell nuclear transfer (SCNT- see Chapter 4) to isolate embryonic stem cells from patients. In discussed in Chapter 3, nuclear transfer technology involves transferring the nuclear genetic material from a patient's own cell into an enucleated oocyte. This "fused" cell is then stimulated to develop into a pre-implanted embryo in order to harvest the embryonic stem cells from the inner mass. Stem cells isolated in this manner would be histocompatible to the patient and therefore could be used for cell replacement therapy. Recent reports by Noggle et al. (2011) and Tachibana, et al. (2013) applying SCNT to human cell systems will probably stimulate a great deal of research to derive patient-specific stem cells.[3]

In 2004 researchers in South Korea claimed to successfully clone a human non-implanted embryo as a source for harvesting embryonic stem cells (Jensen, 2012) (Hwang et al., 2004; Hwang et al., 2005). Hwang claimed to have used extremely fresh eggs donated by South Korean volunteers. When workers in his research institute reported that they were coerced to donate their eggs, the scientific community began to learn about the scientific fraud. All of their data was falsified. Conceptually, Hwang was correct in principle but it took another eight years until Noggle et al. (2011) and Tachibana et al., (2013) were able to apply SCNT technology to generate human embryonic stem cells.

Stem Cells Can Be Obtained from Various Tissues

There are six major tissue sources of stem cells: embryos, fetuses, umbilical cord blood, adult organs, amniotic fluid, and teratocarcinomas. Stem cells from the embryo can either be totipotent or pluripotent, as described earlier in the chapter. From an ethical perspective it is also important to identify whether the stem cells are obtained from "spare embryos" created via IVF, cloned embryos (created for research purposes), or aborted fetuses as the different sources would have different moral implications (see Chapter 7). Stem cells from adults are generally *multipotent* and can be obtained from a variety of sources, including the bone marrow and most major organs. There are a few organs, such as the pancreas, from which stem cells have not been obtained. Another source of adult stem cells is human post-mortem tissue, which can be extracted within 20 hours after death. The main advantage of embryonic stem cells over adult derived stem cells is their capacity to generate a broader range of differentiated cells compared to adult derived stem cells.

Obtaining stem cells from adult or fetal tissue may offer advantages over embryonic stem cells. Human amniotic fluid stem cells and umbilical cord blood, for example, may be important sources for both basic science and regenerative medicine. These stem cells exhibit a high proliferation rate, are self-renewing, and may have a lower frequency of producing tumors than embryonic stem cells

---

[3] http://www.medicalnewstoday.com/medicalnews.php?newsid=70950

(Roura et al., 2012; Cananzi et al., 2009).

Another source for stem cells is teratocarcinomas (see **Textbox 1**), which, historically, were first recognized as yielding pluripotent stem cells. Teratocarcinomas are gonadal tumors. These tumor cells are also one of the main components of human testicular germ cell tumors. One interesting feature of teratocarcinomas is that they contain a wide array of tissues derived from the three primary germ layers that make up an embryo: the endoderm, mesoderm, and ectoderm. Thus they contain a large assortment of tissue types including cartilage, squamous epithelia, primitive neuroectoderm, ganglionic structures, muscle, bone, and glandular epithelia. The differentiated cells of the tumor are formed from pluripotent stem cells present in the tumor. While there is currently limited application for utilizing these cells as sources for stem cell therapy, these cells have provided great insights into the mechanisms of cell differentiation and tumorigenesis.

In 2007 and 2008, scientists claimed a major breakthrough by inducing adult fibroblasts to de-differentiate into stem cells that have pluripotent characteristics. These scientists were able to reprogram mouse fibroblasts into induced pluripotent stem cells (iPS) by genetically overexpressing four genes (oct4, sox2, klf4, and c-myc) and using subsequent drug selection for the reactivation of a marker of pluripotency [Greenbaum 2010]. The process of reprogramming is slow and the frequency of developing into stem cells is low, so it could take up to 20 days to transform fibroblasts into stem cells.

In addition, there are reported side effects of using iPS generated stem cells. Yamanaka et al. (Yamanaka and Blau, 2010) found that 20% of the stem cell-derived offspring developed tumors, presumably related to the activation of one of the transfected genes such as a m-myc (an established oncogene). iPS cells have been obtained from differentiated stomach cells, fat cells, and liver cells and can be obtained even if Myc, which can induce cancer, is omitted . The resulting stem cells do not appear to be substantially different from ES cells. In 2009 and 2011, there were other improvements in iPS technology (Pan et al., 2012) . Non-integrating adenoviral vectors or plasmids, for example, were used to achieve transient expression of reprogramming factors without disturbing the host genome. But such an approach presents two immediate problems: the requirement for prolonged expression of the pluripotency factors to achieve reprogramming, and the difficulty of repeatedly delivering the full complement of factors using a different vector for each one.

The goal of this research was to develop viral-free systems to generate iPS (Drews et al., 2012). A leap of faith must be taken from proof-of-principle in mice to application in humans, and there are still hurdle to overcome. If human stem cells can be generated using iPS technology, patient-specific stem cells could be made without the use of donated eggs or embryos. This technique has an obvious ethical advantage over other techniques because it does not require the destruction of pre-implanted embryos. Yamanaka, who discovered iPS, received the Nobel Prize for his work in 2011.

Textbox 1: Teratoma and Teratocarcinoma

A teratoma is a type of germ line tumor, and also the most common primary brain tumor seen in newborn children. Teratomas account for about 20% of germ cell tumors. They tend to be found in one of two locations: above the pituitary gland in an area called the suprasellar region, and in the pineal region. Teratomas of the ovary and testis have histological similarities but exhibit different biologic behaviors, depending mostly on the site of occurrence and the age of the patient. Thus, most ovarian teratomas are benign, and most testicular teratomas are malignant, with the exception of those occurring in children. A teratocarcinoma is a malignant neoplasm consisting of elements of teratoma and those of embryonal carcinoma or choriocarcinoma, or both. It occurs most often in the testis.

In 1970, Leroy Stevens (1970) made a scientific observation that would profoundly affect stem cell technology decades later. He noticed that the primordial germ cells that gave rise to teratomas in mice testis looked a lot like the cells of early embryos. When he transplanted cells from the inner cell mass of early embryos into testes of adult mice, some of the early embryo cells gave rise to teratomas. These induced-growths looked and acted like spontaneous teratomas. The modern-day term "ES cell" originated from Stevens' name "pluripotent embryonic stem cells," which he used to describe cells from early embryos that could support differentiation. Because These cells became known as embryonal carcinoma, or EC cells because they can give rise to both cancerous and normal cells and could give rise to whole organisms, and not just teratomas (Mintz and Illmensee 1975).

In 2012, researchers in Madrid adapted the iPS technique for of Dr. Shinya Yamanaka to bred genetically engineered mice with the same cocktail of four reprogramming transcription factor genes. By having the mice drink a particular drug, these genes were turned on and embryonic stem cells appeared in multiple tissues and organs in these mice within a few weeks. The researchers extracted these cells and demonstrated through various tests that they were like those in a new embryo containing just 16 cells (Abad et al., 2013). The next step is to explore whether these *in vivo* - generated iPS stem cells are capable of efficiently generating different tissues in vital organs such as the pancreas, liver, heart, bone marrow or kidney. Their research is directed to devise methods for inducing regeneration locally and in a transitory manner for a particular damaged tissue.

There has been considerable progress in converting pancreatic exocrine cells into endocrine β cells using viral and non-viral methods of transfection (Houbracken et al., 2012; Cim et al., 2012). The goals of these studies are to induce cells to go through transdifferentiation without the risk of tumor generation.

Advantages and Disadvantages of Stem Cells from Different Sources

The major medical advantage of embryonic stem cells is their potential to differentiate into any cell of the body. They express strong self-renewal capacity, and can be maintained as stem cells in culture or when frozen. Furthermore, these cells can be easily obtained from fertility clinics. The major disadvantages of embryonic stem cells, apart from ethical considerations, are that they may be rejected if transplanted in an HLA incompatible person, and that they may form tumors more easily than adult- derived stem cells.

Most adult tissues contain multipotent stem cells. The most common source for multipotent stem cells is bone marrow. Bone marrow-derived stem cells can differentiate into a variety of different cell types, aside from blood cells. In addition, the ease by which bone marrow cells can be obtained and our experience using these cells in a variety of treatments (e.g., leukemia) have been a great impetus for exploring this as a source for adult stem cells. Yet, bone marrow-derived cells are not as pluripotent as embryonic stem cells. There have recently been considerable efforts to expand their ability to differentiate into even more kinds of specialized cell types. Another possible disadvantage of using stem cells from bone marrow is that about 10-20% of patients lack a sufficient number of recoverable bone marrow-derived stem cells for therapeutic transplantation because of the patients' disease.

The main advantage of using bone marrow or any adult-derived stem cells is their use in autologous therapy, avoiding the risk of tissue rejection. Adult derived stem cells, however, have some disadvantages in therapeutic applications. One technical hurdle is that adult derived stem cells can only be isolated in low numbers. In mouse bone marrow, stem cells represent only 1 in 10,000 cells. In addition, they are more difficult to isolate than embryonic stem cells, are notoriously slow to grow in culture, and have a restricted proliferation potential.

Another issue with adult derived stem cells is their plasticity, or ability to differentiate into other cell types. Adult derived stem cells from certain organs such as bone marrow, muscle, fat, liver, synovial membranes, and brain, express better plasticity or pluripotency than adult cells from other sources. For example, studies reported (Bellenchi et al., 2012) showed that, even in adult rodent brains, stem cells have the capacity to generate neurons (neurogenesis). This finding may explain why patients taking antidepressants require several weeks before a therapeutic effect is seen. During this time the antidepressants appear to stimulate the generation of new neurons in these patients. This research could lead to developing new compounds that trigger neurogenesis from endogenous adult stem cells in the brain. In fact, a San Diego-based start-up called BrainCells screens drugs that stimulate the proliferation of neural stem cells in the hope of finding new antidepressants or drugs to treat cognitive disorders, such as Alzheimer's.

Since there are several sources of embryonic and adult stem cells, it is critical to assess which type of stem cells will generate the best therapeutic value. To date, the main disadvantages of adult stem cells are that they are: a) few in number, b) difficult to isolate and maintain in culture, c) slow to proliferate, and d) difficult to stimulate to differentiate into various other tissues types. Until we are able to test stem cells from various sources side by side in the laboratory, in a variety of experimental paradigms, the answer as to whether adult embryonic stem cells could serve in a therapeutic mode will remain unresolved.

Stem Cell Differentiation Assessment and Targeting

There are several stages between isolating stem cells and transferring them to patients. In any therapeutic protocol, stem cells must be self-renewing, express the capacity for targeted differentiation, and have the capacity to regulate their numbers for transplantation. Currently, therapeutic applications are focused on four major health problems: diabetes, blood diseases (including AIDS), neurodegenerative disease, spinal cord injuries, and cardiovascular disease. However, the critical stage in the development of these therapies is assessing the capacity of stem cells to differentiate into specialized cells.

Manipulating the extracellular environment can trigger stem cell differentiation into specialized cells. Differentiation into specialized cell types, for example, can be initiated by growing the stem cells at high cell growth densities, placing them on different types of non-proliferating feeder cells, adding specific growth factors, or maintaining these cells on either crude or defined extracellular matrices. Scientists are just beginning to discover the control mechanisms for generating specialized cells. There remains a great deal of future investigation necessary for full identification of all cell culture conditions or chemical factors that regulate stem cell differentiation.

In the laboratory there are several methods to assess the developmental potency of pluripotent stem cells: (1) in vitro differentiation in a Petri dish; (2) differentiation into teratomas or teratocarcinomas, and (3) *in vivo* differentiation when introduced into the blastocoele cavity of a pre-implantation embryo. In the first method, scientists use plasma membrane surface markers to determine whether the embryonic stem cells will differentiate into the target specialized cell. In addition to surface markers, current research also focuses on generating gene expression profiles to characterize stem cells and their differentiated progeny. In the second method, pluripotency is demonstrated when human embryonic stem cells are injected into an animal and form teratomas. The third method involves injecting the human stem cells into a developing animal embryo; pluripotency is assessed by analyzing the tissue distribution of the human cells in the animal that is born. It is important to note that testing human embryonic stem cells in this manner involves creating a chimeric animal, with human DNA throughout its body, a process that may elicit bioethical concerns (for further discussion of human chimeras, see chapter 8).

In many instances, stem cell differentiation leads to a mixed population of undifferentiated cells and differentiated cell types. The differentiated cells and the non-differentiated stem cells must then be separated from one another. Since specialized cells can be identified by the unique surface proteins they express, separation of differentiated versus non-differentiated cells must be done efficiently.

A final obstacle in stem cell differentiation relates to the limited understanding of how to regulate the proliferation of differentiated cells obtained through stem cell technology. In addition, scientists are just beginning to examine how long these stem cell derived differentiated cells maintain their differentiated state. Changes in either cell proliferation or differentiation could have dangerous consequences in the clinical setting.

Potential Therapies Utilizing Stem Cells

Stem cell research has many medical and scientific applications, including cell replacement therapies, drug development, normal development, gene therapy and the study of underlying mechanisms of disease. As stated above, it appears that cell replacement, as opposed to organ development, is the most immediate therapeutic utilization of stem cells.

In several 2012 papers in cardiology, scientists reported the capacity to transform stem cells obtained from various sources into endothelial cells (Clifford et al., 2012; Wang, 2011). These cells were found to integrate into blood vessels following experimental myocardial infarction and improved cardiac function. The mechanisms by which these cells repair the heart are not clearly understood. Despite many promising reports, the use of stem cells in heart failure is in its infancy and will require more research and testing.

Stem cell therapy is being tested for use with a variety of other diseases including cancer (Lou et al., 2012) and diabetes. In Type I diabetes the beta cells of the pancreas, which normally produce insulin, are destroyed by an auto-immune process. The pancreas is an interesting organ because, to the best of our knowledge, it contains no natural stem cells. Scientists envision differentiating embryonic stem cells into beta islet cells capable of producing insulin and then transplanting these islet cells into the diabetic patient. In order for this procedure to work clinically, two major hurdles must be overcome. First, our knowledge of differentiating stem cells into pancreatic islet cells is limited, and much more research is necessary to understand its regulation. Second, there is no guarantee that the diabetic patient's immune system will not destroy the transplanted islet cells in the same fashion that it destroyed its own beta cells. If beta cell destruction in diabetic patients were to occur, it may not occur immediately, rendering stem cell therapy a viable acute method to treat diabetics but requiring periodic renewal transplantation of stem cells to maintain a non-diabetic state. In a 2007 article, scientists were able to use stem cell therapy in conjunction with anti-rejection therapy to treat a small number of patients with Type I diabetes so that they did not require insulin injections (Voltarelli et al., 2007). This was the first time stem cell therapy was effective in taking diabetic patients off insulin. Since then there are several studies examining the use of stem cells to treat diabetes (Zhou and Brown, 2008; Nostro and Keller, 2012).

With many of these stem-cell based therapies, a fear exists that injecting embryonic stem cells into a patient might lead to the formation of a teratoma or cause the cells to differentiate into an undesirable tissue type. Current research is focusing on allowing the embryonic stem cells to differentiate into a still-flexible, progenitor-cell stage before injecting cells into the patient. For unknown reasons these progenitor cells appear to be less likely to form tumors than injecting undifferentiated stem cells.

Another approach to stem cell therapy is to develop medications that enhance endogenous stem cells, found normally in many organs, to proliferate. Since most organs of the human body contain their own stem cells, specific cellular hormones or growth factors could be identified that promote differentiation *in situ*. This type of therapy would not require injection of stem cells into patients; this would allow for broad clinical applications and eliminate most bioethical and religious concerns by eliminating the need for embryos. For example, current evidence suggests that the brain contains endogenous stem cells and a drug that stimulates stem cell proliferation may one day be helpful in treating victims of strokes, Parkinson's, or Alzheimer's disease. Administering cellular hormones that summon the migration of stem cells to sites of injury presents another kind of potential therapy.

Another therapeutic benefit has emerged from stem cell research. Several studies (Potier et al., 2010) show that donor stem cells, using bone marrow transplants, can fuse with resident host tissue cells. Therefore, injecting genetically modified stem cells might constitute a novel means of introducing new genes into the host without the use of viral vectors. The injected stem cells, which contain new genes, would fuse with endogenous cells and allow the expression of these new gene products. The use of stem cells as gene transfer vehicles may lack the clinical problems associated with conventional gene transfer using viral vectors, such as inflammatory side effects and the potential to develop certain forms of cancer.

Cell transplantation in the brain using stem cells may operate in novel ways. In the past few years, there have been reports (Sandner et al., 2012) using stem cells to treat spinal cord-paralyzed rats. The mechanism by which recovery was observed from paralysis remains unclear. At first it was believed that the transplanted stem cells differentiated into new neurons to repair damaged spinal nerves. Now, evidence suggests that the transplanted stem cells stimulate the production of specific growth factors and cytokines that promote regeneration of endogenous nerve (damaged or undamaged) and stem cells (Ruff et al., 2012).

Lastly, stem cell therapy may serve as an effective way to regulate the immune system. For example, it has been shown that murine bone marrow-derived adult stem cells have an immunosuppressive effect on T cell proliferation and in collagen-induced arthritis (CIA). A report in 2010 demonstrated that murine bone marrow-derived MSCs potently inhibit in vitro T-cell proliferation in an IFNγ-dependent mechanism that may in turn suppress several autoimmune diseases (Schurgers et al., 2010) or in neurodegenerative diseases such as Huntington's disease (Razvi, 2010).

While many animal studies serve as models for human diseases and have demonstrated the potential clinical applications of stem cells, translating these studies to humans is often a difficult process. While scientists may be able to cure a specific disease in the mouse, there are many genetic and physiological differences between humans and mice that could account for the failure of their therapeutic applications to humans.

Stem cell lines are also being used in industrial applications such as drug screening (Jensen et al., 2009). Stem cell lines can serve as screening platforms to identify candidate drugs that stimulate stem cell proliferation or differentiation into specific cell types. Stem cells obtained from individual patients may also serve as a better laboratory model to identify drugs that could treat the type of disease that this person is affected with.

When Should Clinical Trials of Stem Cell Technology Begin?

There are several clinical trials in progress or being planned to examine clinical efficacy of stem cell therapies. In 2011, Geron received FDA approval to test stem cell therapy for spinal cord injuries and Advanced Cell Technologies received FDA approval to examine its use in macular degeneration. Other studies are ongoing to examine stem cell therapy in heart disease and neurodegenerative diseases. On the commercial side, a leading regenerative medicine clinic on the West Coast, TeleHealth, is now offering multiple stem cell therapy treatments for arthritis and soft tissue injury such as tendonitis of the shoulder. The injection treatments are covered by insurance, and are offered with Board Certified doctors. This clinic claims that stem cell injection treatments possess the potential for actually repairing the cartilage damage in arthritic joints or tendon damage in an injured shoulder.

Public pressure is certainly one reason that is responsible to initiating these clinical trials. The ethical question is whether the scientific basis to enter clinical trials is justified. In 2013, an expert panel of scientists has issued a report advising the Italian Government against continuing to support a controversial stem cell therapy, deeming it 'unscientific'. The clinical protocols that were considered consisted of using patients' own mesenchymal stem cells, derived from bone marrow, to treat neurodegenerative conditions such as Parkinson's, Alzheimer's, and amyotrophic lateral sclerosis, as well as muscle-wasting disorders. The panel found the submitted protocols incomplete. Records of preclinical studies were not included. Furthermore, data was lacking on the quality of cellular preparation, and an inability to demonstrate the expected expression of proteins in stem cells as they form new neurons. The panel felt that there was not sufficient scientific merit to approve this type of stem cell therapy.

Interestingly, in 2012, Geron stopped its clinical trial of stem cell therapy for spinal cord injuries claiming it was too expensive. In 2013, this company is trying to divest its stem cell research unit even though they funded the monumental work of Thomson et al., (1998) in isolating human stem cells from embryos and maintaining them in culture.

Hisashi Moriguchi, a project researcher at the University of Tokyo, was noted for pioneering work on induced pluripotent stem (iPS) cells. Yet an investigation by staff from the Journal Nature and several stem-cell researchers found that Moriguchi's claim to have cured six heart-failure patients with cells derived from iPS cells was falsified. In addition, he had lied about his university affiliations; and plagiarized key parts of his research papers. He finally convened press conference and admit his lies.

All of these stories highlight the potential gains in medicine that people believe will arise from stem cell therapy. Yet, the public must recognize that translational applications of research into clinical trials is a slow process. The Food and Drug Administration (FDA) is concerned that the hope that patients have for cures not yet available may leave them vulnerable to unscrupulous providers of stem cell treatments that are illegal and potentially harmful. The FDA cautions consumers to make sure that any stem cell treatment they are considering has been approved by FDA or is being studied under a clinical investigation that has been submitted to and allowed to proceed by FDA. As of 2013, the FDA has approved only one stem cell product, Hemacord, a cord blood-derived product manufactured by the New York Blood Center and used for specified indications in patients with disorders affecting the body's blood-forming system.

Before (Aug 2012)   **After (1st Dec 2012)**

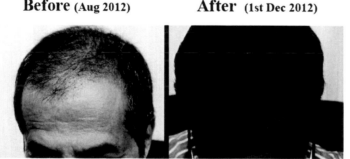

Stem cell hair multiplication results after three and a half months. With this rate patient should have 40,000 plus hair at the end of one- one and a half year.

Non-Medical Applications of Stem cells

Stem cells are being studied as potential treatment modality for a variety of non-medically related conditions. Stems cells are being used for a not-quite-surgical procedure that recontours faces using a mixture of the patient's own fat and stem cells. This procedure is reported to enable the implanted fat cells to better "take hold" in its new location and become part of the face. In addition, these added stem cells appear to increase the blood supply to the skin to enhance its appearance.

Stem cell technology has also enabled scientists at Columbia University to developed a technique to grow human dermal papilla cells in 3-D culture that can induce the growth of de novo hair follicles in human skin, paving the way for a new approach to treating baldness (Higgins et al., 2013).

Commercial companies recognize the potential profits of hair restoration. Histogen, Inc., a company whose focus includes hair restoration, presented clinical evidence at the International Society of Hair Restoration Surgeons (ISHRS) Annual Scientific Meeting in Amsterdam July 22-26, 2009 of using stem cell technology to stimulate hair growth. According to Histogen, HSC is a solution containing naturally secreted embryonic proteins, growth factors than induces new hair follicle formation, hair growth, and hair thickness when injected into the scalp (Meyer-Blazejewska et al., 2011).

Dr. Daniel McGrath in Austin, Texas is an Associate of the American Academy of Cosmetic Surgery and member of the American Society for Laser Medicine and Surgery. He runs a clinic that specializes in hair restoration. He removes a small amount of an individual's blood and the platelet-rich plasma is obtained and mixed with a wound-healing powder called "a-cell", and injected back into the scalp. Finally, the doctor uses some massage and small needles to create tiny wounds, which trigger a healing hair restoring response. Dr. McGrath claims that 80 percent re-growth of hair or regeneration of hair across the board is observed in his patients. It costs about $3,500 for a treatment.

Stem Cells and Your Skin

Discover how Lifeline Skin Care is using this life-changing technology to rejuvenate your skin.

READ MORE ▶

World Stem Cells Clinic in in Cancun, Mexico offers stem cell therapy as its new treatment for Anti-aging (see Textbox). Their therapy is based on the theory that aging is a result of progressive depletion of stem cells, so the introduction of new stem cells and adjunctive treatments has the potential of slowing down or reversing this process. Another serum product is marketed by Lifeline Skin Care based on the unproven concept that human non-embryonic stem cell extracts can renew skin -- by replacing old cells with healthy new ones. These anti-aging stem cell serums are marketed to stimulate the skin's abilities to repair itself.

Textbox 2: Anti-aging Stem Cell Therapy

The World Stem Cells Clinic's team harvest autologous stem cells from your own bone marrow, adipose (fat) tissue or circulating stem cells, within your bloodstream. They also offer allogeneic stem cells from other donors. These cells are harvested in the same way and under the same conditions. They are simply obtained from a donor as opposed to from you. They do not utilize fetal or laboratory-cultured embryonic stem cells. They chose not to use these sources of stem cells to prevent potential complications from contamination or side effects and adverse events such as graft versus host disease (GVHD). After collection, your stem cells are tested and processed at the state-of-the-art and Good Tissue Practice (cGTP) laboratories. Data regarding the source of your stem cells, the amount harvested, and other information is recorded to ensure proper transfusion of your own cell or those of a chosen donor. Following stem cell treatment, World Stem Cells, LLC in conjunction with the The International Cellular Medical Society (ICMS), remains in contact with you and your families to assess the treatment results. Treatment protocols and treatment outcomes – without any identifying personal information – will be openly accessible to all stem cell researchers in the field to promote new technologies, safer stem cell treatment protocols, promote overall patient safety and aid in the advancement of stem cell transplant science. - See more at: http://worldstemcells.com/#sthash.9KnRdTdK.dpuf

---

Research has shown that mesenchymal stem cells that reside in bone marrow are a rich source of adult stem cells. Futures studies will examine whether these stem cells can be used in tooth regeneration and repair (Huang et al., 2009; Mantesso and Sharpe, 2009). Dental pulp stem cells form vascularized pulp-like tissue and are surrounded by a layer of odontoblast-like cells expressing dentin proteins similar to those found in natural dentin. When seeded onto human dentin surfaces and implanted into immunocompromised mice, dental pulp stem cells create dentin-like structures deposited on the dentin surface.

Current Medical Risks and Problems Associated With Stem Cell Therapy

Critical safety issues must be considered in stem cell-based therapies (Thournson et al., 2011). Currently, most related federally funded programs generate embryonic stem cells that are derived from existing or newly established cell lines and are not tissue compatible to the patients. Therefore, patients receiving these transplanted embryonic stem cells will require supplementation of immuno-suppressive drugs to prevent tissue rejection.

There have been reports that show that certain stem cell therapies involving hematopoietic stem cell transplantation have more inherent health risks than ordinary bone marrow transplantation. In addition, the time required for stem therapy to reconstitute the immune system may take several months after autologous transplantation but up to a year or longer after allogeneic transplantation (Wingard et al., 2010).

Tissue rejection can be avoided if patients' own stem cells are used as a source for therapy. As mentioned above, there are several ways in which patients can provide their own stem cells. In addition to pluripotent stem cells obtained from bone marrow, therapeutic cloning offers another way to generate histocompatible stem cells that would not require patients to receive immuno-suppressive drugs. Somatic cell nuclear transfer utilizes technology to transfer a nucleus from a specific cell of a patient and then fuse it with an enucleated oocyte. The resulting zygote would then be allowed to differentiate into a blastocyt *in vitro* and would serve as the source for isolating stem cells from the inner mass.

In addition to tissue compatibility, transplanted pluripotent stem cells can form tumors in animals. Researchers have identified what they call cancer stem cells in blood cancers such as leukemia, breast, and brain cancers (Zhang and Rosen, 2006). In other words, the mutations that drive certain cancers to develop in the body may originate in the body's small supply of naturally occurring stem cells. There is also evidence that cancer stem cells, which only form a small portion of the total tumor, are, in fact, the primary cells that have the capacity to keep the tumors growing (Spillane and Henderson, 2007). Many tumor cells have been shown to exhibit stem cell-like properties, such as reverting back to a less differentiated state and exhibiting the ability to rapidly proliferate. While it remains unclear why a small percentage of the implanted stem cells form tumors, it may be related to differentiation processes that have gone unregulated.

Scientists are trying different approaches to overcome the cancer problems associated with the use of stem cells. One method is to utilize adult-derived stem cells for therapy, as these cells are considered less tumorigenic than embryonic stem cells. Another approach is to transform embryonic stem cells into specialized differentiated cells before transplantation into the patient. The hope is that once the stem cell has completed differentiation, its potential to proliferate uncontrollably will be significantly reduced.

If the stem cell-cancer problem is not overcome in the near future, patients may have to accept that a side-effect of life-saving stem cell therapies is that a proportion of transplanted stem cells may turn into tumors within 10-20 years. Long development times have been observed in several types of cancers, including colon and prostate; these cancers take more than a decade to fully develop from the detection of the earliest cancer nodule. Furthermore, it is unclear what percentage of patients receiving transplanted stem cells will develop stem cell-induced tumors. If stem cells are used to treat a 65-year-old patient who has Parkinson's or Alzheimer's disease, then the risk that the patient might develop cancer within 10-20 years may be one that this patient is willing to take. In contrast, given that stem cell therapies may lead to the development of cancers, their use may not be warranted in a child or young adult candidate.

A third medical risk associated with the use of undifferentiated stem cells is what is called epigenetic instability (Calvanese and Fraga, 2012). The long-term maintenance and continual passing of stem cells that is needed to preserve embryonic stem cell lines can result in aberrant methylation (or silencing) of gene promoter regions. A fourth safety issue is that there may be infectious agents present in the cell-feeder layers used to maintain stem cells. Currently, stem cells are most easily maintained in culture by growing them in chambers where other transformed cells, such as fibroblasts (obtained from other species), serve as feeder layers. The feeder cells supply essential nutrients that stem cells require to maintain their state of self-renewal. In addition, these feeder layers prevent the stem cells from differentiating by secreting a variety of extracellular matrix proteins or cytokines. The human stem cells are physically separated from the cellular feeder layer by semi-permeable membranes. Embryonic feeder cells provide for convenient growth and efficient study of embryonic stem cells in the laboratory but raise the risk of the interspecies transfer of viruses. There is ample evidence that some polio vaccines used during the mass vaccination campaigns of the 1950s and 1960s may have been contaminated with the simian virus SV-40, which has been reported to be associated with a variety of human tumors. SV-40 contamination may have occurred because the vaccine was developed using monkey kidney cell lines (Ferber, 2002). These types of reports suggest that feeder-cell-independent culture conditions, or serum free conditions, have to be developed to prevent infectious agents from contaminating the stem cell preparations. Thus, one goal of embryonic stem cell research is to find a way to derive and culture cell lines without the use of feeder layers or animal serum (Inzunza et al., 2005). In fact, in 2007, Gerecht et al., showed that human stem cells can be maintained on hydrogel (hyaluronic acid) in the absence of any feeder layers (Gerecht et al., 2007).

Conclusions

As of 2013, undifferentiated human stem cells have not cured any disease. To cure diseases, stem cells must be differentiated into more specialized cells that can be transferred to patients. Much more work is needed to understand how or whether stem cell transplants will benefit patients. One

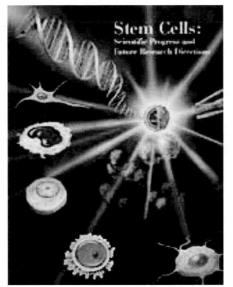

critical unknown is whether the stem cells infused into the animal or patient are proliferating to replace the damaged tissue, or whether these stem cells are merely fusing with existing endogenous cells to affect a therapeutic response. Cell fusion has been observed between adult stem cells obtained from bone marrow and nerves from the central nervous system in animals with spinal cord injuries that were given stem cells. Are the fused cells dead-end products that disappear with time, or are they intermediate steps in the normal process of tissue repair? The capacity of cells to fuse with one another is not unique to stem cells. Fused cells are normally found in several organ systems including the liver, intestine, placenta, skeletal muscle, cardiac smooth muscle, and bone marrow (megakaryocytes). One exciting technology is to encapsulate stem cells in biomaterials that only allows proteins, and not cells, to enter and leave the capsule (Barminko et al., 2011). In this manner, tissue rejection and tumorigenesis are avoided but the release of appropriate cytokines and growth factors that could regulate tissue repair or endogenous stem cell regeneration are maintained.

In summary, stem cell therapy holds exciting promise because it may greatly impact the treatment of a variety of diseases. Stem cell research offers more than just the potential to create new cell transplant protocols or cure disease; in the short term, research into stem cell differentiation will facilitate a better understanding of normal and abnormal cell differentiation, gene regulation, and embryological development from a single cell into a complete organism. The potential for a better understanding of basic biology and the development of new biotechnologies from stem cell research appears quite promising and justifies the investment of money, time and effort in stem cell research.

References

Abad, M., et al., "Reprogramming in vivo produces teratomas and iPS cells with totipotency features." Nature, doi: 10.1038/nature12586. [Epub ahead of print], 2013.

Barminko, J., et al., "Encapsulated mesenchymal stromal cells for in vivo transplantation." Biotechnology and Bioengineering,108:2747–2758, 2011.

Bellenchi, G. C., et al., "Adult neural stem cells: an endogenous tool to repair brain injury?" J Neurochem, Nov 7, 2012.
[http://onlinelibrary.wiley.com/doi/10.1111/jnc.12084/abstract]

Calvanese, V. and Fraga, M.F., "Epigenetics of embryonic stem cells.", Adv Exp Med Biol, 741:231-253, 2012.

Christoforou, N. and Gearhart, J. D.,"Stem cells and their potential in cell-based cardiac therapies." Prog Cardiovasc Dis, 49(6):396-413, 2007.

Cim A., et al., "In vivo studies on non-viral transdifferentiation of liver cells towards pancreatic beta cells. ", J Endocrinol, **214**: 277, 2012.

Clifford D. M., et al., "Stem cell treatment for acute myocardial infarction." Cochrane Database Syst Rev, **2**, CD006536, 2012.

Drews, K., et al., "Human induced pluripotent stem cells--from mechanisms to clinical applications.", J Mol Med (Berl), **90**:735, Jul, 2012.

Evans, M. J. and Kaufman, M. H., "Establishment in culture of pluripotential cells from mouse embryos." Nature, 292(5819):154-156, 1981.

Ferber, D., "Public health. Creeping consensus on SV40 and polio vaccine.", Science, 298:725-727, 2002.

Fernandez, E., et al., "The adult "paraplegic" rat: treatment with cell graftings." Surg Neurol, 65(3):223-237, 2006.

Fischbach, G. D. and Fischbach R. L., "Stem cells: science, policy, and ethics." J Clin Invest, 114(10):1364-1370, 2004.

Gerecht, S., et al., "Hyaluronic acid hydrogel for controlled self-renewal and differentiation of human embryonic stem cells.", Proc Natl Acad Sci U S A, 104: 11298-11303, 2007.

Greenbaum, L. E., "From skin cells to hepatocytes: advances in application of iPS cell technology.", J Clin Invest, **120**: 3102, 2010.

Griffith, L. G. and Naughton G., "Tissue engineering--current challenges and expanding opportunities." Science, 295(5557):1009-1014, 2012.

Higgins, et al., "Microenvironmental reprogramming by three-dimensional culture enables dermal papilla cells to induce de novo human hair-follicle growth." PNAS, October 21, 2013, doi: 10.1073/pnas.1309970110.

Houbracken, I., et al., "Gene delivery to pancreatic exocrine cells in vivo and in vitro." BMC Biotechnol, **12**: 74, 2012.

Huang, G. T., S., et al., "Mesenchymal stem cells derived from dental tissues vs. those from other sources: their biology and role in regenerative medicine." J Dent Res, 88(9):792-806, 2009.

Hwang, W. S., et al., "Patient-specific embryonic stem cells derived from human SCNT blastocysts." Science, 308(5729):1777-1783, 2005.

Hwang, W. S., et al., "Evidence of a pluripotent human embryonic stem cell line derived from a cloned blastocyst." Science, 303(5664):1669-1674, 2004.

Inzunza, J., et al., "Derivation of human embryonic stem cell lines in serum replacement medium using postnatal human fibroblasts as feeder cells.", Stem Cells, 23:544-549, 2005.

Jensen, J., et al., "Human embryonic stem cell technologies and drug discovery." J Cell Physiol, 219(3):513-519, 2009.

Lou, D., et al., "Cao, Selective killing of cancer stem cells by a novel dual-targeting strategy". Med Hypotheses, **79**:430, 2012.

Mantesso, A. and Sharpe, P., "Dental stem cells for tooth regeneration and repair." Expert Opin Biol Ther, 9(9):1143-1154, 2009.

Meyer-Blazejewska E. A., et al., "From hair to cornea: toward the therapeutic use of hair follicle-derived stem cells in the treatment of limbal stem cell deficiency." Stem Cells, **29**:57, 2011.

Mintz, B. and Illmensee K., (1975). "Normal genetically mosaic mice produced from malignant teratocarcinoma cells." Proc Natl Acad Sci U S A, 72(9):3585-3589, 1975.

Noggle, S., et al., "Human oocytes reprogram somatic cells to a pluripotent state.", Nature, 478:70-75, 2011.

Nostro, M. C. and Keller, G., "Generation of beta cells from human pluripotent stem cells: Potential for regenerative medicine." Semin Cell Dev Biol, **23**: 701, 2012.

Pan, G. et al., "Somatic cell reprogramming for regenerative medicine: SCNT vs. iPS cells." Bioessays, **34**:472, 2012.

Potier, E., et al.,"Directing bone marrow-derived stromal cell function with mechanics." J Biomech, 43(5):807-817, 2010.

Razvi, E. S., "Conference scene: Emerging themes in the stem cells space." Regen Med, 5(2):197-200, 2010.

Roura S, et al., "Umbilical **cord blood** for cardiovascular cell therapy: from promise to fact." Ann N Y Acad Sci, 2012 Apr;1254:66-70. doi: 10.1111/j.1749-6632.2012.06515.x.

Ruff, C. A., et al., "Cell-based transplantation strategies to promote plasticity following spinal cord injury." Exp Neurol, **235**:78, 2012.

Sandner et al., B., "Neural stem cells for spinal cord repair." Cell Tissue Res, **349**:349, 2012.

Schurgers, E., et al., "Discrepancy between the in vitro and in vivo effects of murine mesenchymal stem cells on T-cell proliferation and collagen-induced arthritis." Arthritis Res Ther, 12(1):R31,2010.

Shamblott, M. J., et al., "Derivation of pluripotent stem cells from cultured human primordial germ cells." Proc Natl Acad Sci U S A, 95(23):13726-13731, 1998.

Spillane, J.B. and Henderson, M.A., "Cancer stem cells: a review.", ANZ J Surg, 77: 464-468, 2007.

Stevens, L.C., "The development of transplantable teratocarcinomas from intratesticular grafts of pre- and postimplantation mouse embryos," Developmental Biology, 21:364-82, February 1970.

Thomson, J. A., et al., "Embryonic stem cell lines derived from human blastocysts." Science, 282(5391):1145-1147, 1998.

Trounson, A., et al., "Clinical trials for stem cell therapies." BMC Med, **9**:52, 2011.

Voltarelli, J.C., et al. "Autologous nonmyeloablative hematopoietic stem cell transplantation in newly diagnosed type 1 diabetes mellitus.", JAMA, 297:1568-1576, 2007.

Wang, T. W., et al., "Regulation of adult human mesenchymal stem cells into osteogenic and chondrogenic lineages by different bioreactor systems." J Biomed Mater Res A, 2008.
[http://onlinelibrary.wiley.com/doi/10.1002/jbm.a.31914/full]

Wingard, J. R., et al., "Hematopoietic stem cell transplantation: an overview of infection risks and epidemiology." Infect Dis Clin North Am, 24(2):257-272, 2010.

Yamanaka, S. and Blau H. M., "Nuclear reprogramming to a pluripotent state by three approaches." Nature, 465(7299):704-712, 2010.

Zhang, M. and Rosen J. M., "Stem cells in the etiology and treatment of cancer." Curr Opin Genet Dev, 16(1):60-64, 2006.

Zhou, Q., et al., "In vivo reprogramming of adult pancreatic exocrine cells to beta-cells." Nature, 455(7213):627-632, 2008.

Chapter Seven

Bioethics of stem cell research: The web of life's beginnings

Introduction

New biotechnologies often create controversy and challenge our thinking about fundamental principles and values. The major challenge and controversy in stem cell research is defining the beginning of human life - at what point does a human embryo attain the moral status of a human being? The debate concerning the definition of the beginning of human life is several thousand years old and can be found in the writings of Aristotle and in the Jewish Talmud.

Recently, stem cell research re-ignited and transformed this debate. Many scientists and bioethicists argue that an embryo is not simply a community of cells, but possesses human status and, therefore, deserves a set of rights similar to that of any other individual human being. According to this view, human zygotes, embryos, and fetuses have the right to life and should not to be destroyed or discarded. According to this view, the necessity in embryonic stem cell research to harvest cells from and then discard non-implanted embryos would constitute a form of murder.

Others argue that a non-implanted embryo is not a person, and that it should be ethically acceptable, even obligatory, to engage in embryonic stem cell research using this embryo in order to save human lives in need of therapeutic intervention. They argue that personhood including self-awareness, feeling pain or emotions are critical elements for an entity to possess moral rights.[1] All of the above characteristics suggest that an embryo that has not developed any nervous system that cannot feel pain and does not possess self-awareness should not have the status of a human being.

The questionable ethics of destroying embryos led the US Congress in 2001 to enact a broad ban on providing federal funds to support experimentation on human embryos. President Bush modified this ban by removing restrictions for work with existing stem cell lines, but he continued restricting funding for the creation of new stem cell lines. In 2009, President Obama asked the National

---

[1] The problem with this definition is that a comatose person has these attributes but is still considered a person.

Institutes of Health to establish new guidelines to remove some of these restrictions on human embryonic stem cell research. These new guidelines are more liberal than previous ones but still impose many limits on human embryonic stem cell research (**reference**).

This chapter summarizes four different perspectives regarding ethical parameters of stem cell research. The first approach samples viewpoints from different religions on critical issues related to stem cell research. The second approach samples public opinion polls to explore how Americans view and respond to issues related to stem cell research. The third approach explores viewpoints from different classic bioethical and philosophical perspectives. The final approach describes what is viewed as an emerging ethical paradigm: using scientific technology to developed new and innovative methodologies that attempt to respect the multicultural and diverse moral views that underlie these bioethical dilemmas.

Recent successes in transforming adult mouse fibroblasts into pluripotent stem cells through the process of induced pluripotent (iPS) and the use of lineage reprogramming (see Chapter 6) are examples where technology has been developed to defuse the intense debate concerning embryonic stem cell research. Yet, while these successes are exciting, there is a great deal of work that must be done to establish whether these new biotechnologies are as safe and pluripotent as the classical stem cells obtained from the inner mass of the embryo. For the foreseeable future, stem cells from the early embryo will remain the gold standard of stem cells.

Before describing the four different bioethical perspectives set out above, it is important to consider six options currently being debated in the bioethical literature with regard to implementing a policy on human embryonic stem cell research (Walters 2004).

- Option 1- No human embryo research should be permitted.
- Option 2- Research should only be permitted using existing human embryonic stem cell lines.
- Option 3- Research should only be permitted using existing human embryonic stem cell lines or pre-implanted embryos that are no longer needed for reproduction.
- Option 4- Research should be permitted: using: (a) existing human stem cell lines, (b) embryos that have never been implanted into a woman and are no longer needed for reproduction, and (c) embryos created specifically for research purposes via *in vitro*

fertilization techniques and have never been implanted into a woman.

- Option 5- Research should be permitted using: (a) existing human stem cell lines, (b) pre-implanted embryos no longer needed for reproduction, (c) pre-implanted embryos created specifically for research purposes via *in vitro* fertilization techniques, and (d) embryos created via somatic cell nuclear transfer into human eggs (therapeutic/research cloning).

- Option 6- Research should be permitted using: (a) existing human stem cell lines, (b) pre-implanted embryos no longer needed for reproduction, (c) pre-implanted embryos created via any method and (d) embryos created specifically for research purposes including somatic cell nuclear transfer into non-human eggs or zygotes.

Religious Traditions Regarding Stem Cell Research

Religious opinions regarding many bioethical issues are generally diverse and complex. The following represent what appears to be the representative or prominent opinion for each religion discussed, but it is important to recognize that a spectrum of other opinions exists within each faith. For a more comprehensive review of different religious viewpoints see (Waters 2003; Walters 2004).

Jewish Perspective: An embryo requires two conditions to attain the moral status of human life: implantation into a uterus and a 40-day period of embryological development. Thus, a non-implanted embryo or a human embryo during its first thirty-nine days of embryological development does not attain full human status. Nonetheless, destruction of such embryos is considered wasteful and should not be performed unless the purpose is to save human lives. Based on these principles, leading Jewish organizations such as the Rabbinical Council of America, the Union of Orthodox Jewish Congregations, the Conservative Rabbinical Assembly, and the Union of American Hebrew Congregations Assembly all favor the use of pre-implanted embryos that are less than 40 days in embryological development for medical stem cell research and support therapeutic/research cloning (within Options 2-6) (Zoloth, 2002). The use of implanted embryos (or embryos developmentally older than 40 days) as a source for stem cells would not be acceptable, even for medical research.

Islamic Perspective: According to Abdulaziz Sachedina, Professor of Islamic studies in the Religious Studies Department at the University of Virginia in Charlottesville, the consensus among many Muslim theologians is that an embryo in its first twelve days, before implantation, does not constitute a living human being. In addition, according to Muslim tradition, ensoulment (defined as when the soul enters the body) does not take place until after 120 days of pregnancy.   With respect to embryonic stem cell research, Dr. Sachedina proposes that it is permissible to obtain stem cells from excess embryos in IVF clinics. However, it is not permissible to fertilize an embryo to create a cell line solely for research purposes for reasons explained below.   This view is supported by Dr. Shahid Athar, Former Chair of Medical Ethics, Islamic Medical Association of North America.[2]

Dr. Muzammil Siddiqi expands the Islamic perspective on stem cell research as follows: "According to the Shari'ah, we should make a distinction between actual life and potential life....between the fertilized ovum in the dish and the fertilized ovum in the womb of its mother. Indeed, an embryo is valuable... these embryos were developed... in excess of what was required for this purpose [(IVF])... Destroying such embryos is not called and cannot be called abortion" (Weckerly, 2002). He also points out that many Muslim jurists have made a clear distinction between the early stages of pregnancy [first 40 days] and the later stages. Therefore a pre-implanted embryo would not be considered human and there would be "nothing wrong in doing this [stem cell] research, especially if this research has a potential to cure diseases. However, there are strict rules against the misuse of embryos." He believes that Islam distinguishes between using "spare" embryos from *in vitro* fertilization procedures, which would be destroyed regardless of whether or not they were used for research purposes, as compared to the deliberate production of embryos for stem cell research. From this perspective, Islam would sanction Option 3 but would not favor therapeutic cloning. In contrast, a recent Islamic religious legal ruling (called a Fatwa) from Singapore, considered as representing Islam in many parts of Southeast Asia, goes a step further and also endorses therapeutic cloning (Walters, 2004).

Roman Catholic Perspective: St. Thomas Aquinas, the 13th century Roman Catholic theologian, taught that an early fetus did not yet hold the status of personhood. Aquinas believed that "ensoulment" occurred at forty days for males, and at eighty days for females. In addition, Aquinas, following Aristotle, held that a fetus follows a process of "spirit animation consummated with the infusion of the soul," and occurs at quickening - when the mother first feels the baby move in her uterus.   However, as embryologic research and imaging technologies revealed more about fetal development in the late twentieth century,

---

[2] www.IMANA.org; www.ISLAM-USA.com

the Roman Catholic Church began amending this religious perspective. The Declaration of the Pontifical Academy for Life stated the following principles. First, the human embryo, from the moment of the union of the gametes, is human with a well-defined identity. Second, this zygote possesses human individuality and has the right to its own life. Third, cloning is contrary to the dignity of procreation, and of conjugal union; reproduction should occur via normal biological process and not through technology. Fourth, since isolating stem cells from a blastocyst involves destruction of the embryo, it is an immoral act. Finally, the Catholic Church believes that the ends do not justify the means and thus the use of stem cells to develop new therapies is an immoral action if destruction of an embryo occurs in the process. Therefore, research involving embryonic stem cells and any form of human cloning are both considered morally wrong (Ohara, 2003).Therefore, research involving embryonic stem cells and any form of human cloning are both considered morally wrong (Ohara, 2003).

Protestant Perspective: Protestants are divided between conservative and liberal opinions regarding stem cell research. Professor Gilbert Meilaender of Valparaiso University, in his testimony on stem cell research before the National Bioethics Advisory Commission (NBAC), appears to endorse a conservative approach as he stated, "the embryo is, I believe, the weakest and least advantaged of our fellow human beings, and no community is really strong if it will not carry its weakest members." He echoes views of other Protestant denominations that the use of human embryos for stem cell research violates the doctrine of Trinitarian faith.[3] Furthermore, like many Catholic philosophers and theologians, he claims that the use of biotechnology as a "means to an end" is wrong. Thus, embryonic stem cell research and therapeutic cloning are considered unethical.   The United Methodist Church, one of the largest Protestant denominations in the United States, represents a more liberal perspective in stating that existing stem cell lines provide a space to explore the potential of embryonic stem cell research provided that human embryos are not destroyed.[4]

Buddhist Perspective: Buddhism teaches that individual human life begins at conception. By virtue of its distinctive belief in rebirth, moreover, it regards the new embryo as the bearer of a karmic identity, which therefore entitles it to the same moral respect as an adult. Regardless of the potential therapeutic

---

[3] The philosophy of Trinitarian faith posits that all human beings are embodied persons and that a child is not merely given to a husband and wife as a blessing or just as a gift from the Lord. The child and human life is rather viewed within the context of outcome/best interest, not in terms of gift/preservation of life. Thus, destruction of unused embryos would be immoral as it denies the human potential of these beings.
[4] http://www.spiritrestoration.org/Church/religious-leaders-divided.htm

applications, it would be immoral to use as a source of stem cells for research purposes either surplus unwanted or frozen embryos created for *in vitro* fertilization treatment (whether or not these would eventually be destroyed), or human embryos specifically created for research purposes. There may be a distinction between reproductive cloning and stem cell research within Buddhism, in that stem cell research results in destruction of potential life while reproductive cloning, if the technology is appropriately developed, would result in creating life. There are Buddhist scholars who believe that killing of an embryo at any stage violates the tenet that living things should not be harmed. Cloning for reproductive purposes would not violate Buddhist precepts as long as it does not involve the destruction of the embryo (Walters, 2004).

American Perspectives Related to the Beginning of Life

Public opinion polls often vary considerably but can offer a glimpse of the current philosophical values and public ethical concerns of a society. From the polls described below, it appears that Americans are split regarding the ethics of embryonic stem cell research. In 2009, a Gallup poll reported that 51% of Americans surveyed stated that it is more important to conduct stem cell research that might lead to new cures than to avoid destroying human embryos.[5] In addition, the results of this Gallup poll indicated that nearly 80% of respondents favor some restrictions on hESC research, with only 14% favoring no restrictions. Somewhat paradoxically, this same poll indicates that 57% of respondents view hESC research as "morally acceptable," demonstrating that opinions are not easily characterized as either strictly in favor or strictly opposed.[6] In addition, the results of this survey showed that the percent of Americans polled who believe it is morally correct to obtain stem cells from human embryos for medical research increased from 52% in 2003 to about 57% in 2009.

Interestingly, the public views on government funding for stem cell research have remained fairly stable since 2004, with a small majority (about 52%) consistently supporting fewer restrictions on funding, rather than maintaining or strengthening the current restrictions. There have been many polls conducted over the past decade and a number of conclusions can be drawn from all of these polls. Most polls not ask their respondents what motivated their thinking. Second, religious perspectives are diverse with the most common response from religious people being that either conception or the detection of a

---

[5] http://www.gallup.com/poll/116485/Majority-Americans-Likely-Support-Stem-Cell-Decision.aspx
[6] www.gallup.com/poll/21676/Stem-Cell-Research.aspx

fetal heartbeat should be markers for the beginning of human life. Third, the more people heard and became educated about the ethical issues and potential therapeutic applications of stem cell research, the more they supported this research. Finally, Americans are more likely to trust information on stem cell research from scientific researchers than from religious leaders, the media, or government officials.

Ethical Theories Focusing on Stem Cell Research.

Bioethicists have utilized a variety of ethical theories and principles in their discussions of stem cell research. However, unlike religious groups that focus on personhood or when a human soul enters the fetus, bioethicists introduce various theories, such as consequentialist ethics or deontological ethics, which they consider central to stem cell research (Welin, 2002). At the very least, many bioethicists support Option 2, that research should precede using established stem cell lines. There is a diversity of opinions, however, among leading bioethicists across America concerning the use of stem cells derived from embryos that must be destroyed in the process.

Proponents Favoring Stem Cell Research

In general, the proponents of embryonic stem cell research favor Options 3-6 and employ three general ethical principles to support their views: respect for persons/human life/autonomy, beneficence, and justice.

Respect for human life: The interpretation of "respect for human life" or how to define the value of human life is critical in stem cell debates. The proponents of stem cell research claim that the pre-implanted embryo less than two weeks old is merely a community of cells, no different than any tissue or organ part, and does not possess full human status. Arthur M. Caplan, PhD, Chairman of the Medical Ethics Department at the University of Pennsylvania's School of Medicine, presents a novel approach in his discussions of why he supports embryonic stem cell research. He states that isolating stem cells from an embryo protects the potential and/or life of the embryo since its genetic material is stored and maintained in the stem cells and could theoretically be used in nuclear transfer to generate an implantable zygote. He believes that no embryo used to isolate stem cells is actually sacrificed (McGee and Caplan, 2001).

Autonomy: Both the donors and the recipients of the embryonic stem cells should be informed truthfully of the intended aim, as well as probable consequences and risks, of the specific procedure, so that the person receiving the stem cells, or this person's proxy, can act in an informed and responsible manner. A potential prototype in outlining these issues is organ transplantation.

Beneficence: Beneficence applied to stem cell research states that human embryonic stem cell research aims at saving lives through the treatment of disease. This principle is used to support Options 3-6, including therapeutic cloning. Bioethics favoring stem cell research asserts that a utilitarian approach to bioethics applies here or that the ends justify the means (see Chapter 2). Michael Sandel, a bioethicist, highlights this argument from another perspective (Sandel, 2004). He writes that, "if the creation and sacrifice of spare embryos in infertility treatment is morally acceptable, why isn't the creation and sacrifice of embryos for stem cell research also acceptable? Is it appropriate to do a small sacrifice now (e.g., destroy the pre-implanted embryo) for future hopes of developing effective therapies?"

Justice: Justice is another important issue in the application of stem cell technology: who would donate the materials for nuclear cell transfer and the generation of appropriate stem cells, and who would benefit from the research. Currently, cloning technology is envisioned to be an expensive clinical procedure. The proponents of stem cell research believe that the technology and potential to better understand areas of cancer, cell differentiation, and embryological development are worth the high costs of doing this research.

The Opposition to Stem Cell Research

The opponents of embryonic stem cell research (who may support Options 1 or 2, but not Options 3-6) introduce four ethical principles or objections to support their position: dis-respecting human value, nonmaleficence, limitation to human experimentation, and the "slippery slope" argument.

Disrespecting human value: Bioethicists who oppose stem cell research propose an "equal moral status" view of the human embryo to a fully formed human being. This view defines conception as the moment at which an embryo attains moral human status, as a new unique genetic organism has been created that has the potential to develop into a person. This view is similar to that proposed by the Catholic Church and Buddhist tenets but offers a scientific rationale rather than a divine one. Thus, one does not have the moral right to destroy a fertilized egg, let alone a pre-implanted embryo.

Nonmaleficence: "Nonmaleficence" (do no harm) is introduced by opponents to stem cell research to highlight that the destruction of the pre-implanted embryo permanently halts the future development of the embryo into a human being. By introducing this principle, these bioethicists, who usually support in vitro fertilization (IVF) procedures, have now to distinguish between embryonic stem cell research and IVF, since in both instances pre-implanted embryos are destroyed. These bioethicists claim that with respect to IVF, multiple embryos are generated but every embryo, from the moment of its creation, has the potential to develop into a child. Thus, more eggs are fertilized than will be transferred to a woman [in a given cycle], but each embryo is brought into being as an end in itself, not simply as a means to other ends. They view overproduction of embryos in IVF as analogous to what occurs during normal reproduction where over sixty to seventy five percent of conceptions lead to spontaneous miscarriages. With respect to stem cell research, the situation is dramatically different; the creation of embryos in the laboratory for stem cell research currently requires (without exception) their destruction. In other words, an embryo used for stem cell research is being created to be destroyed. From this perspective, bioethicists argue that since the intention to destroy the embryo is involved in this process, it is morally wrong. Furthermore, these bioethicists argue that there is a moral difference between acts of commission and acts of omission, between actively killing an embryo and passively failing to intervene to stop its destruction from other causes.

Limitations in human experimentation: Leon Kass, a renowned member of the President George W. Bush's Council on Bioethics, is outspoken in his opposition to embryonic stem cell research and presents yet another argument. Professor Kass believes that scientific research must have limitations. Scientists should not have the power or authority to engage in any and every research direction they personally deem worthy.[7] In other words, ethical concerns should limit freedom of choice in academic research. This relates to a bioethical mandate that states: it is not what you <u>can </u>do, it is what you <u>should</u> do. As many significant and contentious bioethical issues may not easily or swiftly be resolved, it is better to err on the side of being somewhat conservative, until more information about the risks and benefits of a specific biotechnology is known or decided.

Slippery slope arguments: Opponents of embryonic stem cell research are also concerned with the "slippery slope" argument. As defined in Chapter One, a slippery slope argument means predicting, with or without justification or proof, that one step in a process will inexorably lead to further steps which are generally undesirable or immoral. Several opponents of stem cell research caution that by approving therapeutic cloning, stem cell research will surely lead to reproductive

---

[7] www.aph.gov.au/library/pubs/CIB/2002-03/03cib05.pdf

cloning. The other "slippery slope" fear presented by opponents of stem cell research is that allowing the destruction of embryos to become an entrenched practice would serve to desensitize the scientific establishment, regulating institutions, and indeed society, to the destruction of life in general.

The slippery slope fear is also expressed by members of the disability community who believe that life is not disposable. In other words, the destruction of the embryo devalues human life and its diversity, and that selective destruction of all embryos genetically identifiably vulnerable to genetic diseases can be viewed as part of the larger issue of eugenics and "designer babies." Is it appropriate to abort embryos or terminate pregnancies just because a fetus possesses genes to express cystic fibrosis, Huntington's disease, or Alzheimer's disease?

These opponents of embryonic stem cell research understand the potential value that stem cell research can bring into a clinical setting. However, they argue that there may be credible scientific alternatives to using embryonic stem cells, such as using stem cells derived from adult tissue or from umbilical cord blood, from iPS technology, or from aborted fetuses. These opponents believe that resolving the ethical debate surrounding embryonic stem cell research is too controversial and polarized. They support suspending embryonic stem cell research and exploring the use of non-embryonic stem cells as a less controversial research alternative.

Despite intense debate among bioethicists regarding embryonic stem cell research, there is general consensus on a few issues that place limitations on the directions of stem cell research. Even pro-stem cell advocates propose, for example, that embryonic stem cells produced from donated human embryos should not be used for reproductive cloning but should be permissible in laboratory-based research. As discussed in Chapter 4, reproductive cloning at this point in time should not be done. In addition, virtually all bioethicists agree that combination of human gametes with animal gametes should be prohibited (see Chapter 8).

Scientific Research Responds to Bioethical Concerns

The various bioethical theories and principles, relating to the issue of when human status is attained during embryological development, may be difficult to resolve in a universal manner or with moral consensus in the near future. Indeed this question may be irresolvable because proposed solutions are rooted in multi-cultural, multi-religious, and multi-philosophical values. Yet the debates have triggered new approaches to address these issues and allow for the reformulation of bioethical guidelines (see Chapter 2). Specifically, the scientific community has responded to these dilemmas by striving to develop new technologies that may not conflict with many of the underlying religious and bioethical concerns. Scientists are now trying to develop these technologies in ways that may actually avoid some of the ethical concerns. This represents a fundamental change in the bioethical arena – creating and enhancing a partnership between bioethics and scientific research. The direction of biomedical research now is more influenced by the bioethical issues raised in association with human embryonic stem cell research.

One example of a new platform or collaborative approach involves utilizing induced pluripotent stem (iPS) cell technology (see Chapter 6) as a method to generate embryonic stem cells. The underlying technology of iPS allows researchers to generate pluripotent stem cells from a variety of adult tissue such as the skin, thereby avoiding the necessity to destroy a pre-implanted embryo to obtain embryonic stem cells.

The recent advance by Dr. Douglas Melton at Harvard Medical School using transcription factors to transform one cell type into a different one is another promising technology that avoids the generation of stem cells. As described in Chapter 6, this technology was originally developed to explore new therapies for diabetes, but also has a broad range of potential clinical applications in immunology, heart disease, and neurodegenerative diseases. In addition, this research could lead to better understanding of how to reprogram a cancer cell into a normal cell.

Allocation of Research Funds

A bioethical issue related to embryonic stem cell research that has not received much attention is funding priority. Does the potential of stem cell technology justify its funding as opposed to funding more conventional research programs for diseases that do not involve stem cell research? In 2012, the total budget of the National Institutes of Health was approximately $38 billion. This represents almost one half of the $75 billion allocated by pharmaceutical and biotechnology companies to all biomedical research. In addition, pharmaceutical companies estimate that it takes 10-15 years from conceptualizing a new drug to getting it approved by the FDA, at a cost of approximately $1.5 billion dollars. Many experts in stem cell research predict that costs for clinical applications of stem cells will be even higher, and will require at least another decade of research. One critical ethical challenge is who should fund the clinical studies utilizing stem cells and which diseases should be examined and in which priority?

Research in stem cell differentiation will not only impact potential applications to organ or cell replacement, but will enhance our understanding of basic biomedical principles such as the regulation of gene expression, cellular differentiation, and basic embryology. The pursuit of knowledge for its own sake is a fundamental driving force for many researchers. Even if stem cell research leads to limited clinical applications in the short term (10-20 years), this research has the ability to enrich our understanding of basic processes in biology such as cellular differentiation, gene imprinting, and gene regulation.

The rise of commercially-oriented biotechnology can threaten the valuable pursuit of scientific knowledge for its own sake. Scientists in both academia and industry may try to commercialize their stem cell research even before clinical trials in cell/organ transplant are completed. This aspect of commercialization before clinical implementation was in part responsible for the infusion of huge amounts of funds that went into monoclonal antibody research in the early 1980's. Specifically, it became apparent that monoclonal antibody technology not only had therapeutic applications, but created new diagnostic probes. In fact, the development of a rapid pregnancy test that utilized monoclonal technology provided an immediate revenue stream for companies and universities engaged in this technology. Thus, companies generated profits from this technology even before the first clinically approved monoclonal antibody was marketed in the mid 1990's.[8]

The non-therapeutic commercialization of stem cell technology is not as obvious as other biotechnological discoveries, such as monoclonal technology, but nonetheless might be developed to offset the years of research and investment costs required to bring to market approved therapies from stem cells. It is possible, for example, that embryonic stem cells may be better candidate hosts for vaccine generation than using classical methods of growing viruses in human fetal cell cultures. Another possible commercialization of stem cells, currently in place, involves allowing couples to pay a fee to store umbilical cord blood or fat tissue from liposuction protocols that could be used in the future to obtain stem cells. These stem cells could be frozen for many years and thawed to recover the stem cells if needed for therapy.

Finally, stem cells could also be used very profitably for less serious medical conditions that could receive expedited FDA approval. Each year over

---

[8]http://www.hopkins-arthritis.org/edu/mono_anti.html#application; https://mail.cumc.columbia.edu/owa/auth/logon.aspx?replaceCurrent=1&url=https%3a%2f%2fmail.cumc.columbia.edu%2fowa%2f

one billion dollars are spent to try to correct baldness. At the base of every hair follicle is the hair bulb, where precursor cells become hair. Follicles also contain a structure called the bulge where stem cells are thought to reside. In mouse baldness models it has been shown that these stem cells will differentiate into hair follicles and initiate hair growth (Meyer-Blazejewska et al., 2011). These stem cells not only make hair follicles, but also can generate other skin cells and have a huge capacity to proliferate. Besides treating baldness, transplanting the same stem cells could treat a more significant medical condition - burns. Scientists could isolate and use these stem cells in skin grafts for burn patients, generating better grafts with hairs. Bringing this technology to the clinic and the subsequent approval by the FDA might be much more rapid than the use of stem cells for other therapies and could provide enormous commercial value.

Bio-Legal Issues

There are several issues regarding stem cell research that have legal ramifications. The first is defining the rights of the zygote or the fetus. As stated throughout this chapter, this issue is related to the bioethical issue of when a zygote or embryo attains human status or personhood. In addition, any legal decision must be consistent with current laws on the rights of women to abort fetuses, how unused pre-implanted embryos should be treated, and the use of other fetal cells for biomedical research. For those who want to examine this issue in greater detail, references are provided (Curran, 2009). Another issue is ownership. Who owns embryos or stem cell lines that have already been produced? A case study is provided in **Textbox 1**.

Compensation for women who donate eggs for stem cell research: In 2004, Drs. Hwang and Moon of Seoul National University, South Korea, reported that they had generated eleven human patient-specific embryonic stem cell lines using nuclear transfer technology. As it turned out, their work raised many ethical issues as many of their research results were based on fraudulent data and the coercive use of human subjects for stem cell research. It was revealed that most of the women in their study were lab workers and were under pressure to donate their eggs to be used in generating these stem cells. In contrast, most centers utilized discarded human fertilized eggs to generate embryonic stem cells.

An important question raised in this case is whether these women have any rights in determining how their eggs can be used or whether they could be sold to others inside and outside South Korea? While procuring oocytes and embryos from the excess supply of IVF procedures has a clear precedent, the procurement of oocytes from "non-medical" donors does not have a clear precedent. The women in South Korea donated their oocytes for research purposes that had neither reproductive nor medical purposes. Presumably, these women were aware that procuring their oocytes did have a medical risk. Between 0.3 and 5% of women who undergo ovarian stimulation can experience severe ovarian hyperstimulation, which can cause pain and occasionally lead to renal failure, potential future infertility problems, and even death.

Medical Tourism and Stem Cell Therapies

Medical tourism in which patients travel internationally to gain access to unapproved health care services, such as stem cell replacement therapy, has become increasingly common. As most stem cell therapies are not approved in the United States, numerous patients are going abroad to countries like China, the Caribbean, Latin America, and Russia where such treatments is legal. Individuals travel abroad for such treatments for a variety of reasons. Some are desperate and hope that such treatments could cure illnesses in which no FDA approved therapy has worked. Others read about sports celebrities, including football quarterback Peyton Manning, who have used stem cell therapy to treat their injuries and believe that it works. As of 2013, no reputable published study has demonstrated that any of these medical tourism stem cell clinics offer any healthcare benefits.

Even the use of stem cells for non-medical conditions such as baldness and aging (see previous chapter) drives people to seek such procedures. Horrific cases have been reported. One California woman opted for a relatively new kind of cosmetic procedure at a different clinic in Beverly Hills—a face-lift that made use of her own adult stem cells. A few months later she explained that she could not open her right eye without considerable pain and that every time she forced it open, she heard a strange click—a sharp sound, like a tiny castanet snapping shut After examining her in person at The Morrow Institute in Rancho Mirage, Calif., the attending physician observed that her eyelid drooped stubbornly and that the area around her eye was somewhat swollen. Six and a half hours of surgery later, he surgically removed small chunks of bone from the woman's eyelid and tissue surrounding her eye, which was scratched but largely intact. The clicks she heard were the bone fragments grinding against one another. The stem cells injected to remove her sagging eyes differentiated into bone fragments.[9]

The popularity of international stem cell clinics is of a major concern that the FDA has issues warnings and guidelines on their web site (see

---

[9] https://www.scientificamerican.com/article.cfm?id=stem-cell-cosmetics

http://www.fda.gov/BiologicsBloodVaccines/ScienceResearch/BiologicsResearch Areas/ucm127182.htm). Internet sites offer free advertisement about stem cell clinics that claim to help people suffering from a dizzying array of serious conditions, including: Alzheimer's, Amyotrophic lateral sclerosis, atherosclerosis, autism, brain damage, cancer, cerebellar ataxia, cerebral palsy, chronic obstructive pulmonary disease, Crohn's, diabetes, diseases of the eye, genetic disorders, Huntington's, kidney disease, lupus, muscular sclerosis, muscular dystrophy, Parkinson's, rheumatoid arthritis, spinal cord injury, spinal muscular atrophy, stroke, and Tay-Sachs disease. One issue with stem cell tourism is the number of serious and harmful health risks associated with such procedures.

History: The Master Teacher

The impact of history on bioethical issues: In Chapter 3, one of the new guidelines proposed for resolving bioethical issues involves an historical analysis. Current bioethical debates are of great value to society and to its scientific research institutions.

Bioethical debates can focus on reconciling potential future applications of a new biotechnology with current real medical risks associated with the technology. Several examples of earlier scientific research and the public's response are illustrative. In the 1940's and 50's, nuclear energy was thought to be an answer to solving the need for obtaining cheap and clean energy. The Three Mile Island leak of radioactivity in 1979, as well as other reported leaks in Russia (e.g., Chernobyl) and Japan, confirmed the public's fear regarding safety problems associated with this energy source, and subsequently has limited its practical application. Similarly, public fear associated with the current medical risks or dangers of reproductive cloning (i.e., cloning to produce children- see **Chapter 4**) might also limit its utilization in medicine.

One lesson from scientific history is that science and technology, while often considered value-neutral intrinsically, i.e., neither good nor bad, are rarely morally neutral. In addition, they often pose the problem of dual use, when a technology intended for a specific, benign use by its creator is appropriated by another agent with other and perhaps negative or unintended purposes and applications in mind. Some scientists and philosophers consider the proposition

---

Textbox 1: Bio-Legal issues: A case study

Who has the legal rights to stem cell lines? Does the donor of the embryo have any legal or fiduciary rights? An actual case study is relevant here.

In 1976, Coca-Cola salesman John Moore went to the Medical Center of the University of California suffering from a rare disease called hairy-cell leukemia. His doctor, Dr. David Golde, recommended removing Moore's spleen. Moore agreed and his spleen was removed. Over the next seven years, John Moore returned to UC Medical Center giving samples of blood, skin, bone marrow and sperm, which Golde told him were needed to maintain his health. During this period, Golde noticed that Moore's body was over-producing lymphokines, important components of the human immune system. Without completely consulting Moore, Golde began used samples from Moore's body to create a create what is known as the "Mo" cell line and in 1983, filed a patent application for a "unique T-lymphocyte line and products derived there from these cells." The "inventors" listed on the patent were Golde and Quan. The "Mo" cell line and its derivatives were the basis of commercial contracts with several companies and the University. Mr. Moore sued them in response to their patent for not including himself as an inventor since the cells were derived from his own body.

How would you rule in this case?

One opinion held that Moore's physical body was his own property and that even though it was only tissue obtained from his body, Moore had a proprietary right prior to "discovery" and should be able to benefit financially from its use. Another opinion argued that other, non-economic values, such as dignity and equity, should be considered when debating the market value of human biological materials. Yet another opinion argued that property discourse and market value have no role when it comes to discarded human biological materials.

Does John Moore's attempt to get money from his body represent the exacerbation of human beings' ability to modify themselves and others for short-term profit against their own best long-term interests? In fact, the California Supreme Court ruled in 1990 that Moore's doctor had breached his "fiduciary duty" by not revealing the research and financial interest in his patient's cells. However, the court also denied Moore's claim to ownership of the cells removed from his body. In part, the court argued that since "research on human cells plays a critical role in medical research," granting patients proprietary rights threatened to "hinder research by restricting access to the necessary raw materials." (See Gold, 1996).

---

that there is a built-in moral component imbedded in the core of scientific activity itself. The desire to find the truth is itself a moral impulse, or at least contains a moral impulse. Stephen Hawking commented, "I think that science itself is morally neutral. But scientists themselves need not be morally neutral. They have moral responsibilities".[10]

We are likely entering an era in which new scientific discoveries and technologies are being generated as attempts to solve what appear to be irresolvable bioethical dilemmas. Public response to new technologies also will evolve over time, especially when clear medical benefits are derived from such technology. In vitro fertilization (IVF) provides another useful historical example (Edwards, 2009). IVF is usually the treatment of choice for a woman with blocked or absent fallopian tubes. Religious concerns were raised in 1978 in response to the birth of Louise Brown, the first test tube baby conceived outside the body. In 1978, opinion polls revealed that about 90% of Americans believed it was religiously wrong to create babies via IVF and many considered it a form of "playing God." In 2001, IVF led to the birth of more than 41,000 babies, nearly one percent of the total number of babies born in the United States (Spar 2006). Initially, the procedure offered a 3 to 6 percent chance of pregnancy, but medical and technological advances over the years have increased the rate to nearly 30 percent. Today several medical centers report a rate of success of nearly 50 percent. The primary use of IVF 25 years ago was in cases of fallopian tube disease. Currently, IVF is being conducted if unexplained infertility presents in either the man or the woman. As an example, doctors can take a single sperm from a man with a low sperm-count and insert it directly into the egg to increase the chance of fertilization.

In addition, IVF is used by couples who have a family history of certain genetic diseases, such as Tay Sachs, Huntington's, or cystic fibrosis, to screen out and select only pre-implanted embryos that do not express the defective gene. People often overlook the destruction of defective embryos or embryos when they are in excess of clinical need. Thus, as medical benefits of IVF became apparent, and as society gradually accepted and understood that infertility is a medical condition that is correctable, religious-based concerns appeared to be less important to the general public (Loike, 2001). Today, less than five percent believe there is a religious conflict in utilizing IVF for infertile couples.

With respect to therapeutic cloning or embryonic stem cell research, it is highly unlikely that these technologies will be banned throughout the world. How could countries such as the United States and Great Britain purport to have the best scientific research capabilities if they were to ban stem cell research and rely on other countries (i.e., South Korea, China, or Italy) to examine the potential benefits of therapeutic cloning or stem cell research? Moreover, if either of these

---

[10] http://www.psyclops.com/hawking/resources/cherniack.html

technologies would offer a safe and effective therapy for some of our more pernicious diseases, it is likely that the American public, and, in turn, the federal government, would be inclined to support such therapies.

The final historical example is the use of fetal cells in vaccine development (Hansen and Sladek, 1989; Barnwell, 2003). The use of fetal cells from discarded fetuses has been associated with similar ethical concerns as embryonic stem cells. Yet, cultured fetal cells have been instrumental in evaluating the toxicity levels of drugs and the development of vaccines. Fetal tissue research was responsible for a polio vaccine in the 1950s and later vaccines against rubella, chickenpox, rabies, and hepatitis-A. A human cell line, known as WI-38, was obtained in the 1950s from the lung of an aborted fetus and used for the development of vaccines against chickenpox, rubella, and rabies. Using animal cell lines instead of fetal cell lines poses significant health risks. Undetected animal viruses in animal cell lines, for example, could contaminate human recipients. Millions of people were infected through polio vaccines contaminated with Simian Virus number 40 (SV-40). Undetected in the monkey, these cell lines were used to prepare the vaccines (Poulin and DeCaprio, 2006). While researchers consider SV-40 to be a powerful immuno-suppressor and a cancer-causing virus, the medical side effects of people infected with SV-40 are still being clinically evaluated.

One could rightly argue that undeniably, fetal tissue research resulting in the development of vaccines has already saved tens, if not hundreds, of millions of human lives. It appears that the practical therapeutic benefit of vaccines derived from fetal cells far outweighed the many ethical misgivings. Similarly, the potential therapeutic benefits of embryonic stem cells might be viewed as outweighing the ethical objections.

Conclusions

Determining when a zygote or embryo attains moral human status is one of the many unanswered bioethical conundrums that arise from cloning and stem cell research. Could scientific research ever resolve faith-based issues such as whether the soul exists or when the soul enters or leaves a human body? Currently, we are witnessing an interesting conscious or even unconscious response of scientists to apparently irresolvable bioethical issues, by pursuing new scientific methods that may alleviate the religious and cultural challenges. Many scientists believe that stem cells provide great potential therapeutic applications to fight some of humanity's most pernicious afflictions such as Alzheimer's disease, Parkinson's disease, heart disease, spinal cord injuries, and diabetes, and to create viable methods for organ replacement.

It must be recalled that IVF, fetal cell use, and gene therapy were all born in controversy. However, after decades of research that included clinical setbacks, there is a new understanding and support for applying these technologies to medicine and for recognizing that these technologies promise to have a significant impact on future health care.

Therapeutic cloning and embryonic stem cell research are still in their infancy. Many scientists predict that as clinical applications of stem cells are put into practice there will be a diminished outcry related to ethical objections. Finally, it must be recognized that while the use of stem cells for cell or organ transplantation is the most ethically controversial therapeutic application, there are other ways in which stem cell research may be justified. As mentioned above, understanding basic biological processes for their own sake has been a defining characteristic of scientific research.

Yet, at the end of this discussion, we are still left with a fundamental question: Does science have a right to pursue basic or potential therapeutic knowledge whatever the cost?

CRITICAL THINKING AND CHALLENGES

1. **What are the ethical applications derived from the debates on abortion that might apply to stem cell research?**
2. **Theoretically, new technology has just been developed that allows scientists to reprogram any adult cell into totipotent stem cells. These cells can be differentiated into sperm and ova and upon fertilization in vitro could be implanted into a host mother and develop into a normal baby. Would this technology redefine your concept of when human life begins?**
3. **How would you characterize the ethical issues of transplanting human embryonic stem cells into animals to reconstitute their brains with human neurons?**

   Discussion question: How would you resolve this question, ethically and scientifically- at what point does an embryo attain the status of a human being?

References

Barnwell, J. and Joly, O. "Vaccines." Columbia College Journal of Bioethics, 2:47-49, 2003.

Curran, D.S., "Abandonment and reconciliation: addressing political and common law objections to fetal homicide laws.", Duke Law J, 58:1107-1142, 2009.

Edwards, R.G., "The history of assisted human conception with especial reference to endocrinology." Experimental and clinical endocrinology & diabetes, **104**:183-204, 2009.

Gold, E.R. Body parts: Property rights and the ownership of human biological materials, Georgetown University Press, 1998.

Hansen, J. T. and Sladek, J. R. Jr., "Fetal research." Science, **246**(4931):775-9, 1989.

Hwang, W. S., et al., "Evidence of a pluripotent human embryonic stem cell line derived from a cloned blastocyst." Science, **303**(5664):1669-74, 2004.

Loike, J. D., "Bioethical and legal boundaries of human cloning." American Society of Cell Biology Newsletter, **24**:7-10, 2001.

McGee, G. and Caplan A., "Stem cell research." Hastings Cent Rep, **31**(5):4; author reply 4-5, 2001.

Meyer-Blazejewska E. A., et al., "From hair to cornea: toward the therapeutic use of hair follicle-derived stem cells in the treatment of limbal stem cell deficiency." Stem Cells, **29**:57, 2011.

Ohara, N., "Ethical consideration of experimentation using living human embryos: the Catholic Church's position on human embryonic stem cell research and human cloning." Clin Exp Obstet Gynecol, **30**(2-3):77-81, 2003.

Poulin, D. L. and DeCaprio, J. A.,"Is there a role for SV40 in human cancer?" J Clin Oncol, **24**(26):4356-65, 2006.

Sandel, M.J., "Embryo ethics-the moral logic of stem-cell research." New England Journal of Medicine, **351**:207-208, 2004.

Spar, D. L., "Where babies come from: supply and demand in an infant marketplace." Harv Bus Rev, **84**(2):133-40, 142-3, 166, 2006.

Walters, L., "Human Embryonic Stem Cell Research: An Intercultural Perspective." Kennedy Institute of Ethics Journal, **14**(1):3-38, 2004.

Waters, B. & Cole-Turner, R. God and the Embryo: Religious voices on stem cells and cloning, (Georgetown University Press, 2003).

Weckerly, M., 'The Islamic view on stem cell research." Online. Rutgers Journal of Law and Religion.
http://www-camlaw. rutgers.edu/publications/lawreligion/new_devs/RJLR_ND_56.pdf , 2002.

Welin, S., "Ethical issues in human embryonic stem cell research." Acta Obstet Gynecol Scand, **81**(5):377-82, 2002.

Zoloth, L., "Reasonable magic and the nature of alchemy: Jewish reflections on human embryonic stem cell research." Kennedy Institute of Ethics Journal, **12**:65-93, 2002.

Chapter Eight

Human-animal Chimeras and Respecting Human Dignity

Introduction

Is it ethical to transplant human embryonic stem cells into the nervous system of an animal fetus in order to reconstitute all or part of the animal's brains? This is one of the most contentious issues facing scientists and indeed the public. Such an organism, composed of both human and animal cells, is commonly called a chimera. The word 'chimera' is derived from the Greek name for a mythical beast that had the head of a lion, the body of a goat, and the tail of a serpent. Scientists are creating chimeras in an attempt to benefit humankind, to gain a better understanding of human diseases, and to develop novel therapies. In this chapter we present many examples of human-animal chimera research that have reaped huge scientific and medical benefits without impinging on the "humanness" of the recipients.

Research in stem cell science has had a profound effect on both the science and ethics of chimera research. Research in understanding how to differentiate stem cells into neural cells has elicited proposals to transfer human neural stem cells into fetuses or embryos of mice to study basic brain development (Mueller et al., 2005). Such trans-species forays introduce human central nervous system stem cells into animals during their formative development and may impart human behavioral characteristics or human consciousness. Would it be ethical to use chimeras to study human behavior?

Recent History of Chimeras in Medicine

Apparently, inserting small amounts of human tissue or cells into animals has been reported for decades without ethical outcry (Huther, 2009). Researchers, for example, have transferred human material such as embryonic stomachs, intestine, tracheas, and lungs into the bodies of mice (Angioi et al., 2002). Researchers also have transfused human blood and transplanted skin stem cells into postnatal mice (Raychaudhuri et al., 2001) and into fetal sheep (Narayan et al. 2006).

In the late 1980s, Dr. Irving Weissman from Stanford University transplanted human bone marrow cells into a mouse strain that lacked its own immune system (McCune et al., 1991). The stem cells from the human bone marrow were not rejected by the host mice and differentiated into a nearly complete human immune system. These human-mouse chimeras have proven to be extremely valuable in studying a variety of human diseases such as AIDS. HIV, the virus that causes AIDS, does not normally infect mouse cells but will infect human cells in the immune system of these human-mouse chimeras. From these animal chimeric models, a great deal of information has been obtained on how the AIDS virus infects and replicates in human immune cells within a living animal. In addition, these human-mouse chimeras serve as important models to study potential new therapies for fighting AIDS.   Recently, scientists have repopulated a mouse liver with human liver cells and now are using this animal model to both gain a better understanding of liver development and to examine drug metabolism within human livers (Meuleman et al., 2005). These human-mouse chimeras are also being used to study the pathology of hepatitis viral infection (Chayama et al., 2011).

Organ transplantation is another potential application of sheep-human chimera research that is being investigated by Esmail Zanjani, at the University of Nevada at Reno (Almeida-Porada et al., 2007). Dr. Zanjani found that about halfway through a sheep's fetal development, there is a window of time where their immune system does not reject any foreign cells. Thus, the sheep fetuses can accept human stem cells and incorporate them into various organs where the stem cells develop and multiply. When born, these sheep chimeras will contain millions of human cells in specific organs including their blood, livers, and kidneys. The location of the human stem cells that are transplanted determines which organs develop human cells. Thus, a patient in need of a liver transplant could have his bone marrow--derived stem cells injected into a specific location within a sheep fetus. Once born, this sheep would have a liver that is composed of primarily human cells and genetically compatible for transplantation into the bone marrow donor.[1] Currently, livers from these human-sheep chimeras contain 80% human cells. The overall goal is to generate human livers with a minimal number of sheep cells to reduce tissue rejection.

Research has also is beginning to develop human-pig chimeras. Dr. Nakauchi and colleagues are exploring the idea of implanting human pluripotent stem cells into pig embryos genetically engineered to be incapable of developing their own pancreases. These cells could be either embryonic stem cells or iPS cells (derived from a patient's own skin) and would develop into human

---

[1] http://www.timesonline.co.uk/tol/news/world/asia/article6222361.ece

pancreases in the pig fetus. The human cell containing pancreas would then be harvested after the pig is born and islet cells would then be isolated for transplantation into human type 1 diabetes patients.[2] Their work is based on animal studies showing that they can generate pancreases for one pig species in apancreatic embryos of a different pig species (Matsunari, et al., 1013). Pig organs are similar in size to humans, so it should be possible to harvest a human organ grown for transplantation when it is the right size for an intended recipient. If the approach succeeds, Nakauchi and others say, it might be applied to other organs, including kidneys and hearts.

In addition, there are several reports of transplanting human embryonic stem cells or neural cells into animal embryos or fetuses. Ourednik et al. (Ourednik et al., 2001), for example, transplanted human neural cells into the developing fetal brain of Old World monkeys. Other groups have transplanted human embryonic stem cells into chicken embryos and human neural stem cells into fetal sheep (Almeida-Porada et al., 2005).

Scientific Objectives in Human-animal Chimeric Research

Before discussing the neuro-ethics of trying to reconstitute a human brain in an animal, we should address whether such experiments are scientifically informative and whether these experiments will lead to new therapies. There are several broad biomedical applications, which may emerge from the research in human-animal chimeras:

- *To understand basic biological principles regarding cellular differentiation*, e.g., how precursor stem cells differentiate into the various cells that comprise brain and the nervous system. The human brain is one of the most fascinating organs and is comprised of about one hundred billion cells. Thus, creating novel human-animal chimeras could provide models to study human physiological systems previously possible only in human subjects. This will enable scientists to examine all the parameters that regulate human stem cell development within an animal environment rather than in a Petri dish.
- *To understand basic principles of cancer*. When does transplanting human stem cells into mice result in only benign tumors and when are malignant tumors formed (Erdo et al., 2003; Bulic-Jakus et al., 2006)?
- *To examine how specific genes function by transplanting genes across species.* Specifically, if you transfect a human gene into an animal that lacks that gene, you now have a method for analyzing how genes or DNA

---

[2] http://www.sciencemag.org/content/340/6140/1509.long

sequences, only found in human beings, play a role and function in human development. This technology can be used to study how certain genes influence intelligence or human behavior.

- *To help understand how human organs are formed and help identify problems when organ formation becomes defective.* While the idea of studying human brain transplants is not within the immediate future, scientists are trying to use chimeras to understand how brain size is regulated during development and how human neural networks or circuits are formed during development.

- *To develop an assay to assess stem cell plasticity.* Transplanting human embryonic stem cells into non-human blastocysts could serve as a method to test the potential for global incorporation into host tissue in vivo (Brivanlou et al. 2003).

- *Understanding behavior.* One of the most debated issues in using human-animal chimeras is whether or not creating chimeras with human neurons or nerve tissue will result in talking mice or mice with a human consciousness. There is at least some evidence that transplanted neural cells can indeed transfer behavioral characteristics. Dr. Evan Balaban, at McGill University in Montreal, took small sections of brain from developing quails and transplanted them into the developing brains of chickens. The resulting chickens exhibited vocal trills and head bobs unique to quails, suggesting that the transplanted parts of the brain contained the neural circuitry for quail calls. It also offered astonishing proof that complex behaviors could be transferred across species (Balaban, 2005).

While it remains unclear whether or not human-animal chimeras will offer a model for examining human neural/behavioral development, these chimeras certainly would provide proof of principle that human cells can contribute to tissue formation or repair of damaged tissue in a comparable nonhuman animal. It is not the primary objective of these experiments to transfer emergent psychological characteristics from humans to animals and <u>certainly not from animals to humans</u>. Yet, similar to the human-mouse blood chimeras, such a model could provide an excellent system to study human neurological diseases.

Distinguishing Between Chimeras and Cross-bred Hybrid Animals.

It is critical to differentiate between a hybrid and a chimera animal. Hybrids are created by breeding two different species via normal mating or in vitro fertilization. Each cell and organ of a hybrid animal contains the combined genetic information of each of the different parent-species used in the cross breeding procedure. Interspecies hybrids often have serious genetic anomalies that do not allow them to survive to birth; or they may be abnormally large, as in the hybrid liger, offspring of a male lion and female tiger. Many are also born sterile because each parent contains a different number or chromosomes, as in the mule (e.g., the product of mating a male <u>donkey</u> with a <u>female horse</u>). A human-monkey hybrid, therefore, would be difficult to create since humans have forty-six chromosomes, while chimpanzees and gorillas have forty-eight chromosomes.

In contrast to a hybrid, a chimera is a cellular mosaic composed of cells from two different species. Each cell of the chimera only contains the genetic information of one of the original species, not a mixture as found in hybrids. Therefore, unlike hybrids, chimeras should have the capacity to mate with another animal providing that the germ cells (sperm and eggs) of the two mating pairs are derived from identical species.

Using gene vectors to transfect animal embryos with human genes is another method to create chimeras. Tissue-specific promoters are included in these gene vectors to directly express these genes in specific tissues or cells of the target animal. But as general transfection methods are not 100 per cent efficient, only a fraction of the embryonic cells will contain the human genes. Technically, these transgenic animals could be viewed as chimeras.

Ethical Concerns Related to Human-animal Chimeras

There has been little public outcry over transplanting human blood cells or human skin cells into mice. Research attempts to reconstitute a human brain in animals, however, has generated a moral concern among scientists, the religious community, and the public alike. Is it ethical to transplant precursor human nerve stem cells into a mouse or non-human primate fetus with the intention of creating a human brain or nervous system? Response to this challenge by United States scientists has been slow but deliberate. In April 2005, the National Academy of Sciences established ethical guidelines for scientists who want to transplant human embryonic pre-neural stem cells into animal fetuses (NAS, 2005). The National Academy of Sciences, a self-elected group of scientists, advises the United States government on a broad variety of health and scientific issues. The Academy's recommendations are nonbinding but are taken seriously within the scientific and governmental sectors.

Why did the Academy consider the bioethical issue of human-animal chimeras? Dr. Irving Weissman of Stanford University proposed several years ago to insert human neural stem cells into the brain of a mouse embryo whose own neural stem cells were dysfunctional. This was in an effort to understand how human neurons develop in the brain in hopes of developing stem cell therapies that could lead to curing Parkinson's or Alzheimer's disease. His research team and other scientific groups had already succeeded in developing mice with one percent of their brains containing human cells. However, before continuing with these experiments, Dr. Weissman asked Stanford University to convene an ethics committee to advise him on the ethics of these types of experiments. Stanford University understood the complexity of this proposal and felt that it should be presented to the National Academy of Sciences.

The resulting landmark report by the National Academy of Sciences in May 2005 lists more than thirty major guidelines covering everything from accurate record-keeping to prohibitions against certain experiments, as well as outlining the need to establish a system of local and national oversight panels for reviewing stem cell research.[3] The guidelines are intended to enhance the integrity of all human embryonic stem cell research, regardless of who allocates the research funds. For example, the Academy advises against growing normal or chimeric embryos past 14 days in culture. The fourteen-day limit was chosen since it is the time when nervous system development initiates in the fetus and when the fertilized zygote implants into the uterus. The Academy also recommended against inserting human stem cells into non-human primate embryos, at least for the time being until science gains more information about the risks and benefits of this new biotechnology. It also recommended that no chimeric animals should be allowed to mate in order to avoid the remote possibility of human conception in such circumstances. Another recommendation by the Academy was that all human embryos should be donated, not bought or sold.

With respect to Dr. Weissman's proposal, the Academy advised him to go ahead with the first part of his experiments to see in the mouse fetus, whether the architecture of the human-mouse brain was mouse-like or human-like after implanting human neural stem cells into a fetal mouse. Dr. Weissman's proposed experiments would be valuable in beginning to understand how the human brain is formed during development. The National Academy of Sciences would revisit Dr. Weissman's proposal after he obtained his initial results.[4]

---

[3] http://dels.nas.edu/bls/stemcells/guidelines.shtml

[4] http://www.pbs.org/newshour/bb/science/july-dec05/chimera_8-16.html);
http://tigger.uic.edu/depts/ovcr/research/protocolreview/escro/policies/NAS_Guidelines.pdf

Ethical Concerns Related to Human-animal Chimeras

The most common ethical concerns with respect to human-animal chimeras are: a) tampering with natural law, b) violating the integrity of species, c) disrespecting human dignity, d) unnecessary cruelty to animals and e) an unknown consequence. On the other hand, studying human-animal chimeras may also enhance our understanding of human evolution.

Tampering with natural law: From a scientific perspective, tampering with natural law is unethical when it results in harming animal life, the environment, human individuals, or society. Some ethicists also believe in the Aristotelian theory that asserts that every living thing has an inner tendency to reach its appropriate end or goal (*telos*) by exercising certain characteristic biological functions. According to traditional natural law theorists, the very fact that a living entity pursues a particular kind of life through certain biological processes is its own justification (Crowe, 1977). Thus, transplanting human cells, tissues, and organs into nonhumans in ways that change their normal function would violate the natural teleology of these beings.

Often scientific experiments are conducted that tamper with or create biological situations not normally found in nature. The purposes of engaging in these types of experiments are to develop a greater understanding of basic biological principles, to subsequently apply these principles to develop new therapies, and to expand basic science in scientifically purposeful and highly significant ways not otherwise obtainable. Good examples include expressing the human gene for speech in transgenic mice as is reconstituting a human immune system also in transgenic mice. Nonetheless, the creation of artificial biological systems to examine how specific genes or cells function within a whole animal can be extremely important and are generally considered ethically acceptable. The reason there was no public outcry in response to human-mouse chimeras expressing a human immune system is due to the importance it brought to our understanding of how this mouse model could be used to study a variety of human diseases such as AIDS.

As of 2012, scientists are not proposing to use human-animal chimeras to study human behavioral characteristics. Experiments are being proposed, however, to use chimeras to study early human neural circuitry. The mechanism by which early neural precursor cells differentiate and form the first circuits is a critical issue in the neurosciences. While animal models are extremely important in examining these questions, studying human cells in animal models can be an even better model. In addition, we have very little knowledge related to the regulation of brain size or brain architecture across species. Human-animal chimeras serve as an important tool to examine these types of issues.

One concern among bioethicists is that chimeric technology could be used to modify the behavior of animals or human beings. In general, every academic institution in the United States requires approval for all studies using animals. Therefore, it is unlikely that any institution would approve of experiments in which either human embryonic stem cells or human brain slices were transferred to animal fetuses in order to examine human behavior. It is agreed at this time to accept recommendations from the National Academy of Sciences that prohibit the implantation of animal fetuses or embryos containing human neural stem cells into animals. This prohibition is designed to prevent the development into whole organisms. Scientists can continue to study early human neural circuitry in an animal embryo within the confines of a Petri dish.

Violating the integrity of species: One obstacle in elaborating the ethical issues related to human-animal chimeras is how scientists define a species, because many essential physical and behavioral characteristics are often non-specific to a particular species. Also, science now has the capacity to alter, via genetic engineering, the physical and behavioral characteristics of plants, animals, and human beings.

The history of classification is of interest. Aristotle was one of the first thinkers to classify organisms based on defined criteria. He referred to similar biological organisms as members of a "natural kind," who share physical characteristics or properties common to all of them. Karl Linnaeus, viewed as the father of biological taxonomy, utilized visible appearances and structures to group animals into distinct species. In the twentieth century, Ernst Mayr incorporated the concept that members of the same species are able to propagate together and generate fertile offspring. One of the problems raised by his view, however, is that asexually reproducing organisms, such as bacteria, or the five percent of interbreeding birds that are taken to be of different species, do not fit into such a classification system. Even a genetic approach to try to classify species has yet to yield an acceptable model.

Many studies have tried to identify unique human characteristics such as opposable thumbs, bipedality, culture, complex language (written and spoken), humor, utilizing makeup, utilizing fire, cooking, dressing and our larger brain size to differentiate our species from all others. Yet, many of these characteristic can also be found in other creatures. Chimps have rudimentary culture, parrots speak, and some rats giggle when tickled.

Research efforts are in progress to try to identify unique genetic sequences in humans that may confer human characteristics. FOXP2, for example is a human gene that appears to regulate motor control of speech. There is a mouse analogue of FOXP2. Homozygous mice lacking this gene failed to emit ultrasonic sounds when separated from their mothers, had severe motor defects, and died young (White et al., 2006). How this mouse analogue relates to the human form will be of great interest.

At least 50% of the human genome consists of mobile elements that are more commonly called "jumping genes." Barbara McClintock won the Nobel Prize in 1983 for predicting the existence of mobile elements - pieces of DNA that translocate from one location in the genome to another. These jumping genes could account for developmental differences among individuals of a given species (Ostertag and Kazazian, 2005). These mobile elements may play a critical role in creating the uniqueness of individuals within a population because they are active in neural differentiation and could affect neuronal development and diversity of brain function in humans.

The controversies associated with establishing defined criteria to identify Homo *sapiens* complicate how ethicists and scientists debate the generation of chimeras. Nonetheless, the outward characteristics may play a primary role. Generating an animal with any visibly recognizable human characteristics will probably be universally targeted as defining whether a chimera is human or animal, irrespective of the underlying genetic composition.

Human Dignity

Any discussion on the ethics of reconstituting a human brain in animals has to incorporate the role of human dignity in these debates. Human dignity has to do with the worthiness of embodied human life, and the worth of our natural desires and passions, our natural origins, our sentiments and aversions, our loves and longings. Kant proposed that human beings have an unconditioned and incomparable worth or dignity because they are moral agents whose actions can be imputed to them. Human dignity is the dignity of mankind and empowers human beings in an unparalleled fashion. Dignity is manifested in individual persons' capacities to set goals for themselves and achieve them in the practical sphere. Human beings are autonomous, and possess the rights to legislate laws, models of conduct, and ethical standards. A violation of human dignity not only includes the loss of control over one's own choices but also it infringes on the infinite value of human beings.

Major religions of the world emphasize the infinite value of human life and that human life must be preserved almost at all cost. Producing animals with human characteristic elicits concerns related to the dignity of such organisms. If an organism is created that potentially infringes on human dignity, it will be met with universal criticism, even if medical benefits could emerge from these organisms.

Concern for the Welfare of Animals:

Currently, science does not have sufficient experience generating chimeras to assess whether or not the chimeras suffer. Yet, several human-mouse chimeras with a reconstituted hematopoietic (blood) system developed life threatening tumors (Kroon et al., 2001). Thus, animal experimentation creating chimeras must take into account the welfare and potential for animal suffering as well as accessing whether these types of experiments offer unique scientific paradigms for medical research that outweigh the known and unknown risks and concerns.

Application of these Ethical Concerns to Chimera Research

The ethical issues related to tampering with biological processes are often difficult to justify from a secular moral perspective. By its very nature, evolution tampers with existing biological entities and offers opportunities for both intra- and inter-species development. The major concerns in chimera research are the dual-use issues of safety and usefulness or risks verses benefits. Will this research lead to breakthroughs in biology or medicine or rather will the insertion of different genes into bacteria or viruses generate pathogens that could bring about pandemic disease?

The issue of defining *Homo sapiens* as a unique species is a scientific challenge. We have seen that so far there exists no definitive criterion to characterize *Homo sapiens*. Yet, some, like Jamie Shreeve, propose that creating human-animal chimeras with human visible parts is unethical because "human appearance is something we should reserve for humans" (Shreeve, 2005). The ethical challenge is twofold: are human beings defined based on function or is there a minimal amount of genetic or cellular material that has to be transplanted into an animal in order to be considered a human being? Clearly, few would argue that an anencephalic infant (a baby born with most of its brain missing) still retains human status.

The remaining issue regarding these human-animal chimeras with transplanted human neural stem cells is "human dignity." As we have described, human dignity is associated with other moral principles such as autonomy or respect for persons, beneficence, and justice. Human dignity is degraded and demeaned when human beings are subjected to violent acts such as murder, torture, enslavement, abuse, rape, and acts that injure a person physically, psychologically, and spiritually. Encasing human components in a nonhuman body to be used as experimental subjects is viewed by most as denigrating human dignity.

Conclusions

Many ethicists, including those who worked on the National Academy of Sciences proposal, agree that there should be limits on certain types of experiments based on their potential affront to human dignity (NAS 2005; Robert, 2006). Scientists will have to consider in good conscience that it is not what they can do but rather what they should do. Are the experiments ethically and scientifically justified? The challenge for future chimeric researchers attempting to reconstitute a human brain into animals should ensure that they conduct experiments that are morally acceptable and have the potential to generate meaningful medical benefits (Karpowicz et al., 2005; Robert, 2006).

There are no clear answers to the ethical considerations of generating human-animal chimeras. The fact that scientists have already been able to use human-animal chimeras to better understand viral diseases like AIDS suggests that research which examines early human neural circuitry may be beneficial. One vital lesson, implicit in the National Academy of Sciences recommendations, is that, at this point in time, research should proceed with caution. Before scientists begin to allow animal fetuses containing human neural stem cells to develop into viable organisms, the research should first focus on in vitro studies. This will also provide time for our society to engage in meaningful dialogue and to debate and explore the profound ethical, social, and legal issues that emanate from these technologies. One lesson that can be derived from the history of science is that ethical issues require sufficient time to be discussed and are never quickly resolved.

As Albert Einstein remarked "concern for man himself and his fate must always form the chief interest for all technical endeavor... in order that the creation of our minds shall be a blessing and not a curse for mankind. Never forget this in the midst of your diagrams and equations..." [5]

---

[5] http://www.inesglobal.com/News/Einstein/Einstein.html.

References

Almeida-Porada, G., et al., "In vivo haematopoietic potential of human neural stem cells." Br J Haematol, 130(2):276-283, 2005.

Almeida-Porada, G., et al., "The human-sheep chimeras as a model for human stem cell mobilization and evaluation of hematopoietic grafts' potential." Exp Hematol, 35(10): 1594-1600, 2007.

Angioi, K., et al., "Xenografted human whole embryonic and fetal entoblastic organs develop and become functional adult-like micro-organs. " J Surg Res, 102:85-94, 2002.

Balaban, E., "Brain switching: studying evolutionary behavioral changes in the context of individual brain development." Int J Dev Biol, 49(2-3):117-124, 2005.

Brivanlou, A. H., et al., "Stem cells. Setting standards for human embryonic stem cells." Science, 300(5621): 913-916, 2003.

Bulic-Jakus, F., et al., "Of mice and men: teratomas and teratocarcinomas." Coll Antropol, 30(4):921-924, 2006.

Chayama, K., et al., "Animal model for study of human hepatitis viruses." J Gastroenterol Hepatol, 26(1):13-18, 2011.

Crowe, M.B., The Changing Profile of the Natural Law, (Martinus Nijhoff Publishing, 1977).

Dobson-Stone, C., et al., "Investigation of MCPH1 G37995C and ASPM A44871G polymorphisms and brain size in a healthy cohort." Neuroimage, 37:394-400 2007.

Erdo, F., et al., "Host-dependent tumorigenesis of embryonic stem cell transplantation in experimental stroke." J Cereb Blood Flow Metab, 23(7):780-785, 2003.

Goldstein, R. S., et al., "Integration and differentiation of human embryonic stem cells transplanted to the chick embryo." Dev Dyn, 225(1):80-86, 2002.

Huther, C. Ludwig-Maximilians-Universität München Ph.D. Thesis, 2009.

Kroon, E., et al., "NUP98-HOXA9 expression in hemopoietic stem cells induces chronic and acute myeloid leukemias in mice." Embo J, 20(3):350-361, 2001.

Matsunari, H., et al., "Blastocyst complementation generates exogenic pancreas in vivo in apancreatic cloned pigs." Proc Natl Acad Sci U S A. 110(12):4557-62, 2013.

McCune, J., et al., "The SCID-hu mouse: a small animal model for HIV infection and pathogenesis." Annu Rev Immunol, 9:399-429, 1991.

Meuleman, P., et al., "Morphological and biochemical characterization of a human liver in a uPA-SCID mouse chimera." Hepatology, 41(4):847-856, 2005.

Mueller, D., et al., "Transplanted human embryonic germ cell-derived neural stem cells replace neurons and oligodendrocytes in the forebrain of neonatal mice with excitotoxic brain damage." J Neurosci Res, 82(5):592-608, 2005.

Narayan, A. D., "Human embryonic stem cell-derived hematopoietic cells are capable of engrafting primary as well as secondary fetal sheep recipients." Blood, 107(5):2180-2183, 2006.

NAS Guidelines for Human Embryonic Stem Cell Research, National Academy of Sciences, 2005.

Ostertag, E. M. and Kazazian H. H., "Genetics: LINEs in mind." Nature, 435(7044):890-891, 2005.

Ourednik, V., et al., "Segregation of human neural stem cells in the developing primate forebrain." Science, 293(5536):1820-1824, 2001.

Raychaudhuri, S.P., et al., "Severe combined immunodeficiency mouse-human skin chimeras: a unique animal model for the study of psoriasis and cutaneous inflammation." Br J Dermatol, 144:931-939, 2001.

Robert, J.S., "The science and ethics of making part-human animals in stem cell biology.", Faseb J, 20:838-845, 2006.

Shreeve, J., "The other stem-cell debate: to test the potential curative powers of human embryonic stem cells, biologists want to inject them into lab animals. Creating such chimeras makes perfect sense, to a point: a sheep with a human liver? O.K. A mouse brain made up of human cells? Maybe. But a chimp that sobs?" N Y Times Mag: 42-47, 2005.

White, S. A., et al., "Singing mice, songbirds, and more: models for FOXP2 function and dysfunction in human speech and language." J Neurosci, 26(41):10376-10379. 2006.

Figure 1. Classical image of a chimera

Figure 2. Contemporary image of a chimera

Chapter Nine

Molecular Genetics and its Sovereignty of Human Disease

Introduction

The overall objective of molecular genetics is to better understand how genes and regulatory elements of the genome function in response to various developmental and environmental cues. Rapid advances in mathematical, computational, and molecular biology along with new technologies in DNA microarrays will revolutionize genomics in the next few decades. Out of the almost 9 million known species, only several hundred completed genomes from different organisms have been sequenced,[1] and around 30,000 genomes from different human volunteers have been mapped as of May 2012,[2] and whose data is being complied in ENCODE: The human encyclopedia. ENCODE is a public research consortium launched by the US National Human Genome Research Institute in September 2003, whose primary objective is to find all functional elements in the human genome.

The term genetics, coined by William Bateson in the early 1900's, comes from the Greek term "to generate" and is the science of biological heredity and variation. In 1866, Gregor Mendel, an Austrian monk, published the results of his decade-long investigations into the inheritance of "factors" in pea plants. He suggested that every cell contains pairs of "factors" and that each pair determined a specific trait. The members of each pair segregated from each other in the process of sex-cell formation so that a gamete contained one member of each pair. The segregation of each pair was independent of the segregation of other pairs of factors. It wasn't until 1909 that a Danish botanist, Wilhelm Johannsen, introduced the word "gene" to characterize Mendel's "factors."

---

[1] http://ngs-brescia.blogspot.com/2012/02/do-you-know-how-many-species-are-there.html

[2] http://blogs.discovermagazine.com/gnxp/2011/11/how-many-human-genomes-have-been-sequenced/#.UL4O-uTpfTo

Prelude to Genetics and Disease

As a prelude to any discussion of genetics and disease, it is important to highlight several basic principles of genetics and its relation to diseases.

The first principle is that chromosomes are composed of nucleic acids and proteins. DNA sequences can also be divided into genes where each gene encodes the information necessary to synthesize one or several proteins. The location of a gene on a chromosome region is called a locus. At any given gene locus, DNA sequences may differ from one individual to another in some small ways. These different DNA sequences within a gene locus are termed alleles. In most populations of animals and plants, 10-20% of the genes are composed of multiple alleles. There are several processes by which different alleles develop. One process is through mutations such as a point mutation, where one nucleotide is replaced by another nucleotide. Another process involves a section of DNA eliminated or translocated from one chromosome location to another location on the same or different chromosome.

The second principle is that every human being has mutations in their genes and these mutations can occur at almost any location within the whole genome. This means that there are no individuals with a "perfect" human genome. Some of these changes have no major phenotypic expression in that organism. Other mutations can lead to disabling conditions, to specific disease states, or to death.

The third principle relates to the heterogeneity of response to genetic mutations and the consequences of genetic changes. Cells have a remarkable ability to edit their DNA to ensure that mutations do not occur at a high frequency. Even when mutations do occur, these changes have no perceptible effects because the genetic code is redundant. A point mutation that has no effect at all on the protein being coded for is called a silent mutation. Changes in the DNA sequence that **do not** have profound effects on protein function occur if the changes do not dramatically change the three dimensional structure of the protein.

Sometimes alterations of DNA sequences by snipping or swapping nucleotides can result in a fatal condition because the coding sequence will lead to a structurally or functionally defective protein that is critical to sustaining life. For example, gene mutations responsible for Tay-Sachs disease express themselves in a narrow range such that most individuals with Tay-Sachs present similar lethal clinical symptoms. In contrast, individuals with cystic fibrosis express a wide range of disease severity because there are many types of mutations in the gene encoding the transporter protein involved in the disease. Thus, allelic heterogeneity implies that there are many places on the gene which can be mutated and not all mutations have the same impact on phenotypic or disease expression.

Genes also vary a great deal with respect to how much they can be changed without the changes harming the organism. Some genes, such as those that encode the basic components of metabolism, replication, transcription, and translation machinery, are hard to mutate without harming an organism. We see very little variation in those gene sequences from one organism to another. Such genes are said to be conserved.

Some changes in alleles or DNA sequences can be favorable and promote a healthier life. As an example, there are several alleles that encode for the protein apoE which is a ligand for the LDL receptor. It is a critical membrane protein in cholesterol regulation. In Italy there is a community near Milan whose residents are less likely to develop atherosclerosis because of a fortunate mutation in one of their forebearers. Their apoE isoform, referred to as apoE2 appears to protect them from developing atherosclerosis. In addition, an individual that expresses this type of apoE also has been shown to be an important determinant of Alzheimer's disease. Individuals with the apoE4 isoform have a higher rate of atherosclerosis, heart disease, and Alzheimer's disease.

The fourth principle is that epigenetics can regulate genes and their functions. As mentioned earlier, epigenetics involve methylation or acetylation of either nucleotides or DNA associated proteins, such as histones. These modifications can either turn on or turn off gene expression.

The final principle in basic genetics is that understanding of any genetic process or phenotype will often require a complete understanding of how each region of the DNA operates within the whole human genome. For example, there are genes that increase the chances of getting lung cancer in smokers and yet there are many heavy smokers whose genetic makeup enables them to never come down with lung cancer.

Mechanisms by Which Parental Genes Impact the Health of the Offspring

On a basic level, each parent donates one chromosome to the child and, in turn, donates one gene for each of the 20,000 genes or so encoded in Human DNA. Over 60% of the genes can alternatively splice to form several protein products. This accounts for the over 200,000 different proteins expressed in human beings. The nature of each contributed gene influences the health of the child in various ways. If a genetic disease is inherited in a dominant manner, such as Huntington's disease, then one parent donating this gene to the fertilized egg will result in a child that will eventually be stricken with this neuron-degenerating fatal disease. Statistically, each child in a family where only one parent carries an abnormal copy of the gene for Huntington's disease (or any other dominant gene), has a fifty percent chance of inheriting the gene for Huntington's disease.

However, most genetic diseases are recessive disorders. To be affected by a recessive disorder requires that an individual must possess two abnormal or mutated copies of a gene. Therefore, each parent must donate one copy of the abnormal gene to the child. Cystic fibrosis and Tay-Sachs are examples of recessive disorders. A person who obtains only one abnormal copy of a gene for a recessive condition is known as a carrier. A carrier of a genetic condition will not develop the disease and should not have any health-associated abnormalities due to the presence of a recessive gene.

The predisposition of many human diseases such as heart disease, Alzheimer's disease, and cancer, are influenced by multiple genes in a complex fashion. It should be noted that being genetically predisposed to a disease does not necessarily mean that an individual will suffer from that disease. It simply means that there is an increased risk of developing the disease. Of great concern is a woman who tests positive for a genetic mutation in BRCA1 who may have a 55 to 85 percent chance of developing breast cancer by age 70, and a 40 to 60 percent chance of developing ovarian cancer. Yet, only about 10-20 per cent of all breast cancers diagnosed have a family history of the disease. Since many of these diseases are regulated by environmental factors and other genetic factors, it is often difficult to precisely predict the susceptibility of an individual contracting such diseases.

Genetic Testing and Screening

There are several types of genetic tests available to the developing fetus or new-born baby to identify genes that affect the health of the child. Pre-implantation Genetic Diagnosis (PGD) is done in pre-implanted embryos, allowing the couple to select an embryo that does not contain the gene causing the specific disease. Dr. Mark Hughes developed PGD in the mid-1980's with Robert Winston and Alan Handyside as a screen to test which embryos will develop cystic fibrosis. PGD is performed on an embryo created via in vitro fertilization (IVF) that has developed to the 8 stage. Using micro-manipulation techniques, one of the cells is removed and tested for a specific mutation using

PCR (polymerase chain reaction) to screen for a specific DNA segment. Sometimes, chromosomal aberrations, as seen in Down's syndrome, are detected in this removed cell using fluorescence *in situ* hybridization technologies. Using PGD, embryos are selected that do not express two defective genes or even an embryo that does not express one defective gene (such an embryo will develop into a child who will be a carrier for the recessive disorder) and one or two of these embryos are implanted into the woman. In 2007 over 700 healthy babies were born using PGD.[3] The list of diseases that now can be screened using PGD is over one hundred and includes cystic fibrosis, Down's syndrome, Duchenne muscular dystrophy, Huntington's disease, certain forms of early onset Alzheimer's disease, sickle-cell disease, and Tay-Sachs disease (Murphy, 2012). PGD can also be used for sex selection. As of 2011, the error rate for misdiagnosis varied between 0.5-2% depending on which diseases were screened (Harper, and SenGupta, 2012). Some of the errors result from a rare phenomenon that the cell removed from the 8 cell embryo may not be representative of the other cells. This phenomenon is called mosaicism. In other words, one cell would appear to lack the genetic defect whereas the remaining cells in the embryo would be abnormal or vice versa.

There appears to be a misnomer in calling this test Pre-implantation Genetic Diagnosis. In fact, this test is in reality a way to screen pre-implanted embryos for specific genetic mutations. Therefore, it should be renamed Pre-implantation Genetic Screening (PGS) or Pre-implantation Genetic Testing (PGT).

Prenatal diagnostic testing is another way to assess reproductive risk. Prenatal diagnostic testing involves testing the fetus before birth to determine whether it has a certain hereditary or spontaneous genetic disorder. The most common tests used to detect abnormalities in a fetus include ultrasonography, chorionic villus sampling (CVS), amniocentesis, and percutaneous umbilical blood sampling. CVS involves removing a small amount of tissue called the chorionic villi, which is located on the outside of the fetal gestational sac and will later become the placenta. The chorion, as fetal tissue, shares its genetic makeup with the fetus, not the mother. The chorion has many small, finger-like projections on its outer surface, and a few of the cells from the chorion may be carefully removed without disturbing the pregnancy. The chorionic villi cells may be used for chromosome analysis or other genetic testing. The chorionic villi cannot be used to test for open neural tube defects. CVS is available from 10.0 to 13.3 weeks of pregnancy. The CVS may be performed trans-abdominally by

---

[3] http://www.genome.gov/10004766

guiding a thin needle through the abdominal wall to the chorionic villi, then withdrawing a small amount of this tissue.

Most genetic tests are offered primarily to couples with an increased risk of having a baby with a genetic abnormality (such as Down's syndrome) or a chromosomal abnormality (particularly when the woman is aged 35 or older). In Sardinia, for instance, where beta thalassemia is a relatively common genetic condition, prenatal genetic screening programs have produced striking results. Following fetal diagnosis of homozygous beta thalassemia, most couples decide to terminate the pregnancy. Overall, since the introduction of widespread genetic education, counseling, and screening programs in Sardinia, "the incidence of beta thalassemia major has been reduced from 1 of every 250 live births in 1975 to 1 of every 4000 in 1996, with 94% of the cases prevented" (Cao et al., 1997). Notable reductions in incidence due to targeted prenatal testing are reported for other disabling conditions as well, such as Tay-Sachs disease among Ashkenazi Jews, spina bifida in Britain, and Down's syndrome in the United States (Eng et al., 1997; Harper, and SenGupta 2012).

Newborn genetic screening is aimed at identifying infants who have genetic conditions that can be helped by early intervention. In many cases, this early intervention means the elimination or reduction of symptoms that would have left an unscreened individual with a lifetime of disability. Historically, this type of screening was strongly influenced by a genetic disease called Phenylketonuria (PKU). PKU is a genetic metabolic disorder that is easily treated by restricting certain foods from the diet; if left untreated, however, the disorder causes severe mental retardation. PCR is a common method for screening newborn babies for PKU.

Carrier screening is usually carried out in adults and involves identifying unaffected individuals who carry one copy of a gene for a recessive disease condition. The most common tests in carrier screening are cystic fibrosis, Tay-Sachs, and sickle cell trait. As a case in point, since carrier screening has begun for Tay-Sachs, the incidence of babies born with this disease has decreased dramatically in New York City alone (Kaback et al., 1993). It is unusual to see a baby with this condition after 2000. Individuals can also undergo pre-symptomatic testing for predicting adult-onset disorders such as Huntington's disease or for estimating the risk of developing adult-onset diseases which have multifactorial etiologies like cancers, ischemic heart disease, asthma, diabetes, and Alzheimer's disease.

Huntington's Disease- a Lesson in Scientific Calvinism

Huntington's disease (HD) provides an interesting model for in-depth analysis of genetic predisposition to disease because DNA analysis of any individual can predict not only who will develop Huntington's disease, but also the age of onset and the level of neural degeneration. John Calvin, the famous Christian theologist, never conceived of this level of determinism or predestination. Calvin had argued theological determinism – that people are fated from the start, and there is nothing to be done. The destiny that Calvin had talked about seemed to have manifested itself in some extent in modern scientific determinism, reflected in the discovery of Huntingtin gene.

Interest in HD emerged in the late 1970's when Woody Guthrie's terrible death from the disease led his widow to join efforts with Dr. Milton Wexler, a clinical psychologist and psychoanalyst whose wife and three brothers-in laws all died of the disease, to start an organization to combat Huntington's chorea. Dr. Wexler's daughters, Nancy Wexler, of Columbia University, and Alice Ruth Wexler were determined to identify the gene responsible for HD and formed the Huntington's Disease Foundation and joined the organizational committee. In 1979, they heard of a community in Venezuela that had high incidences of HD and went there to collect blood samples. By 1983 Nancy Wexler and her colleagues reported a genetic marker close to the affected gene which led them to finally identify the gene in 1993. This is one of many examples where personal motivation was instrumental in making a major scientific discovery.

Huntington's disease is characterized as one of several polyglutamine diseases located on gene 4 of the human genome. Mutations in this gene from either the maternal or paternal side results in Huntington's chorea or HD. The function of the normal allotype is not entirely known but the gene contained several CAG repeats. The expanded CAG repeats in exon 1 of the Huntingtin gene translates into an abnormally long polyglutamine amino acid sequence in the Huntington protein. This gene is primarily expressed in both cells of the central nervous system (CNS) and in non-neural cells as well. The expression of a defective gene in non-neural cells raises a fundamental problem — why are almost all of the symptoms of HD neurological? The function of normal Huntingtin gene is not well understood but may play a role in the intracellular trafficking of proteins, energy metabolism, oxidative stress or regulating inflammation (Aronin and Moore, 2012).

In the normal population, the length of the polyglutamine sequence in this gene locus is polymorphic, generally ranging from about 10 to 36 consecutive glutamine residues. An individual's destiny, sanity, and lifespan hang by the thread of this repetition. Individuals with less than 35-36 repeats in this DNA region are perfectly normal. Individuals with 39 or more repeats develop HD and begin declining in health by mid-life. The health decline begins with a slight deterioration of intellectual faculties, followed by jerking limbs and descends into deep depression with occasional hallucinations and delusions. It takes about 15-20 horrifying years to run the course of HD before termination[4]. Table I shows how the number of CAG repeats precisely determines average age of onset. In general, longer expansions correlate with earlier onset, and a more severe disease progression.

At least nine inherited other neurological disorders are caused by trinucleotide (CAG) repeat expansion, including Kennedy's disease, dentatorubro-pallidoluysian atrophy, and six forms of spinocerebellar ataxia. These are all adult-onset diseases with progressive degeneration of the nervous system that are universally fatal. The genes responsible for these diseases appear to be functionally unrelated. The only known common feature is a CAG trinucleotide repeat in each gene's coding region, resulting in a polyglutamine tract in the disease protein. Understanding the molecular mechanisms by which the CAG repeats causes neurological dysfunction is under intense investigation and to date there is no consensus on how these CAG repeats cause the disease symptoms.

The wild type huntingtin protein is normally cleaved and stays in the cytoplasm of all cells. In contrast, mutant huntingtin protein enters the nucleus, loses its anti-apoptotic function, and generates toxic products. Several studies (Kazantsev et al. 2002; Sanchez et al. 2003) have shown that pathogenic and non-pathogenic polyglutamine (polyQ) peptides can be induced to form fibrillar aggregates in vitro. However, these fibrillar forms of polyQ peptides Q20 and Q42 only cause cell death when they localize to the nucleus and not when restricted to the cytoplasm, indicating that polyQ aggregates are toxic to cells when they localize in the nucleus. The expanded polyQ sequence is able to trigger neuronal cell death by enhancing reactive oxygen species and inducing nitric oxide generation, cytochrome c translocation, suppression of ubiquitin-proteasome system, and activation of various caspases. A recent demonstration that aggregation inhibitors delay neurodegeneration and rescued lethality supports the belief that aggregated polyQ has toxic effects and causes neuronal death associated with HD.

---

[4] Dr. Nancy Wexler has also reported individuals from Venezuela who symptoms appear in children at age 10. Wexler, N. S., J. Lorimer, et al. (2004). "Venezuelan kindreds reveal that genetic and environmental factors modulate Huntington's disease age of onset." Proc Natl Acad Sci U S A **101**(10): 3498-503.

Table I: Observed Age of Onset by CAG Repeat Size		
CAG Repeat Size	**Median Age at Onset (Years)**	**Range of Age of Onset (95% Confidence Interval) (Years)**
39 repeats	66 yrs	(59-72) yrs
40 repeats	59 yrs	(56-61) yrs
41 repeats	54 yrs	(52-56) yrs
42 repeats	49 yrs	(48-50) yrs
43 repeats	44 yrs	(42-45) yrs
44 repeats	42 yrs	(40-43) yrs
45 repeats	37 yrs	(36-39) yrs
46 repeats	36 yrs	(35-37) yrs
47 repeats	33 yrs	(31-35) yrs
48 repeats	32 yrs	(30-34) yrs
49 repeats	28 yrs	(25-32) yrs
50 repeats	27 yrs	(24-30) yrs

Although the exact mechanism by which huntingtin protein aggregates are toxic to neurons is not clear, it is believed that they may disable transcription factors and disrupt the ubiquitin-proteasome system. Symptoms of the HD will set in when these precipitates have reached a critical size or have resulted in a critical number of neural blocks.

Treating patients with HD is difficult and frustrating since there are no really effective therapies. Several classes of medications have been used to ameliorate the various symptoms of HD, including typical and atypical neuroleptics, dopamine depleters, antidepressants, antiglutamatergic drugs, GABA agonists, antiepileptic medications, acetylcholinesterase inhibitors, and botulinum toxin. In addition, surgical approaches including pallidotomy, deep brain stimulation, and fetal cell transplants have been used for the symptomatic treatment of HD. The selected therapy must be customized to the needs of each patient, minimizing the potential adverse effects.

Despite the conventional wisdom that genetic diseases such as HD are unresponsive to environmental factors, recent studies indicate that life style, exercise, and diet can at times delay the onset of HD. The impact of environment to disease has been termed "environmental enrichment" and has been used to improve neurological function as well as motor performance in animal models with neurological deficits. Scientists reported positive neurological benefits from increased social interaction, sensory stimulation, exploration, and physical activity improved survival in mice models of Huntington's disease (Wood et al., 2010). While the mechanisms by which these environmental factors affect the disease remain unsolved there is evidence that environmental factors stimulate endogenous stem cells in the regions of the brain that HD strikes and make contribute to the delay of onset.

Genes that Affect Intelligence, Personality, and Sexuality

Unlike genes that are directly responsible for diseases like Hungtinton's Disease, there are genes that in combination with environmental factors influence human health and behavior. For example, it has been known for a long time that certain human behavioral characteristics are rooted in our genetic background and mimic behaviors observed in other members of the animal kingdom. However, studying genes that affect behavior creates its own unique set of scientific problems. The majority of behavioral genetics studies have focused on genes that influence criminal tendency, cognitive ability, novelty seeking, mental disorders, addiction to drugs or alcohol, and sexual behavior. Most geneticists interpret current scientific data to show that these behavioral traits are complex in their pattern of inheritance and involve a combination of many genes interacting with environmental factors.

Genes that influence intelligence have been a keen interest in major research centers around the world. A variety of methodologies have been employed to examine the genetic contribution to cognitive ability (intelligence or I.Q.). Yet, there are inherent problems studying the genetics of intelligence since these studies requires the investigators to define intelligence in a measurable and definitive fashion. For example, is IQ a sufficient measure of intelligence? The problem of cognitive assessment may in part be responsible for the scarcity of well-designed studies to characterize specific genes that contribute to the development of intelligence. Furthermore, intelligence is often seen as a highly complex trait, with many possible influential genetic factors. Therefore, the precise genetic and epigenetic polymorphisms underlying normal-range intelligence differences remain mysterious and vastly undefined (Deary et al., 2010; Haggarty et al., 2010).

Studying the genetic role of intelligence also highlights how environmental factors may account for the difficulties in identifying specific genes. Specifically, it is difficult to sort out environmental verses genetic or epigenetic factors that influences behavior, in part because genes that regulate aspects of behavior appear to be highly responsive to environment stimuli. Traditional research strategies that include studies of twins and adopted children, are often used to distinguish between biological and environmental influences on specific behaviors (nature vs nurture). Many of these studies have not yielded sufficient results to dramatically expand our understanding of how environment and genetics interact to affect behavioral characteristics.

The inability to positively identify intelligence genes via genome-wide scans or using state-of-the art technologies are leading some scientists to propose that genes do not play a major role in determining intelligence. Rather, environment and maternal effects may be the critical parameters that account for intellectual abilities (Ho, 2013).

Evidence for a genetic component in behavior arises from observations that certain behavioral characteristics, such as aggression or intelligence, run in families. In addition, over the last few years geneticists have modified mouse behavioral patterns by inserting or disabling specific genes. There are several examples where genetic alleles affect behavior in the areas of autism, schizophrenia, and bipolar disorders. While these methods will surely enhance the search for specific genes associated with behavioral characteristics such as sexual preference and basic personality traits, the success has been difficult and to date remain elusive.

Genes and Sexual Preferences

In addition to searching for genes that influence intelligence there has been a great deal of effort to examine the role of genes in sexual behavior. Such studies have been going on for decades and usually involve trying to identify sexual patterns among monozygotic twins, dizygotic twins, or adoptive siblings. Many studies have focused on homosexual behaviors and several papers utilize two lines of evidence that homosexuality is influenced by polymorphic genes: (i) twin studies indicate that there are both genetic and environmental factors that contribute to the expression of the homosexual phenotype (Ramagopalan et al., 2010), and (ii) male homosexuality appears to be inherited more frequently from the matrilineal lineage. These studies suggest the existence of polymorphic, heritable maternal effects and/or polymorphic X-linked genes influencing male homosexuality. In some studies the researchers found that of the relatives, 52% (29/56) of monozygotic twins, 22% (12/54) of dizygotic twins, and 11% (6/57) of adoptive brothers were homosexual. Thus, heritability of homosexuality was considered to be substantial under a wide range of assumptions about the population base rate of homosexuality and ascertainment bias. However, the rate of homosexuality among non-twin biologic siblings, was significantly lower than would be predicted by a simple genetic hypothesis and by other published reports. From the rates of homosexuality observed in monozygotic and dizygotic twins, ordinary siblings, and adoptive brothers and sisters of homosexual men and women, overall heritabilities of 31 to 74% for males and 27 to 76% for females were estimated. The observation that male homosexuals usually have more gay brothers than gay sisters, whereas lesbians have more gay sisters than gay brothers, suggested that the factors responsible for familial aggregation are at least partially distinct in men compared to women.

Hamer et al. (Hamer et al., 1993; Mustanski et al., 2005) performed one of the most complete and largest studies in an attempt to identify a gene for homosexuality. In 1993, he studied pedigree and linkage analyses of 110 families of homosexual men. Increased rates of same-sex orientation were found in the maternal uncles and maternal male cousins of these subjects, but not in their fathers or paternal relatives, suggesting X-linked transmission. Linkage analysis using DNA markers in a selected group of 40 families in which there were 2 gay brothers and no indication of nonmaternal transmission demonstrated a correlation between homosexual orientation and the inheritance of polymorphic markers on the X chromosome in approximately 64% of the sib-pairs tested. The linkage to markers on Xq28 on the tip of the long arm indicated a statistical confidence level of more than 99% that at least 1 subtype of male sexual orientation is genetically influenced. In these studies, sexual orientation was assessed by the Kinsey scales, which ranged from zero for exclusive heterosexuality to 6 for exclusive homosexuality. Hamer (LeVay and Hamer, 1994) emphasized that the findings of his study should not be interpreted as 'medicalizing' homosexuality because sexual preference should be viewed, he insisted, as a behavioral variable. His studies were consistent with the observation that homosexuality seems to run in the female line. Gay men shared the same version of this marker 75% of the time while straight men shared a different version 75% of the time.

In 2005, Hamer and his colleagues examined a genome-wide scan of male sexual orientation and did not find strong linkage to Xq28. Rather, several regions on chromosome 7 such as 7q36 provided strong linkage. Candidate genes in this region include vasoactive intestinal peptide receptor type 2 which functions as a neurotransmitter and as a neuroendocrine hormone required for the development of the hypothalamic suprachiasmatic nucleus in mice. One reason why this is an interesting candidate gene is that there are earlier reports that this area of the hypothalamus is enlarged in homosexual men. While this group found other candidate genes on chromosome 8 that are involved in sexual development, they are re-analyzing the linkage results to Xq28.

What motivated Hamer's research in the genetics of homosexuality? Hamer hoped that scientific research would help dispel some of the myths about homosexuality that in the past years have clouded the gay and lesbian community. Hamer also recognized that educating the public about genetics and behavior would eventually improve our understanding of the natural rights of individuals and human diversity.

If there are genes that influence gay behavior, then it will be important to understand how this trait provided an evolutionary advantage since by its intrinsic nature gay couples do not procreate. Yet, it is possible that the historical social anti-gay attitude of many cultures applied pressure on gay adults to bear children. In addition, there are suggestions that genes that confer gay tendencies may in fact offer evolutionary advantages in heterosexual individuals such as making them more loyal, considerate or empathic (Wilson and Rahman, 2005). Genes that promote same-sex bonding may also reduce aggression within social communities and encourage resource sharing which may have provided an evolutionary benefit.

There are many theories how genes could orient sexual behavior in humans (Hatemi and McDermott, 2012). One proposed by Dr. Glenn Wilson (Wilson and Rahman, 2005) is that these genes regulate testosterone absorption. These receptors play a critical role in male fetus development. Testosterone absorption is thought to be critical in the male brain development. Thus, male fetuses that absorb less testosterone develop brains whose circuitry is more feminine and are therefore more attracted to male partners.

Emanuele et al., in 2007 (Emanuele et al. 2007) examined whether genes affect human romantic bonding and found a significant association between a certain neurotransmitter genes (the dopamine D2 receptor gene, DRD2-TaqI A genotypes) and a specific style of love characterized as EROS (a loving style characterized by a tendency to develop intense emotional experiences based on the physical attraction to the partner). These associations were present in both sexes.

Genes and Violent Behavior

Behavioral genetic research has analyzed thousands of sibling pairs. In conclusion, it pointed to the "inescapable conclusion" that genetic factors do contribute, to a certain degree, to the etiology and cause of violence (Ferguson, 2010). Some conclude from these that approximately 50% of the variance in antisocial phenotypes is the result of genetic factors.[5]

Examining genes that regulate violent behavior has been supported by both academic centers as well as governmental agencies that monitor terrorism and the rate of crimes committed within a specific society or country. Violent behavior is clearly affected by social and possibly genetic factors (Tuvbald, 2011). The NIH has been examining both of these areas over the last several decades. This research points to the importance of a nurturing social environment in childhood, good early education, and success in academic areas. Peer influence, whether positive or negative, is of critical importance in predicting violent behavior. Yet, many twin and adoption studies indicate that child and adolescent antisocial behavior is influenced by both genetic and environmental factors, suggesting that genetic factors directly influence cognitive and temperamental predispositions to antisocial behavior. These predisposing child factors and socializing environments, in turn, influence antisocial behavior. Research also suggests that for some youth with early onset behavior problems, genetic factors strongly influence temperamental predisposition, particularly oppositional temperament, which can affect experiences negatively. When antisocial behavior emerges later in childhood or adolescence, it is suspected that genetic factors contribute less, while such youths tend to engage in delinquent behavior primarily because of peer influences and/or have experienced abuse in the home.

Based on genetic analysis, several studies have suggested that genes coding for the Monoamine oxidase (MAOA) and Tryptophan hydroxylase (TPH) enzymes are linked to specific cases of violent behavior. These genes code for certain enzymes that are responsible for the metabolism or synthesis of three neurotransmitters (serotonin, norepinephrine, and dopamine) that have been associated with the onset of aggression or violence. Serotonin is one neurotransmitter that is responsible for different moods, appetite, sexual activity, homeostasis, and sleep. Norepinephrine regulates stress and moods in the brain. Dopamine regulates emotion, the "pleasure center" of the brain, and motivation.

One problem with associating MAOA encoding genes and behavior is that in the literature there are scores of behavioral characteristics that have been ascribed to this gene. The same polymorphisms of these genes are said to predict variation in other behavioral and physical traits. The idea that a one or

---

[5] http://www.sciencedirect.com/science/article/B6VH7-4VWB1FV-1/2/1f82d13f59a9a1736288374849e8372f.

two genes could be responsible for so many disparate behaviors is biologically implausible.

Epigenetics

No chapter in the genetics of disease can omit discussing epigenetics. Epigenetics is a hereditable process but differs from Mendelian genetics. In Mendelian genetics changes in the base pair sequence of a gene can be a critical determinant of its activity. Epigenetics is the study of changes in gene activity that is caused by chemical modification of specific base pairs or proteins that govern gene expression. It can be viewed as the software of the genome. What scientists have learned over the past several decades is that these changes can be passed down to at least one successive generation. Epigenetic regulates gene expression by orchestrating a set of chemical reactions that switch parts of the genome off and on at strategic times and at specific DNA locations. The epigenetic changes include DNA methylation and histone modification, which regulate high-order DNA structure and gene expression. Epigenetic regulation of gene activity involve a structure called an epigenome that sits on top of the genome, just outside it (hence the prefix epi-, which means above). The epigenome consists of chromatin, a protein-based structure around which the DNA is wrapped whose activity can be regulated by post-translational modifications and methylation of specific bases such as cytosines. In general chromatin and DNA methylation results in gene silencing. It is through epigenetic marks that environmental factors like diet, stress and prenatal nutrition can make an imprint on genes that is passed from one generation to the next. As James Watson said in 2003 "you can inherit something beyond the DNA sequence. That's where the real excitement of genetics is now."

At first glance epigenetic trans-generational inheritance of acquired characteristics is reminiscent of a theory of genetics proposed by Jean-Baptiste Lamarck (e.g., a giraffe through evolutionary processes, has a long neck because he must reach the highest branches to obtain food). In fact, the current underlying mechanisms of epigenetics provide scientific evidence how environment can trigger heritable changes. There is ample evidence in animals and even in human beings that environmental factors shape health and disease via epigenetic mechanisms that mediate gene-environment interactions. According to Dr. Moshe Szyf, a leading geneticist, epigenetics is a physiological mechanism by which the genome senses the world and changes itself (Narain, 2012).

Conclusions

The genetic composition of an individual can have profound effects on health, behavior, and disease. In some situations such as Huntington's disease, the nature of the defect can predict age of onset and severity of the disease. In other situations, environment, diet, and life experiences may alter disease onset and progression. Studying the role of genetics in behavior is compounded by a variety of factors including the complex interaction between genetics and environmental factors. Moreover, it can be difficult to precisely measure human behavior because there are so many variations. This chapter outlined various methods for diagnosing genetic-based diseases and behavioral characteristics and by searching for specific genes that influences these diseases and behavior. In part, the overall goal of these studies is: a) to reduce the probability of a child being born with a genetic-based disease or abnormal behavior characteristics and b) to understand how genetic factors contribute to disease and behavior in helping design new therapeutic interventions.

References

Aronin, N. and Moore, M. "Hunting Down Huntingtin.", New England Journal of Medicine, **367**:1753-1754, 2012.

Cao, A., et al., "Molecular diagnosis and carrier screening for beta thalassemia.", JAMA, 278: 1273-1277, 1997.

Charney, E. and English, W., "Candidate genes and political behavior." American Political Science Review, 1:1-34, 2012.

Charney, E. and English, W., "The Voting Gene.", Scientific American Magazine, 307:14-14, 2012.

Deary, I. J., et al., "The neuroscience of human intelligence differences." Nat Rev Neurosci, **11**(3):201-11, 2010.

Emanuele, E., et al., "Genetic loading on human loving styles." Neuro Endocrinol Lett, **28**(6): 815-21, 2007.

Eng, C. M., C. Schechter, et al. (1997). "Prenatal genetic carrier testing using triple disease screening." JAMA, **278**(15):1268-72.

Ferguson, C. J., "Genetic contributions to antisocial personality and behavior: a meta-analytic review from an evolutionary perspective." J Soc Psychol, **150**(2):160-80, 2010.

Haggarty, P., et al., "Human intelligence and polymorphisms in the DNA methyltransferase genes involved in epigenetic marking.", PLoS One, **5**(6):e11329, 2010.

Hamer, D. H., et al., "A linkage between DNA markers on the X chromosome and male sexual orientation." Science, **261**(5119):321-7, 1993.

Harper, J.C. and SenGupta, S.B., "Preimplantation genetic diagnosis: State of the ART 2011.", Human genetics, 131:175-186, 2012.

Hatemi, P.K. and McDermott, R., "The genetics of politics: discovery, challenges, and progress." Trends in Genetics, 28(10):525-33, 2012.

Ho, M.W., "No genes for intelligence in the fluid genome." Adv Child Dev Behav.;45:67-92, 2013.

Kaback, M., et al., "Tay-Sachs disease--carrier screening, prenatal diagnosis, and the molecular era. An international perspective, 1970 to 1993. The International TSD Data Collection Network." JAMA, **270**(19):2307-15, 1993.

LeVay, S. and Hamer D. H., "Evidence for a biological influence in male homosexuality." Sci Am, **270**(5):44-9, 1994.

Mustanski, B. S., et al., "A genomewide scan of male sexual orientation." Hum Genet, **116**(4): 272-8, 2005.

Narain, C., "Changing behavior with epigenetics.", Nature Neuroscience, 15:1329-1329, 2012.

Ramagopalan, S. V., et al., "A genome-wide scan of male sexual orientation." J Hum Genet, **55**(2):131-2, 2010.

Tuvblad, C., et al., "The genetic and environmental etiology of antisocial behavior from childhood to emerging adulthood.", Behavior genetics, 41:629-640, 2011.

Wilson, G. & Rahman, Q. Born gay. The psychobiology of sex orientation, 2005.

Wood, N. I., et al., "Responses to environmental enrichment differ with sex and genotype in a transgenic mouse model of Huntington's disease." PLoS One, **5**(2): e9077, 2010.

Figure 1. Genetic sequencing (from NIH.gov)

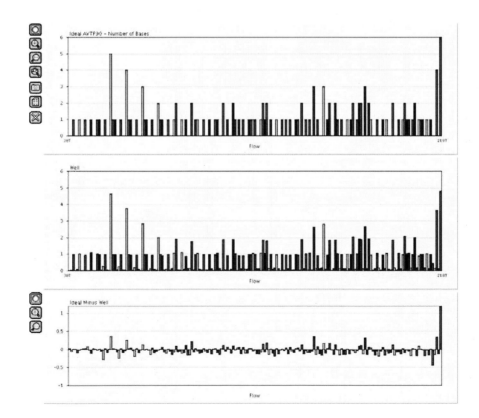

Chapter Ten[1]

Genomics and Personalized Medicine

Introduction

Personalized medicine is designed to synthesize an individual's clinical history, family history, genetic makeup, epigenetic makeup, and environmental experiences to individualize the prevention and treatment of disease. The field largely emerged at the turn of the twenty-first century with the first full sequencing of the human genome and is gaining popularity as the costs of genomic sequences is dropping. In 2009, the cost to sequence an individual is about $1000 in comparison to the billion dollars it cost to sequence the first human genome in 1999 (Oberweis 2009).

The overall expectation and hope is that the including of an individual's unique genetic profile will improve the health care provider's ability to understand, predict, prevent, detect, diagnose, and treating the illness with a more accurate selection and dosing of medicines (National Human Genome Research Institute). In addition, the hope is that personalized medicine will help control or even reduce health care costs and spur economic growth.

While seemingly promising, personalized medicine also faces challenges that must be addressed to gain the full benefits of this technology, especially in the areas of: assessing the genomic information and translating it to the patient, patient and provider education, the role of direct-to-consumer companies in the field, high up-front innovation costs, insufficient insurance reimbursements, and legal frameworks.

Benefits

Before mapping the criticisms and problems challenging the emerging field, it is important to summarize some of the potential benefits of including individual genomic analysis in the diagnosis and treatment of disease. First, the emerging field promises improved abilities to classify diseases according to their molecular signatures, perhaps most evident in the field of oncology. Cancers like melanoma, for instance, are no longer seen as just melanoma (Ginsburg and Willard 2009). Melanoma tumors can now be sub-classified by their genetic

---

[1] Some of the material contained in this chapter was obtained from Loike, J.D. and Miller, J. Personalized Medicine, Encyclopedia of Bioethics, In Press 2013.

mutations (e.g., *BRAF*, *BRAF* wild type, or *c-KIT* genes; Curtin, Fridlyand, Kageshita, et al. 2005). Similarly, breast, brain, leukemia, and certain types of lung cancers can also be sub-classified by the tumor's molecular designation (Ausborn, Le, Bradley, et al. 2012; Horton and Huntly 2012; Gokmen-Polar and Badve 2012; Northcott, Dubuc, Pfister, et al. 2012). It is important to note, however, that WGS use in cancer care is not a one-time application. Patients may require repeated monitoring as they are treated with the therapies indicated by the_genomics of their cancer. Secondary and tertiary sampling of recurrent cancers may prove to be essential in understanding how the genome of the patient's specific cancer has changed, and what new therapeutics might be more effective for treating their disease, when their first therapy fails.

Second, intimately related to classifying the pathological signature of a disease, genomic based personalized medicine is enabling the development and delivery of targeted drugs to treat an individual's particular type of disease, based on its specific genetic demarcation. In general, genetics-based tests can potentially identify whether a particular cancer patient will improve with "hormone therapy alone, avoiding the expense and toxic effects of chemotherapy, or whether a more aggressive treatment is needed" (Personalized Medicine Coalition 2011). For example, it is now possible to select the appropriate treatment for melanoma patients according to the genetic mutations and biological drivers of their particular tumor (Dancey, Bedard, Onetto, et al. 2012). It is also possible to assess *HER2* expression levels in breast cancer patients to determine whether to administer Herceptin treatment (Moelans, de Weger, Van der Wall, et al. 2011). Patients with chronic myeloid leukemia who have failed standard therapies are also incorporating their personalized genomic analysis to help select the next phase of treatment. Moreover, studies have shown that skin-cancer patients carrying the *BRAF* gene are significantly more likely to respond to a targeted treatment, contrasted with a very low response in patients given a standard treatment (Mandalà and Voit 2013). This practice, called pharmacogenetics or pharmacogenomics, is becoming more routine in clinical practice, especially in oncology and cardiology.

In a similar fashion, pharmacogenomics can also be helpful in revealing when small populations are likely to experience serious side effects from particular drugs. Such was the case with irinotecan, a drug used to treat colorectal cancer, which is now understood to cause severe deleterious side effects in patients with a genetic variation in the UDP-glucuronosyltransferase gene (*UGT1A1*; Innocenti and Ratain 2003). Pharmacogenetics can help doctors better understand if certain populations are more prone to toxicity from particular drugs because of gene mutations.

Third, pharmacogenetics also can predict the how patients will metabolize therapeutic drugs in the most efficacious manner. The genetic predisposition to drug metabolism can direct proper drug dosing, by recognizing how individuals metabolize drugs at different rates. Slower drug metabolizers may "have trouble inactivating a drug and eliminating it from their bodies," putting them at risk for overdose toxicity. Faster drug metabolizers may eliminate a drug before drug efficacy has been established. Studies have shown that failures to consider individuals' genetic makeups when dosing drugs can result in unnecessary adverse outcomes and drug reactions that could lead to death (Leon-Cachon, Ascacio-Martinez, and Barrera-Saldana 2012). The effectiveness of the anticoagulant warfarin is a classic example: patients differ in their clinical responses because of their genetic-driven capacity to metabolize this drug.

Fourth, many experts theorize that personalized medicine can help control overall health care costs in two ways. Individuals with the gene *apoE3* are more prone to develop atherosclerosis and Alzheimer's disease as they age as compared with individuals expressing the *apoE2* genotype (Huang 2010). Knowing the genetic predisposition of an individual, in advance might allow the patients to start taking statins earlier in life before clinical symptoms of heart disease appear. Second, delivering individualized drug therapy is associated with avoiding a host of unnecessary and costly health outcomes including adverse drug reactions that result in costly hospitalizations, the use of costly medicine when cheaper and similarly effective substitutes are available, and the use of medicines to which patients will likely be unresponsive. One study, for example, showed that "upfront *KRAS* testing to limit cetuximab therapy to patients with wild-type *KRAS* tumors can result in drug cost savings of $604 million" (Sipkoff 2009).

Similarly, personalized medicine may also help spur economic growth. The US Presidential Commission for the Study of Bioethical Issues (US Presidential Commission 2012) has acknowledged that advances in scientific and medical innovation generally have positive economic impacts. The Human Genome Project, responsible for enabling the field of personalized medicine, is credited with enriching individuals in 2010 to the tune of $244 billion in personal income. It also created more than 300,000 jobs within the United States alone that same year. Reports further estimate that the human genome project has yielded a positive total US economic impact of nearly $800 billion (Akst 2011). Experts note that it is difficult to think of a similar medical innovation sponsored by the US government that has generated such similar positive economic growth.

Criticisms and Challenges

While the emerging field of personalized medicine holds much promise, it is not without its criticisms and challenges. Indeed, critics largely see the benefits attributed to the field as hyperbole. Skeptics and proponents alike tend to agree there are seven significant challenges that need to be overcome for personalized medicine to advance more fully.

First, critics argue that personalized medicine is neither novel nor truly personal. The field does not represent a new era of medicine, but rather the same old medicine operating with a larger variable set, claim many critics. Moreover, critics view the practice not as "personal," in the sense of being personalized to the individual patient with a particular disease, but rather as targeted to "sociodemographic groupings" (Langanke, Brothers, Erdmann, et al. 2011). As a result, some would dub the practice "stratified medicine rather than personalized medicine" (Langanke, Brothers, Erdmann, et al. 2011).

Second, skeptics note that the nature of and risk factors contributing to disease and a disease's response to treatments are more complex than proponents of personalized medicine may publicly extol. Regarding disease risk factors, they are not exclusively genetically based; they tend also to include environmental, epigenetic, and psychosocial and behavioral variables such as smoking, exercise habits, sun exposure, experiences of stress, and overall mental health (Hansson 2010). Cancers, for example, are more strongly associated with lifestyle variables than genetic heritability (85% of cancers; Hansson 2010). Similarly, the onset of type 2 diabetes is attributed primarily to lifestyle factors (Hansson 2010). Similarly, diseases do not necessarily react linearly to personalized therapies. Tumors, for instance, are often resilient entities that may not respond to a single targeted drug (Hansson 2010). Many targeted therapies will be more effective if administered in combination with other pharmacogenomic drugs or, as some are used now, with existing conventional drugs.

Furthermore, whole gene sequencing is not the whole story with regard to personalized medicine. The emerging understanding of epigenetics will eventually have to be integrated into personalized medicine. Epigenetics, as discussed in Chapter 9 is the study of the mechanisms by which heritable changes in a phenotype occur in the absence of any alterations in the DNA sequence. Epigenetic mechanisms determine whether a cell will serve as a neuron, cardiomyocyte, leukoctye, or cancer cell. Epigenetics also elucidates how environment impacts heredity. In the future, epigenetic profiling of cancers will help elucidate better diagnostics and specific therapies to treat this devastating disease. In general genomics presents a static picture of the patient. In the future genomic analysis will be integrated with transcriptomic data (showing potential changes in messenger RNA levels), with proteomic data (showing the actual levels of protein), and with metabolomic data (showing the products of enzymatic and signaling cascades) to completely understand the current patient state (Altman 2013).

Third, as with any diagnostic test, genomic analysis will have to be re-assessed as to it accuracy in application to the diagnosis and treatment of disease. Therefore, experts in genomics will be needed to help assess the results and evaluate the genetic data in conjunction with other biological markers and clinical symptoms.

Fourth, proponents worry that without reforms to current regulatory and reimbursement structures, the field may have a very limited future. Companion diagnostics, for example, are essential to the field as they test individuals for specific genetic mutations known to be responsive or unresponsive to particular targeted therapies. Currently insurance companies do not necessarily cover these types of diagnostic tests. Without a commercial market, there may be little incentive to develop these essential tests, let alone spend millions to clinically test them. Moreover, there is no comprehensive process or pathway within the FDA or other governmental entity to review and approve many of the necessary diagnostics that accompany targeted therapies.

Fifth, genetic testing kits are marketed directly to consumers by groups like 23andMe, and AncestryDNA, with limited quality controls and consumer privacy protections (Korn 2012). Regarding quality concerns, researchers have sent animal DNA samples labeled as human samples to select direct-to-consumer genetic testing companies for testing, only to have companies return "a sundry (of) findings and interpretations and complete failures to distinguish the animal from a human sample" (Korn 2012). What security protocols can be instituted to insure that the person sending the samples is in fact, the same person from which the sample was obtained from? Along with quality concerns, there remain many unresolved legal questions regarding who owns the collected genomic data and what privacy protections these companies can or should assure consumers (Korn 2012). It is also unclear how much license these companies have to use the materials they collect and what kind of informed consent, if any and from whom, is required for subsequent usage of genomic collections (Korn 2012).

Sixth, translating the medical knowledge gleaned from personalized medicine (e.g., regarding the causes, prevention methods, and treatments for diseases) into tangible public and patient health benefits is a formidable challenge. In the first place, many patients may not want to know about their disease risks and possible preventive care options (Cornetta and Brown 2013). Before personalized tests were available for Huntington's disease, 60 percent to 75 percent of people at risk wanted such a test. Now that it is available, only 3 percent to 21 percent actually take the test. In addition, even if a patient is tested and informed of disease risks, will the patient comprehend the nature of disease risk or pre-disposition to disease? Will patients understand how to engage preventative measure to reduce risk or how to modify their behaviors accordingly. They may not change their diet, exercise, smoking, sun-tanning, and the like to minimize impacts of a disease (Hansson 2010). Will patients elect to undergo controversial medical procedures (e.g., prostatectomy or mastectomy) in response to learning that they may carry genes that increase their risks for certain cancers.

Seventh, on the issue of cost-effectiveness, experts argue that the up-front implementation costs for the field are still quite high and that health economical study data verifying cost-effectiveness remain scarce (Lunshof 2005). Indeed, the complexity of confounding variables in personalized medicine makes it necessary to study large sample sets. Many of these sets contain biosamples and medical records that are expensive to access and maintain, and their use raises significant medical privacy concerns. Moreover, drugs that have accompanying genetic tests are commonly more expensive than drugs that do not. Companies justify the higher prices for these drugs because pharmacogenomics limits their markets and because these drugs are supposed to be safer and more efficacious. Without genetic testing a drug may have a market of 100 percent of a population with a particular disease; pharmacogenomics, however, may limit the market to a subset of the populations that has a particular molecular signature. Market forces can be a disincentive for companies to innovate in the field of personalized medicine, which raises its own set of ethical issues.

Ethical Considerations

Advancing the field of personalized medicine requires the collection of vast amounts of genetic data and therefore "widespread public participation and individual willingness to share genomic data and relevant medical information" (US Presidential Commission 2012). This raises immediate ethical and legal considerations regarding how best to protect the privacy of individuals (and of blood relatives as well) providing their genomic and medical information (Fox 2012).

Interestingly, there is some incoherence between the legal and ethical norms guiding the use of this data. The US Presidential Commission for the Study of Bioethical Issues currently recommends that genomic research follow the traditional research principles outlined in the Belmont Report (US National Commission 1978): respect for persons and related subprinciples of public beneficence, responsible stewardship, intellectual freedom and responsibility, democratic deliberation, and justice and fairness (Lunshof 2005, Knoppers and Avard 2009).

In contrast, legally, much of personalized medicine research falls outside of the scope of traditional human research subject protections, such as the US Common Rule (US Department of Health and Human Services) because it is believed that the information being used and accessed has been sufficiently stripped of personal identifiers. It has been argued that de-identified information is like a fingerprint—it "does not have a name or address encoded directly in it. To discover the suspect's identity, one must link the print to a database containing both traditional personal identifiers and fingerprints in order to know which person to arrest [a debatable assumption to which we will return later]" (US Presidential Commission 2012).

Notwithstanding this potential incoherence, most stakeholders agree that providing some level of privacy and confidentiality for patients' health care information is a basic ethical responsibility that falls under the principle of respect for persons (US Presidential Commission 2012). However, there is no consensus on how to define how much privacy protection to afford, only that the principle (like many sub-principles), is not an absolute value (US Presidential Commission 2012).

Patients, for example, generally want high levels of privacy. They often want only their immediate caregivers to have access to their records without explicit consent (Scott 2011, 32–33; US Presidential Commission 2012). Reports indicate that patients worry about a series of social harms that can result from unauthorized access to and use of this sensitive data. They fear that the release of negative information could lead to social stigma and discrimination, disruptions to "their home, family, and community life," psychological harm, and other social disadvantages such as missed opportunities for employment, long-term health care, disability and health insurance, "financial backing or loan approval(s), educational opportunities, sport eligibility, military accession, or adoption eligibility" (US Presidential Commission 2012). These risks can also accrue to individuals' blood relatives. However, it should be noted that "the number of documented cases of discrimination on the basis of genetic test results is small" (US Presidential Commission 2012).

Researchers, in contrast, frequently want low privacy protections. They tend to argue that mandating routine informed consent to access medical records slows medical progress and increases costs and red tape. They further note that mandating consent can invalidate research results by creating a selection bias, by including only patients that can be located and are willing to provide consent (Humber and Almeder 2001).

At the same time some experts believe that medical privacy is simply impossible to maintain (Scott 2011). Indeed, re-identifying a person from de-identified data is a relatively straightforward process. Forensic techniques challenge the possibility of total anonymity in general for genomic research. An individual can be identified from a data set by, for instance, matching their genetic data with publicly available single nucleotide polymorphisms (SNP) data. It is also possible to re-identify an individual from longitudinal and transactional information in data sets by looking at the number of times a patient visits a hospital, the length of their stays, the time since their previous clinic visit, and/or diagnostic codes (El Emam 2011). Most of this information is currently available in most data sets. Once a person is re-identified, "the rest of the genotypic, phenotypic, and other information linked to that individual in public records would also become available" (Lin, Owen, and Altman 2004). Various methods have been tested to increase privacy protections and to mitigate re-identification risks. However, to date the tested methods have mostly complicated data analysis without increasing privacy protections (Lin, Owen, and Altman 2004).

Experts also note that there are unavoidable trade-offs inherent in balancing individual patient privacy rights with public health goals and between prioritizing the patient (a goal of bioethics) and maximizing profits for institutions (a consideration of business ethics). In general, most agree that the benefits that result from medical research and progress outweigh minimal intrusions into patients' medical privacy—even though the burdens of privacy intrusions accrue mainly to the individual and the benefits are reaped largely by the public (US Presidential Commission 2012, 36). One means for balancing competing ethical claims between the principle of respect for persons (and its sub-principle of respect for privacy) and the need to advance public health, is to maintain a robust informed consent process. Informed consent can help ensure that individuals are aware of and provide permission for the foreseeable consequences of their decision to share their personal information. The importance of informed consent is not unique to personalized medicine, but there are some unique considerations. The US Presidential Commission on Bioethics (2012) recommends that the consent process in personalized medicine should clearly:

- Define what genome sequencing is and include information about "how data will be analyzed, stored, and shared," including who has access to the data;
- Identify what will or will not be shared with them, including what "types of results the patient and participant can expect to receive", including whether the sequencing results and incidental findings will be returned to subjects and the process for doing so;
- Explain "the likelihood that the implications of some of these results might currently be unknown, but could be discovered in the future"; and
- Classify potential future uses of the data and control if any they have over future uses.

Typically only a very broad general consent is sought for the collection and deposit of new biosamples. Researchers using precollected data and blood or DNA samples are generally not required to obtain informed consent from the original patient or individual sourcing the biosamples and data (Hansson 2010). US regulations currently allow repositories to use an opt-out approach to the informed consent process. By contrast, German regulatory requirements require an explicit informed consent that bars the use of an opt-out model. Opt-out methods have the benefits of being more cost-effective and contributing to higher participation rates than opt-in methods. For this reason, participation bias may be lower in opt-out research studies (Langanke, Brothers, Erdmann, et al., 2011). However opt-in methods may better protect the autonomy of individuals sourcing the data and biosamples.

Legal Landscape and Standards

The gathering of personal data and information and the corresponding need to develop protective legal measures to ensure the security and privacy of gathered information is not new. Census and tax systems have long collected and stored personally identifiable information. However, personally identifiable health information is understood to be different from census and tax information and not as well protected. Despite US congressional hearings covering medical privacy that date back to 1971, no uniform federal laws have emerged to comprehensively protect medical information—let alone to specifically ensure genetic privacy (Scott 2011).

The Health Insurance Portability and Accountability Act of 1996 (HIPAA) is the major US federal law guiding medical privacy issues. It protects health information, if it is considered identifiable, for living people (not post death) in a few specific areas, namely for "health plan(s), health care clearinghouse(s), or a health care provider(s) that transmits any health information in electronic form." De-identified data or data falling outside these categories, indeed much of the genomic data used in personalized research, are not necessarily protected by HIPAA.

The Genetic and Information Nondisclosure Act of 2008 (GINA) is the most prominent federal protection guiding the use of genetic information. Driven in part by the successes of the Human Genome Project, the US congress passed GINA to prohibit employers and health insurers from discriminating against individuals based on the results of genetic tests. GINA only provides protections against employment and health insurance discrimination risks. It does not regulate discrimination risks in other contexts, such as by life, long-term care, and disability insurers (US Presidential Commission 2012). Nor does it regulate concerns pertaining to "access, security, and disclosure of genetic or whole genome sequence information across all potential users" (US Presidential Commission 2012). The Act allows states to individually adopt more robust guidelines. As a result, "the level of protection afforded to an individual's genetic information differs widely from state to state" (US Presidential Commission 2012).

There are three main sets of standards under HIPAA and the associated Privacy Rules of 2003 available to guide the data de-identification process: the Safe Harbor Standard, the Limited Data Set, and the Statistical Standard (El Emam 2011). Of these three sets of standards, data custodians tend to prefer the Safe Harbor standards for their simplicity and for their international applicability (international guidelines have tended to rely on the Safe Harbor standards; El Emam 2011). The standards mandate the removal of eighteen specific personal identifiers from data sets ranging from geographic subdivisions smaller than a state, elements of dates except years, telephone numbers, electronic mail addresses, social security numbers, medical record numbers, health plan beneficiary numbers, vehicle identifiers and serial numbers, and Internet protocol address numbers, to full-date photographic images (Narrative Inquiry). While the standards are generally well received by custodians, they are not without their disadvantages and critics.

Some critics quip that the standards are too strict and hinder research. For example, mandating the removal of dates and geographic locations from data sets can make investigating singular events in particular locations at specific times impossible (think epidemics and environmental exposures; Langanke, Brothers, Erdmann, et al. 2011). Others worry that the standards are too lax, that not enough information is required to be removed (such as certain types of genetic, longitudinal, and transactional data and free-form notes) to prevent individuals from being reidentified (El Emam 2011). They note that the Safe Harbor standards fail to require the removal of, for example, free-form notes from data sets that can include references to specific injuries, parents' professions, and places of employment—all of which might easily identify a person when matched with public information from social networking sites (El Emam 2011).

Conclusions

In 2013 the methods of whole genome sequencing (WGS) and epigenetic analyses were expected to improve and the costs to dramatically decrease within ten years, which was expected to help these technologies become part of routine medical care. Personalized medicine holds great promise in improving current methods for understanding, predicting, preventing, detecting, diagnosing, and treating illness. For these potential benefits to fully burgeon, the high up-front innovation costs, insufficient reimbursement and legal frameworks, and other challenges outlined above must be addressed. Personalized medicine is not the answer to every health care challenge, but it is a piece of the puzzle available to be included in evidence-based medicine.

References

Akst, J. "Billion Dollar Babies of the Human Genome." The Scientist, May 14. 2011

Altman, R. "Personal Genomic Measurements: The Opportunity for Information Integration." Clin Pharm and Therap 93 (1): 21–23, 2013.

Ausborn, N., et al., "Molecular Profiling to Optimize Treatment in Non-Small Cell Lung Cancer: A Review of Potential Molecular Targets for Radiation Therapy by the Translational Research Program of the Radiation Therapy Oncology Group." Int J Radiation Oncol: Biology Physics 83 (4): e453–64, 2012.

Cornetta, K., Gunther Brown, C. "Balancing Personalized Medicine and Personalized Care." Acad Med 88 (3): 309–13, 2013.

Curtin, John A.; Jane Fridlyand; Toshiro Kageshita; et al. "Distinct Sets of Genetic Alterations in Melanoma." NEJM, 353 (20): 2135–47, 2005.

Dancey, J. E., Bedard, P.L., Onetto, N., Hudson, T.J. "The Genetic Basis for Cancer Treatment Decisions." Cell 148 (3): 409–20, 2012.

El Emam, K. "Methods for the De-Identification of Electronic Health Records for Genomic Research." Gen Med 3:25, 2011.

Fox, J. L. "Commission Calls for Genomic Privacy." Nature Biot 30 (11): 1017, 2012.

Ginsburg, G. S., and Willard, H.F. "Genomic and Personalized Medicine: Foundations and Applications." Transl Res 154: 277–87, 2009.

Gokmen-Polar, Y., and Badve, S. "Molecular Profiling Assays in Breast Cancer: Are We Ready f   or Prime Time?" Oncology 26 (4): 350–57, 361, 2012.

Hansson, M. G. "Taking the Patient's Side: The Ethics of Pharmacogenetics." Pers Med 7 (1): 75–85, 2010.

Huang, Y. "Mechanisms Linking Apolipoprotein E Isoforms with Cardiovascular and Neurological Diseases." Curr Opin Lipid 21 (4): 337–45, 2010.

Humber, J. M., and Almeder,R.F. Privacy and Health Care. Totowa, NJ: Humana Press. 2001.

Innocenti, .F, and Ratain, M.J. "Irinotecan Treatment in Cancer Patients with UGT1A1 Polymorphisms." Oncol 17 (5 Suppl 5): 52–55, 2003.

Knoppers, Bartha Maria, and Denise Avard. "'Principled' Personalized Medicine?" Pers Med 6 (6): 663–67, 2009.

Korn, D. "Interview: A Perspective on Personalized Medicine: Dr David Korn." Pers Med 9 (3): 259–63, 2012.

Langanke, M., Brothers,K.B., Erdmann, P., et al. "Comparing Different Scientific Approaches to Personalized Medicine: Research Ethics and Privacy Protection." Pers Med 8 (4): 437–44, 2011.

Lin, Z., Owen, A.B., Altman, R.B.. "Genetics: Genomic Research and Human Subject Privacy." Science 305: 183, 2004.

León-Cachón, R.B., Ascacio-Martínez,JA., and Barrera-Saldaña, H.A. "Individual Response to Drug Therapy: Bases and Study Approaches." Revista de Investigación Clínica 64 (4): 364–76, 2012.

Lunshof, J. "Personalized Medicine: How Much Can We Afford? A Bioethics Perspective." Pers Med 2 (1): 43–47.,2005.

Mandalà, M., and Voit, C. "Targeting BRAF in Melanoma: Biological and Clinical Challenges." Crit Rev Oncol/Hem., forthcoming. Published online 14, 2013. doi: 10.1016/j.critrevonc.2013.01.003, 2013.

Moelans, C. de Weger,r.,van der Wall,e., van Diest, P. "Current Technologies for HER2 Testing in Breast Cancer." Crit Rev Oncol/Hem. 80 (3): 380–92, 2011.

National Human Genome Research Institute. "Personalized Medicine." http://www.genome.gov/Glossary/index.cfm?id=150.

Northcott, P. A., Dubuc, A.M., Pfister, S., Taylor, M.D. "Molecular Subgroups of Medulloblastoma." Expert Rev Neurother 12 (7): 871–84, 2012.

Oberweis, J. "The Next Big Thing: Personalized Medicine." The Oberweis Report. Forbes, May 28, 2009. http://www.forbes.com/2009/05/28/illumina-life-genomics-personal-finance-guru-insight-nih-genes.html.

Personalized Medicine Coalition. 2011. The Case for Personalized Medicine. 3rd ed. Washington, DC: http://personalizedmedicinecoalition.org/sites/default/files/files/Case_for_PM_3rd_edition.pdf.

Scott, C. "Is Too Much Privacy Bad for Your Health?: An Introduction to the Law and Ethics of Medical Privacy." In Privacy and HealthCare, edited by James M. Humber and Robert F. Almeder, 26. Totowa, NJ: Humana Press. 2011.

Sipkoff, M. "Who's Tackling Rampant Overutilization? Health Plans!" Managed Care, Dec 2009. http://www.managedcaremag.com/archives/0912/0912.utilization.html?page=11.

US Department of Health and Human Services. Federal Policy for the Protection of Human Subjects ("Common Rule"). http://www.hhs.gov/ohrp/humansubjects/commonrule/.

US National Commission for the Protection of Human Subjects of Biomedical and Behavioral Research. 1978. The Belmont Report, Washington, DC: US Government Printing Office.

US Presidential Commission for the Study of Bioethical Issues. 2012. "Privacy and Progress in Whole Genome Sequencing." Washington, DC: http://www.bioethics.gov/cms/sites/default/files/PrivacyProgress508.pdf.

Figure 1. Medical History. A family history is a record of medical information about an individual and their biological family. Human genetic data is becoming more prevalent and easy to obtain. Increasingly, this data is being used to identify individuals who are at increased risk for developing genetic disorders that run in families. (obtained from NIH.gov).

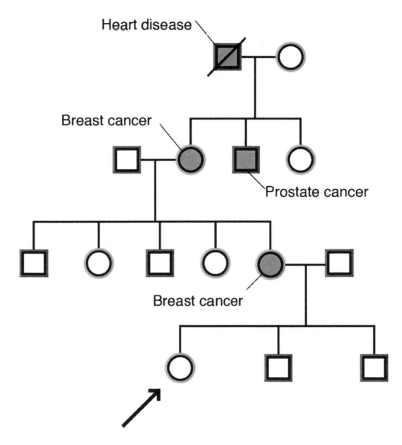

Chapter Eleven

Women's Reproductive Technology

Introduction

Assisted reproductive technologies (ARTs) have improved and expanded a woman's ability to control her lifestyle and career path. Although generally marketed towards young infertile women, ARTs currently allow women of all ages to manage their reproductive futures more effectively. This chapter delves into the technical and scientific details of three distinct areas of evolving reproductive technologies: cryopreservation of embryos and oocytes, donation of reproductive organs and tissue, and medical regulation of menses. Where appropriate, the next chapter will briefly examine selected bioethical implications of these expanded technologies.

The process of *in vitro* fertilization (IVF) stems from research conducted in the early 1950s by Chang (Chang, 1951) and Austin (Austin, 1951), who independently reported that mammalian sperm must spend some time in the female reproductive tract before the sperm acquire the ability to fertilize eggs. The phenomenon underlying the acquisition of fertilization capability is called sperm capacitation (Austin, 1952), and established one critical step in order to use sperm to fertilize an egg in vitro for IVF.

Cryopreservation of Embryos, Oocytes, and Ovarian Tissue

Human cryobiology, the science of life at low temperatures, has rapidly developed, beginning from the freezing of animal spermatozoa in Italy during the 1770s, up through the current freezing of ovarian tissue for fertility purposes (Dittrich et al., 2011). Following the first birth from a frozen embryo in 1983 (Leslie, 2007) and the subsequent current boom of IVF, clinical applications of cryopreservation of human sperm, eggs, and embryos have become commonplace in fertility clinics around the world. It is estimated that more than five million babies have been born using ARTs[1] and approximately 400 babies are born each year using frozen embryos.[2] One unintended consequence of ART is that hundreds of thousands of frozen embryos remain in storage pending decisions for their final destiny (Lyerly and Faden, 2007).

---

[1] http://www.huffingtonpost.co.uk/2012/07/02/health-ivf-five-million-babies-1978_n_1642231.html

[2] Http://www.prweb.com/releases/FirstFrozenEggBabyReunion/WestCoastFertilityCenters/prweb8848857.htm

Vitrification: Freezing and preserving human sperm has been in place for over 50 years (Edgar and Gook, 2012). Embryos are frozen in the lab through a process called vitrification that can result in successful pregnancies after freeze-thawing the frozen embryos. Successful "freezing" of embryos is a challenging technique that requires precise cooling and solidification of cells without causing the formation of ice crystals inside cells or tissues that can lead to cell damage or cell death. In 2012, a new cutting-edge technology is developing to freeze and preserve the human oocyte or egg (Mertes et al., 2012). The difficulty in freezing human eggs is that it is the largest cell in the body and has the largest water content.

Normal freezing of cells in an aqueous solution or buffer is a lethal event. A historical twist in cryopreservation occurred by way of an accidental finding when Polge and his colleagues reported that freezing cock spermatozoa at -80°C in an aqueous buffer containing glycerol maintains their viability for extended periods of time (Polge et al., 1949).

Vitrification cools living systems faster than the time required for ice formation and results in a glass-like solidification of the cells. Specifically, this process involves immersing cells in liquid nitrogen vapors at a specific cooling rate of 120°C per minute. This method has been shown to be effective for pre-embryos, defined from the time of conception to the 14th day (Kuleshova and Lopata, 2002) and is now a common practice in many fertility clinics in the United States (Leslie, 2007). Embryos derived from oocytes (eggs) cryopreserved by the vitrification method are reported to produce an on-going pregnancy as effective as a pregnancy from fresh oocytes.[3]

Freezing oocytes: Freezing oocytes poses more challenges than freezing embryos. In 1986, Chen reported the first pregnancy using cryopreserved oocytes (Chen, 1986). Like embryo cryopreservation, the main biophysical challenge to freezing oocytes has been avoiding intracellular ice formation but a different process had to be developed. At present, freezing oocytes differs from embryo freezing by utilizing a method that slowly freezes the oocyte and then rapidly thaws it (Mertes et al., 2012). Cryopreserved storage of mature metaphase II oocytes may make oocyte donation safer by allowing enough time to screen the donors for any genetic disease, circumventing potential legal and ethical problems derived from the generation of surplus embryos.

The lower success rate using frozen oocytes and the higher costs for this procedure compared to classical IVF were catalysts for the American Society for

---

[3] http://www.sciencedaily.com/releases/2010/06/100630071142.htm

Reproductive Medicine (ASRM) to endorse freezing oocytes only in a limited situations: to preserve the fertility of cancer patients (Leslie, 2007). One study in 2010 showed that only about 7% of frozen oocytes produced viable babies (Scaravelli, 2010). A specific problem with using frozen oocytes is that the best success rates occur in woman under the age of 35. Factors that also contribute to success are the number of eggs retrieved and the clinic's ability to provide comprehensive and cutting edge technologies. Advocates for oocyte freezing claim that the rate for frozen oocyte success have been and continue to improve to be on par with the success rate of using fresh oocytes.

Hyperstimulation of the Ovaries and Associated Health Risks

In order to retrieve mature eggs from a woman to be used for classical IVF or cryopreservation, hyperstimulation of the ovaries has been necessary. This process involves a seven to ten-day regimen of medications in which hormones the female body normally produces are injected in much larger doses (Bothwell, 2007). Fertility drugs are prescribed and self-injected, resulting in the simultaneous ripening of multiple eggs instead of the normal ovulation of one egg per month during a menstrual cycle. At a precisely indicated time, determined by the woman's blood hormone levels and ultrasound of her ovaries, as many as 12-20 eggs can be retrieved in a ten-minute procedure. The woman is put under light anesthesia and a needle is guided through the vaginal wall by ultrasound to the ovary where the eggs can be collected.

There are short-term medical risks associated with the surgical procedures and anesthetics involved in egg retrieval. These risks include infection, hemorrhage, pain, aspiration, and psychological effects. Psychological stresses include acknowledging the fact that there are fertility problems. The planning and long period of time involved with IVF requires the disruption of work or school, as well as the rigorous schedule of a prolonged process as opposed to a one time medical procedure. Additional stress may be due to the costs associated with IVF that are significant with an average price of $12,000. If additional assisted reproductive technologies needed, the cost will be higher. Intracytoplasmic sperm injection (ICS), for example, where a single sperm is injected directly into an egg, may be cost an additional $1,000 to $1,500 while PGD genetic testing of embryos, may be around $3,000 or more.[4]

One particular serious short-term risk is associated with the hormone treatment needed to stimulate the production of mature oocytes. The risk of ovarian hyperstimulation syndrome (OHSS) affects a small proportion of women

---

[4] http://infertility.about.com/od/ivf/f/ivf_cost.htm

(approximately 3-6% for moderate cases of OHSS) (Bothwell, 2007). Yet for some women, OHSS can cause life-threatening complications including blood clots, kidney failure, shock, and pulmonary edema (fluid buildup in the lungs). In a small number of cases, OHSS could necessitate removal of the ovaries (Klein and Sauer, 2010).

Long-term risks are more difficult to assess. In the 1980s, clomiphene citrate was used instead of gonadotropin hormones to stimulate ovulation and one study found that this type of treatment significantly elevated risks of ovarian cancer when treatment exceeded twelve cycles (Pearson, 2006). Currently, insufficient data are available to document clear, long-term risks associated with the process of oocyte donation. Controversial and dated studies have proposed many complex and convoluted factors that complicate the determination of any concrete links between donation and harms to the donor's health (Sunkura, 2012). It is vitally important for reproductive specialists to study the long-term effects of fertility drugs when their use is so commonplace in IVF practice. The concern is heightened that women engaging in multiple cycles of hyperstimulation of the ovaries may be at increased risk of certain cancers such as ovarian cancer, or onset of early menopause. Despite this obvious need for data, no epidemiologic studies have appeared in the literature following women who have had repeated cycles of hyperstimulation of the ovaries, particularly those women who serve as egg donors over multiple cycles. Is there a difference in health risks between women serving as egg donors who do not go on to having a pregnancy versus women who use IVF to produce a pregnancy? These critically needed studies of both populations of women should examine the health of the woman as well as the health of the offspring. Epidemiologic studies should be conducted but as IVF is a relatively new procedure, it is important to recognize that researchers have had only about a decade to study significant numbers of women and any possible adverse effects. Since there is no registry of women who donate their eggs for fertility or research and since cancers often do not appear until ages 50 or 60, any associations will remain inconclusive until the necessary data are obtained (Gadducci et al., 2012).

Because OHSS is a serious medical risk, several clinics have used a variety of techniques to reduce the danger. Withholding Human Chorionic Gonadotropin combined with cycle cancellation is considered the safest option, but it also carries adverse emotional and financial implications. Withholding hormonal treatment for several days (coasting) has been shown to diminish the incidence and severity of OHSS without compromising pregnancy rates. In 2010 and 2011, several clinics have reported the use of Gonadotropin-releasing hormone agonist (GnRHa) to trigger final oocyte maturation. Data from these clinics indicate that this procedure was safer than that of coasting in patients at high risk for OHSS (DiLuigi et al., 2010; Imbar et al., 2012).

The intense pressure from infertile couples wanting to have children and needing eggs (their own or a donor's), coupled with the financial successes of many fertility clinics, are likely to have limited the number of studies that have been carried out to examine the associated medical risks of egg donation. Implementation of expensive long-term follow-up studies will require government mandates. But who will fund these studies? More details about the barriers to study the links with cancer are found in the next chapter.

New Technologies to Obtain Oocytes

An exciting 2006 development made possible by advances in freezing technology has been the cryopreservation of ovarian tissue. The experimental technology, discovered in the mid-1990s, and used with young pre-menstrual girls about to undergo chemotherapy, entails removing and slicing one ovary into sections, and either: 1) freezing hundreds of primordial follicles or 2) transplanting the sections back into the body, perhaps under the skin of the arm or abdomen (auto transplantation). Years later, after chemotherapy, if the woman wishes to become pregnant, two procedures can be initiated. In the first option, the immature follicles are matured *in vitro* and then used in IVF technology. The second option is to transplant the tissue grafts back into the remaining ovary. Currently, ovarian tissue transplantation is only approved for patients undergoing cancer treatments due to its unknown success rates and experimental status (Whitworth, 2006). As of recent report in 2011 (Dittrich et al., 2012), transplantation of frozen/thawed ovarian tissue has yielded 17 live births, and it is expected that in the near future more and more cancer patients who have been cured of their disease will be requesting reimplantation of cryopreserved ovarian tissue.

As a result of the uncertainties of the medical risks associated with hyperstimulation of the ovaries, biotechnologies are being developed that will allow the physician to obtain **immature** oocytes **without** hormone treatment. In addition, freezing mature eggs or embryos is not an option for girls who have yet to reach puberty. A better way of preserving their fertility is to freeze slices of ovarian tissue that contain small immature eggs, and subsequently maturing these eggs so that they can be used in IVF treatment.

In 2012, new technologies have the potential to improve the efficiency of using immature oocytes for IVF. Scientists have shown that phosphatase and tensin homolog deleted on chromosome ten (PTEN) is a negative regulator of phosphatidylinositol 3 kinase (PI3K), and functions in oocytes to specifically suppress the primordial follicle activation. A chemical which inhibits PTEN can trigger the maturation of small eggs from mice to form healthy, mature eggs (Adhikari et al., 2012). Scientists are now examining this process in human immature oocytes.

As of 2007, over three hundred healthy babies have been born from an immature oocyte that was allowed to mature in the laboratory, freeze, and then thaw (Huang et al., 2007). Therefore, this new assisted reproductive technology that utilizes immature eggs may offer a safer procedure than IVF. Additionally, it may benefit many women who do not have the opportunity to utilize assisted reproductive 'fresh' egg technology. In addition to children with cancer, older cancer patients who may not have time to undergo fertility treatment before chemotherapy, or women with medical conditions such as hormone-sensitive breast cancer, or women who have adverse response to ovarian stimulation may find this technology helpful.

Frozen vs. Fresh Embryos

Pre-implanted embryos: Embryonic and oocyte cryopreservation have revamped the standard IVF procedure which was to repeatedly pursue fresh cycles of IVF, with their inherent risks, until there was a successful implantation and pregnancy. Many women, especially over the age of 35 who undergo IVF, do not conceive after their first round of treatment and cycles must be repeated (Wang et al., 2008). Improvements in cryotechnology have modified this practice to now include implanting fresh embryos in the initial cycle and then cryopreserving the excess embryos. These high quality embryos are kept in reserve in case they are needed for additional cycles. Cryopreservation avoids the need to repeat fertility hormone treatment and retrieval of fresh eggs. Using fresh then frozen embryo transfer and having the ability to distinguish high quality embryos (standards which are necessary in cryopreservation), has increased the success of IVF (Hinckley et al., 2008). Unfortunately, not all women produce quality embryos that meet the standards to be cryopreserved. As a result, they must repeat fresh embryo transfer cycles until a successful pregnancy results. In this situation where there is a lack of high quality embryos to cryopreserve, the repeat transfer is associated with significantly reduced implantation and pregnancy rates (Wang et al., 2008).

Risks to the Fetus using Cryopreservation Techniques and ART

Long Term Assessment of Health Risks and Follow-Up Research: The increasing rate of infertility and the intense desire of infertile couples to have children are driving the development of new technologies in ART. Because of these medical and social pressures, the ART of cryopreservation is evolving so rapidly that long-term health effects have not yet been accurately assessed. While there is little that can be done to slow the development of new ARTs, large scale clinical trials are still needed to assess the safety and efficacy of these new procedures for both the mother and child.

One means to gain more insight into the medical effects of such techniques includes follow-up research involving children who have been born utilizing ART or cryopreservation techniques, A few countries have used their population-based health registries to assess the health of children born via IVF that will establish the scientific premises for such medical procedures.

In Sweden, for example, national archives have documented IVF births from all fertilization clinics in the country since 1982. Details such as age of mother at the time of treatment, intracytoplasmic sperm injection (ICSI) technology usage, and other possible confounders in the analysis of delivery outcome are recorded. There has been several health risks reported from these studies. Some immediate risks of IVF, as opposed to natural and spontaneous conception, have been noted, including increased rate of neonatal diagnoses, still birth and infant mortality, and congenital malformations. A few studies have shown an association between IVF born children and cancer risks. However, no concrete cause and effect links have been made to date. At present, the increased health risks and harms of IVF to the unborn fetus remain to be properly investigated and weighed against the medical and psychological benefits of this technology.

Similar research should also be conducted that involves the newer, technological realm of cryogenic methods as there is also a sufficient level of concern extending to the health of a child using cryogenic techniques. To date, little differences in outcome, however, have been seen in the immediate birth effects when comparing different IVF methods including ICSI with cryopreservation. The slight discrepancies may be a result of the composition of groups of women treated.

Potential Risks of IVF

As of 2013, over 5 million babies have been born via IVF. What are the medical risks to the child? Several reports (see Wen, et al., 2012) reviewed and pooled epidemiological data assessing the risk of birth defects after ART and compared the risk difference of birth defects after intracytoplasmic sperm injection (ICSI) and IVF. Their results show a small but significantly increased risk of birth defects in infants conceived by ART. However using ICSI did not increase the risk of birth defects as compared with IVF. It is important to recognize that an increase in birth defects may also result from the underlying infertility (especially female infertility) in the couples seeking treatment. It is often difficult to distinguish whether the infertility problems or the ART procedures or some combination is responsible for the increased risk of birth defects.

There are also reports that IVF (see Vermeiden and Bernardus, 2013) or ICSI is associated with imprinting disorders. Imprinted genes are transcribed from only one specific parental allele, either the maternally derived copy or the paternally derived copy. This monoallelic expression of imprinted genes is associated with epigenetic modifications and DNA methylation and is parent-of-origin specific. Imprinted diseases are quite rare and arise from aberrant methylation of a specific gene causing the disease. For example, imprinting of H19 (maternally expressed) is reciprocal with the imprinting of IGF2 (paternally expressed). Hypermethylation of H19 is associated with the Beckwith-Wiedemann syndrome (BWS) and hypomethylation with the Silver-Russell syndrome (SRS).

Research is ongoing on quantifying the medical risks to women undergoing IVF. Pregnancies resulting from in-vitro fertilization (IVF) have significantly higher rates of requiring induced labor or caesarean section. However, it is to be assumed that these complications and unfortunate developments are not caused by extracorporeal fertilization itself, but rather are due to the frequency of multiples and to the risk factors of the women involved. These women are, on average, older and there are often more problems with cycle irregularities, uterine anomalies and obesity than in the total collective of all pregnancies. The methods of modern reproductive medicine often bring a higher rate of multiple pregnancies. The clinical problem of multiple pregnancies is, above all, the raised rate of premature births and intrauterine growth retardations that contribute to the significantly higher rate of morbidity and mortality for these children. The slightly higher rate of congenital defects after IVF and intracytoplasmic sperm injection (ICSI) are also attributed more to the risk profile of the parents and less to the techniques themselves. The most important and easy-to-avoid complication is the multiple pregnancy, and it should be our goal to lower this rate even further.

Egg Donation for Infertility or for Research

At the University College London in 1958, Dr. Anne McLaren and John D. Biggers carried out the first transfer of an embryo from one mouse to another. Their research has extrapolated into human embryo transfer allowing for the introduction of surrogate mothers as well as egg and sperm donation (Surani and Smith, 2007; Renfree and Short, 2008). The first child conceived from a donor egg occurred in 1984 only seven years after the first baby was born via IVF (Orenstein, 2007).

Much has changed since then in donor and recipient characteristics as well as in the procedure's acceptability within medicine and society. Donor eggs are in high demand as many women are either not able to produce quality oocytes, have a family history of a heritable disease (e.g., Huntington's disease), or are older so their eggs are considered of lower quality. Approximately 12 percent of IVF attempts currently utilize donor eggs. The majority of recipients are in their 40s due to the finding that while eggs have a "shelf-life" and become increasingly problematic with age, the definitive age for uterine reproductive capability is yet to be determined. As of 2006, successful pregnancies have been experienced beyond menopause to over 60 years. The knowledge that their eggs can be preserved or they can receive a donor egg has provided younger women with the potential to safely and successfully delay having children (Orenstein, 2007). The ethics of egg donation and commercialization of eggs is discussed in Chapter 11.

Health Risks of Egg Donations: Similar issues regarding health risks and bioethical concerns emerge from egg and embryo donations obtained from younger women. Many of the medical risks are a result of hormonal hyperstimulation as described above. More research has to be done on the health risks of younger women donating eggs. However, many egg donors are difficult to identify, raising difficulties in following up over years if any developments such as cancer or infertility result from their donations. Anecdotal cases of cancer have led to an effort to establish a national registry of donors to track their future medical history. There are numerous barriers to setting up a registry including cost, preference of donors to remain anonymous, coupled with a lack of motivation by physicians and clinics to establish a registry (Schneider, 2008).

Another potential health danger of egg donation to the child is *inadvertent consanguinity.* This can result when two or more different families have offspring from the same donor and the offspring, and unaware of their genetic backgrounds, two of these offspring marry and attempt to start their families. Awareness of the known and speculated health risks of increasing numbers of donations has prompted publication of health guidelines. The American Society for Reproductive Medicine (ASRM) has recommended a limit of six stimulated cycles as the maximum for oocyte donation based on health risks (Pearson, 2006; Practice Committee of American Society for Reproductive Medicine, 2008).

With anonymous donation, there is no standard procedure on future contact by the donor child, and with no donor registry, the risk of interbreeding of half-siblings remains a possibility.

Pre-implantation Genetic Diagnosis **(PGD)**

As discussed in Chapter 9, a single cell obtained from either a pre-implanted eight cell embryo or from a previously frozen embryo can undergo a procedure called pre-implantation genetic diagnosis (PGD).[5] Generally used by women over 35 or couples that have a history of a genetic disease, PGD significantly increases the probability of having a normal, healthy child by screening out embryos found to have disease genotypes. More than two hundred diseases can be evaluated using this technique including Tay Sachs, cystic fibrosis, trysomy 21, hemophilia, fragile X, and many more.

Regulation of Menses and Birth Control

The historical evolution of menses in women clearly demonstrates the impact of new technologies related to menstruation. Two hundred years ago, most women did not use barrier contraception since from marriage at an early age, through their forties, they were either pregnant or nursing. Presently, an American woman will usually have 400 menses through a lifetime, not an unusual number. In contrast, a study done of Dogon women in Mali, where contraceptives are not used and there is a culture of pre-industrial sedentary agriculture, revealed that the median number of menses per lifetime is around 100 (Strassmann, 1997; Renteria, 2008). Menstrual periods have become much more common in women. This is a result of two life-style patterns, First, women and families have limited the number of children they want to three or fewer, and second, many women choose not to breast feed their babies.

Menstrual periods can have a significant and deleterious impact on many women's quality of life ranging from slight discomfort to major health concerns for those who experience menstrual-related conditions or disorders such as dysmenorrhea and fibroids (Archer, 2006). Although certainly not true of all women's cycles, common symptoms of menses can include varying degrees of bloating, headaches, irritability and mood swings, tender breasts, etc., and can promote morbidity and suffering (Archer, 2006).

---

[5] There is some question whether PGD is better termed as pre-implantation genetic **testing** rather than **diagnosis**. This procedure does not necessary diagnose a genetic disease but rather screens for embryos carrying the genes for such diseases.

While the majority of women do not require medical treatment for symptoms of menstruation, some do seek diagnosis and therapy that result in significant health care costs. In a National Hospital Ambulatory Medical Care survey, 12% of emergency room visits were attributed to gynecological disorders and 65% of women who do have menstrual disorders have contacted a physician for treatment. Other economic losses attributed to natural, monthly cycles of menstruation are time lost from work, decreased productivity, and personal costs associated with purchasing necessary feminine hygiene products (Archer, 2006).

Oral contraceptives: Oral contraceptives work by preventing ovulation, hindering sperm and egg contact by thickening the cervical mucus and reducing the build-up of the uterine lining. Women who take "the pill" do not experience uterine lining thickening which normally occurs in preparation for egg implantation, and have thin, un-implantable linings that are shed between menstruation cycles as a result. 'Withdrawal bleeding,' the term for this uterine shedding, tends to be shorter and lighter than a regular menstrual period and serves no medical function (Seval et al., 2011). Oral contraceptives are available as combined oral contraceptives (COC), containing both estrogen and progestin, or progestin only pills (POP).   Aside from   some potential health risks associated with oral contraception, one recognized behavioral change is that oral contraception can dramatically inhibits a woman's libido resulting is her lack of desire to engage in marital relations (Battaglia et al., 2012).

A national poll revealed that three out of five women preferred not to have monthly periods, and that one out of three would chose never to have them (Seval et al., 2011). Until recently, medical professionals advised their patients on methods to avoid monthly cycles of menstruation by skipping the week of placebo pills and continuing onto a new monthly packet of pills. Dr. Steven Goldstein stated, "Scientists who invented birth control pills back in the '50s thought that women would be more likely to take them if they included a period week." This would help reassure women of their continued fertility and, importantly, that they were not pregnant (Seval et al., 2011).

To respond to women who desire to limit their menstrual periods, new pills on the market are extended-cycle oral contraceptives that can prolong cycles of menstruation from the conventional 28 days to 91 days -- and just recently -- up to a year (Seval et al., 2011). The 91-day extended-cycle oral contraceptives, Seasonale and Seasonique are COCs containing the hormones ethinyl estradiol and levonorgestrel to result in a mere four menstruations per year. In May of 2007, a new contraceptive called Lybrel was FDA approved that delays menses (eliminates periods) up to a year through low dose, continuous hormones and works like other established COCs (Seval et al., 2011).

One concern associated with extended cycle and continuous oral contraceptives relates to the ability of women to monitor their fertility and pregnancy status. With these new forms of birth control, women may unknowingly become pregnant as they no longer are able to rely on menstruation to indicate their fertility or pregnancy status. Consequently, women may continue to take hormones during pregnancy which is tied to a higher incidence of complications such as tubal pregnancy (Atiyeh and Stern, 2007).

Does the acceptance of extended-cycle birth control "minimize the complex interplay of hormones and their many roles in {women's} bodies...[or] gloss over the still unknown long-term effects of menstrual suppression?" (Houppert, 2007). Two, one-year studies have evaluated the continuous method of oral contraceptive, deeming "the extended pill" safe and effective (Anderson et al., 2006). Similarly, the adverse effects in a two-year study of the 91-day cycle of Seasonale were typical of regular, monthly-cycle oral contraceptives. Since the release of continuous-use Lybrel in 2007, and extended-cycle Seasonale in 2003, however, there has not been a passage of time significant enough to allow researchers to evaluate the long-term effects that could occur, including possible disorders such as diseases of the gallbladder, venous thromboembolic disorders, and certain cancers.

Menopause: A Symptomatic Dilemma: Menopause is a natural phase in the onset of aging in women where ovulation and menses cease terminating their reproductive capability. Many women undergoing menopause can experience a wide variety of discomforts including hot flashes and night sweats, vaginal dryness, sleep disturbances, mood disorders and depression, sexual dysfunction, and reduced quality of life. The onset of menopause is preceded by a period of irregular cycles of menses, usually occurring in the early 40s and ending by the mid-50s. Normally, this period lasts on average of 1 to 3 years, although some women report having symptoms up to 10 years. This menopausal transitional period is related to the decrease in ovarian follicles to a critical level, resulting in endocrine changes which are characterized by hormone instability. Raised FSH (follicle-stimulating hormone) levels are shown to indicate late reproductive aging and are associated with a possible increase in estrogen and a decrease, not only in ovarian follicles, but also menstrual cycle length. The precise mechanisms causing these symptoms to present in menopausal women are under intense investigation (Mihm et al., 2011). Further studies of hormonal changes in pre-menopausal and menopausal women aim to describe the relationship between hormonal fluctuations and clinical features, to characterize the fluctuations linearly or mathematically, and to understand the physiology of the transition. Such research would facilitate a better understanding of menopause, creating the opportunity for safe, effective relief and treatment for women (Pearson, 2002; Mishra et al., 2010).

There are myriad products on the market that claim to relieve the distressing symptoms of menopause. Most common are hormone treatments that deliver doses through the skin and vagina via patches, gels, and sprays, as well internally released doses by vaginal rings. The landmark Women's Health Initiative has included studies that have found hormone replacement therapy can be harmful (Reid, 2003). Some of the health effects related to hormone treatment were increased incidence of stroke, breast cancer, heart attack, neurological disease, and the risk of blood clots. In response, doctors have begun recommending low-dose treatment options that shorten the duration and dosage of hormones to the smallest effective dose. Doctors still lack evidence proving the safety of low-dose treatment. Although many medical options are available to women, they face difficult and often conflicting information concerning safe and effective relief of menopausal symptoms.

Many women have also turned to more natural remedies such as bio-identical (natural, not synthetic) hormones including estradiol, progesterone, and multivitamins. In addition, women turn to complementary and alternative medicinal natural herbs such as black cohash in an effort to find relief from menopausal symptoms.

The variability in reproductive aging in women signified by the delayed age of onset of menopause has become a studied topic in the late 20th and 21st centuries. Of interest is the impact of delayed childbearing and ART availability. Since bearing children is no longer the biological destiny of a woman, it has now become an issue that involves careful consideration and planning. In particular, the regard to the desire to have children, when to bear children, and even the desired genetic makeup of the child, all now possible through IVF and PGD technologies. Genetics, environment, seasonal environment, lifestyle, prior oral contraceptive and other hormone use, and fertility have been implicated as contributing factors to the variability in menopausal onset and completion. Studies have documented significant heritability for age of menopause and found later onset in women with higher socioeconomic status who are non-smokers and have healthy diets (Pearson, 2002).

Safety Concerns related to hormone replacement therapy in menopausal women: As mentioned above, both protective effects and increased malignancy risks have been associated with hormonal replacement therapy (HRT) for menopausal women. The outcomes depend on duration of therapy and type of therapy. Up until recently, higher dosage hormone therapy was in vogue to relieve the troubling symptoms. However, in 2007 the Women's Health Initiative (WHI) found an association between long-term hormone replacement therapy and increased breast cancer risk but also found a decreased incidence of colorectal cancer. Therefore, a decline in the incidence of breast cancer has occurred, which is often attributed to the immediate decreased use of hormonal therapy. This is directly a result of the increased number of women now refusing hormonal therapy for menopause (Ravdin et al., 2007) and is seen in many countries in Western Europe

Alternatively, transdermal therapy, compared to oral intake, continuously delivers controlled doses of hormones through the skin into the systemic circulation, avoiding gastrointestinal and hepatic metabolism that is associated with a lower incidence of breast cancer (Corrao et al., 2008). There is also the option of low-dose hormone therapy. But one problem persists: with low-dose hormones, when the prescribed medication regimen concludes, symptoms often resume (Rabin, 2007). Women are caught between a rock and a hard place where the so called 'safe' but still unproven substitute for regular hormone therapy is 'low-dose' hormone treatment, which ultimately results in the same dose exposure when continued over a longer duration anyways.

Therefore, it is important to take medical conditions into consideration when advising patients. Hormone therapy can relieve these symptoms, but may increase the chance of heart attack, stroke, breast cancer, and blood clots.

Hormone replacement therapy is also prescribed for pre-menopausal women who have undergone a hysterectomy accompanied by removal of the ovaries. A significant population has undergone a hysterectomy-almost one third of women in the United States by the age of 60. Typically after surgery, there is a dramatic decrease in circulating endogenous sex hormones, which subjects the woman to hormone withdrawal and related symptoms. Estrogen replacement therapy relieves vasomotor symptoms such as hot flashes. Combined therapy with progesterone can be considered for estrogen-responsive endometrial cancer or endometriosis but also involves a greater risk of breast cancer. Hormone therapy requires careful consideration based on individualized risk/benefit analysis and can be an intense dilemma for many women.

Conclusions

In this chapter we have presented several novel technologies, some still being developed, that are used to stimulate or prevent ovulation, to preserve the oocyte and embryo, and to relieve related function or dysfunction of the female reproductive system. While the benefits of research, development, and experimentation in these technologies are numerous, they are far from being proven to be 100% effective or safe. Risky medications and technologies are still available to the public. The goal of reproductive bioethics is to stimulate dialogue between health professionals and bioethicists across numerous disciplines to address a healthy balance and analysis of the known and unknown benefits and risks of medical and research technology. Ultimately, the goal is to develop products that will improve the welfare of the women who place their trust in the safety of advancing reproductive science.

In this chapter we have described the brief significant advances in the treatment of fertility and other issues in women's reproductive lives. The next chapter will delve in greater detail the profound and contentious ethical, legal, social, economic, and policy issues that are generated by the impressive advances in reproductive technologies.

References

Adhikari, D., et al. "The safe use of a PTEN inhibitor for the activation of dormant mouse primordial follicles and generation of fertilizable eggs.", PLoS One, 7:e39034, 2012.

Anderson, F. D., et al., "Long-term safety of an extended-cycle oral contraceptive (Seasonale): a 2-year multicenter open-label extension trial." Am J Obstet Gynecol, **195**(1):92-6, 2006.

Archer, D. F., "Menstrual-cycle-related symptoms: a review of the rationale for continuous use of oral contraceptives." Contraception, **74**(5):359-66, 2006.

Austin, C. R., "Observations on the penetration of the sperm in the mammalian egg." Aust J Sci Res, B **4**(4):581-96, 1951.

Austin, C. R., "The capacitation of the mammalian sperm." Nature, **170**(4321):326, 1952.

Atiyeh, K, and Stern, B., "Full Stop: The End-of-Line for Periods?" Columbia University Journal of Bioethics, 6:17-20, 2007.

Battaglia, C., et al., "Sexual behavior and oral contraception: A pilot study." The Journal of Sexual Medicine, 2012. [http://onlinelibrary.wiley.com/doi/10.1111/j.1743-6109.2011.02597.x/full]

Bothwell, L., "Ethical Issues at Play in Oocyte Donation." Columbia University Journal of Bioethics, 6:31-33, 2007.

Chang, M. C., "Fertilizing capacity of spermatozoa deposited into the fallopian tubes." Nature, **168**(4277):697-8,1951.

Chen, C, "Pregnancy after human oocyte cryopreservation. ", Lancet, 1:884-886, 1986.

Corrao, G., et al., "Menopause hormone replacement therapy and cancer risk: an Italian record linkage investigation." Ann Oncol, **19**(1):150-5, 2008.

DiLuigi, A.J., et al., "Gonadotropin-releasing hormone agonist to induce final oocyte maturation prevents the development of ovarian hyperstimulation syndrome in high-risk patients and leads to improved clinical outcomes compared with coasting." Fertil Steril, 94:1111–1114, 2010.

Dittrich, R., et al., "Live birth after ovarian tissue autotransplantation following overnight transportation before cryopreservation." Fertility and Sterility, 97: 387–390, 2012.

Edgar, D.H. and Gook, D.A. "A critical appraisal of cryopreservation (slow cooling versus vitrification) of human oocytes and embryos." Human Reproduction Update, 18:536-554, 2012.

Gadducci, A., et al., "Fertility drug use and risk of ovarian tumors: a debated clinical challenge. " Gynecological Endocrinology, ; 29(1):30–35, 2013.

Hinckley, M. D., et al., "Improved Success With Frozen Embryo Transfer in Gestational Carriers Compared With Fresh Transfer." Fertility and Sterility, **89**(4, Supplement 1):S22-S22, 2008.

Houppert, K. (July 17, 2007). Final Period. The New York Times.

Huang, J. Y., et al., "Retrieval of immature oocytes followed by in vitro maturation and vitrification: a case report on a new strategy of fertility preservation in women with borderline ovarian malignancy." Gynecol Oncol, **105**(2):542-4, 2007.

Imbar, T., et al., "Reproductive outcome of fresh or frozen–thawed embryo transfer is similar in high-risk patients for ovarian hyperstimulation syndrome using GnRH agonist for final oocyte maturation and intensive luteal support.", Human Reproduction, 27:753-759, 2012.

Klein, J.U. & Sauer, M.V. "Ethics in egg donation: past, present, and future." Semin Reprod Med, 28:322-328, 2010.

Kuleshova, L. L. and Lopata A., "Vitrification can be more favorable than slow cooling." Fertil Steril, **78**(3):449-54, 2002.

Leslie, M., "Melting opposition to frozen eggs." Science, **316**(5823):388-9, 2007.

Lyerly, A. D. and Faden, R. R., "Embryonic stem cells. Willingness to donate frozen embryos for stem cell research." Science, **317**(5834):46-7, 2007.

Practice Committee of American Society for Reproductive Medicine, "Repetitive oocyte donation." Fertil Steril, **90**:S194-5, 2008.

Mertes, H., et al., "Implications of oocyte cryostorage for the practice of oocyte donation." Human Reproduction, 27:2886-2893, 2012.

Mihm, M., et al., "The normal menstrual cycle in women. ", Animal Reproduction Science, 124:229-236, 2011.

Mishra, G. D., et al., "A life course approach to reproductive health: theory and methods." Maturitas, **65**(2):92-7, 2010.

Orenstein, P., "Your Gamete, Myself." The New York Times **Volume**, DOI, (July 15, 2007).

Polge, C, et al., "Revival of spermatozoa after vitrification and dehydration at low temperatures. " Nature, 164:666, 1949.

Pearson, E. V. P., "The Variability of Female Reproductive Ageing." Human Reproduction Update, **8**(2):141-154, 2002.

Pearson, H., "Health effects of egg donation may take decades to emerge." Nature, **442**(7103):607-8, 2006.

Rabin, R., "For a Low-Dose Hormone, Take Your Pick." NYTimes.com **Volume**, DOI:, 2006.

Ravdin, P. M., et al., "The decrease in breast-cancer incidence in 2003 in the United States." N Engl J Med, **356**(16):1670-4, 2007.

Reid, R. L., "Hormone therapy: the Women's Health Initiative has caused confusion and concern." Fertil Steril, **80**(3):491-3, 2003.

Renfree, M. and Short, R., "In memoriam Anne McLaren." Int J Dev Biol, **52**(1):1-2, 2008.

Renteria, S. C., "To bleed or not--a new dogma or a real choice in contraception?." Rev Med Suisse, **4**(176):2246-50, 2252, 2008.

Scaravelli, G., et al., "Analysis of oocyte cryopreservation in assisted reproduction: the Italian National Register data from 2005 to 2007. Reprod Biomed Online, 4:496-500, 2010.

Schneider, J., "Fatal colon cancer in a young egg donor: a physician mother's call for follow-up and research on the long-term risks of ovarian stimulation." Fertil Steril, **90**(5):2016 e1-5, 2008.

Seval, D.L., et al., "Attitudes and prescribing patterns of extended-cycle oral contraceptives. " Contraception, 84:71-75, 2011.

Strassmann, B., "The Biology of Menstruation in Homo Sapiens: Total Lifetime Menses, Fecundity, and Nonsynchrony in a Natural-Fertility Population." Current Anthropology, **38**(1):123-129, 1997.

Sunkara, S.K., "Risk of early menopause following IVF treatment." In Assisted Reproduction Techniques: Challenges and Management Options, pg 7-8, 2012.

Surani, A. and Smith J., "Obituary: Anne McLaren (1927-2007)." Nature, **448**(7155): 764-5, 2007.

Vermeiden, J.P., Bernardus, R.E. "Are imprinting disorders more prevalent after human in vitro fertilization or intracytoplasmic sperm injection? " Fertil Steril, 99(3):642-51, 2013.

Wang, J. G., et al., "Cryopreservation of supernumerary high quality embryos predicts favorable outcomes for patients undergoing repeated cycles of in vitro fertilization." Fertil Steril, **89**(2):368-74, 2008.

Wen, J., et al., "Birth defects in children conceived by in vitro fertilization and intracytoplasmic sperm injection: a meta-analysis." Fertil Steril 97(6):1331-7, 2012.

Whitworth, A., "New options expand possibilities for fertility preservation in cancer patients." J Natl Cancer Inst, **98**(19):1358-60, 2006.

Figure 1. **Newborn screening** (obtained from NIH.gov).

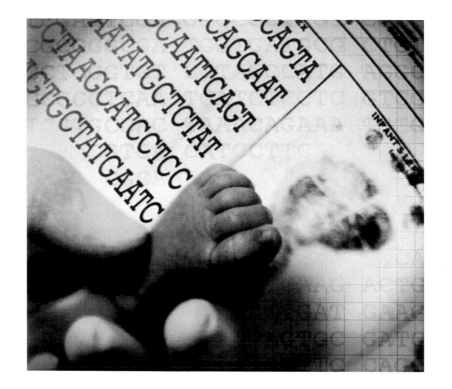

Chapter Twelve

Women's Reproductive Technology:

Ethical and Social Standpoints

Introduction

"World's Oldest New Mom Dying After IVF Pregnancy at Age 72"

-Fox News 06/16/2010

Assisted reproductive technologies have been designed and developed in order to introduce safe and effective methods for enhancing fertility. However, as discussed in the previous chapter, these technologies may potentially pose serious medical and life-style challenges for the mother, child, egg donor, the In Vitro Fertilization (IVF) recipient, and the immediate and extended family of the couples engaged in reproductive medicine. The article headlined above (Cappon, 2010) describes a successful IVF procedure conducted on a post-menopausal woman who gave birth at age 72. While making headlines, this procedure raises the question of whether applying fertility technology to a post-menopausal woman is ethical. Follow-up research on similar births by women over the age of 50, aims to evaluate the developmental capacity of the newborn child and the physiological and psychological health of the aging mother in raising the child (Ameratunga et al., 2009).

In addition to the physiological and psychological consequences of giving birth later in life, there are added bioethical challenges related to the burgeoning assisted reproductive technologies (Marten, 2006; Cutas, 2007).   Recently, bioethicists have become concerned with the over-regulation and over-medication of women's bodies when attempting to regulate their menses.

Actions that appear to be as simple as freezing one's own gametes, spawn ethical debate regarding the potential disintegration of the family unit, the pressure on women in balancing work and family, the reproductive rights of women, and safety issues related to this technology. These bioethical dilemmas are in addition to long- standing debates including when human life begins and at what point the destruction of a pre-implanted or implanted embryo constitutes a moral violation of human life (see Chapter 7).

This chapter discusses unique ethical dilemmas focused on women's issues and related to three areas of reproduction: gathering and storing eggs, egg and embryo donation, and regulation of menses. All of these situations may require re-examination of the most basic terms such as 'motherhood', to incorporate the possibility of a genetic (biological) mother, birth mother (gestational or surrogate), as well as a social (adoptive) mother.

Assisted Reproductive Technologies (ART) and Cryopreservation

Assisted reproductive technologies (ART) assists couples and individuals, suffering from infertility, in providing a miraculous solution to their problems. These biotechnologies also evoke practical and ethical dilemmas that need to be addressed, such as the ethical and legal concerns regarding the structure of family and the right to privacy. The degree of government regulation in these technologies is also critical. Too much regulation in ART may deny many a chance at producing offspring. Too little regulation may make these technologies prone to misuse, lead to possible social and economic coercion, legal actions, and a plethora of unforeseen medical risks.

Religious perspectives on ART and Cryopreservation: Cryopreservation allows women to freeze their unfertilized eggs and subsequently thaw them for future use in IVF. Producing successful deliveries by freezing embryos for future use has a success rate between 10-28% (Hirth et al., 2010). From an ethical perspective, there are several issues that need to be addressed. Some religions, such as Catholicism and Buddhism, maintain that an embryo, even in a frozen state, cannot be destroyed or discarded because it is considered a human being (see Chapter 7) (Bredkjaer and Grudzinskas, 2001; Leslie, 2007). Many Islamic (Serour, 2008) and Judaic scholars (Loike et al. 2009; Loike and Tendler, 2010) maintain that a pre-implanted embryo that is less than 120 days old (in Islam), or 40 days old (in Judaism), has not reached religious personhood and can be used in IVF to obtain stem cells for therapeutic purposes, or for biomedical research as the embryo. The critical ethical dilemma concerns the fate of these embryos as it is estimated that there are over 400,000 of these frozen embryos stored in IVF clinics in the USA (Mundy, 2010). Undeniably, the religious debate concerning the process of ART remains controversial.

Legal disputes: A preserved embryo has co-owners who together can cause legal disputes in determining its fate. This situation has led many couples and families to seek ownership rights through the court system. The successful use of frozen oocytes for reproduction ('success' refers to live births resulting from reproductive technologies), rather than embryos, may reduce the future number of embryos to be frozen while also reducing related legal disputes (Tucker et al., 2004; Walker, 2008; Borini and Coticchio, 2009), as oocytes are then defined as exclusively owned by the woman donor.   However, the prospect of such legal dispute may undermine the perceived social acceptance of ART and cryogenic techniques as part of family life.

Social Concerns on Age of Motherhood

We began this chapter with the ethics of engaging in ART in order to facilitate older women who desire to be pregnant and experience motherhood. With the advancement of ARTs, older populations of women (over 35) eager to

---

Case Study #1:

Amy, at twenty-five, marries her high-school sweetheart, Ben. They are both engineering students graduating with honors, sealing jobs with firms straight out of school. They soon decide to start a family. Amy, however, was born with defective fallopian tubes. Therefore, the couple decides to use IVF. After the second cycle of the treatment, Ben dies tragically in a car accident. Devastated, Amy cannot emotionally handle the loss of her husband and discontinues the IVF treatment with the stored frozen embryos.

Three years later, Amy has fallen in love with a colleague, Jeffrey, and they marry. He wants to start a family with her right away but she has some reservations. She is still affected by the death of Ben and considers the possibility of finally having his baby using the frozen embryos saved from their earlier attempts at IVF. Amy's first complication is deciding which man's baby she wants to have.   She will again have to try IVF, this time with Jeffrey's sperm.   While it would be easier on her to use the embryos she created with Ben, she has just learned that Ben's father was recently diagnosed with Huntington's disease and the diseased allele has a 50% chance of being passed on to Ben and if so, then there is a 50% chance of the allele being passed on to the frozen embryo. Lastly, Amy wants to go to law school and become a partner in a law firm, and is therefore considering the possibility of waiting to have children using cryopreserved oocytes.

What are Amy's choices when taking into consideration the current status of cryopreservation and pre-implantation genetic diagnosis?

What ethical debates arise from her situation?
- Extending her biological clock
- Embryo viability
- Frozen egg technology
- Genetic screening of embryos
- Baby's quality of life
- Genetic privacy

Who are the individuals affected in her decision-making and how?

---

exercise their extended reproductive rights have emerged. Older women have participated in clinical fertility research that continues to produce pregnancies and live births (Kort et al., 2012).

The scientific community accepts that the quality of a woman's natural reproductive declines with age, which correlates to decreased ovarian reserve (reduction in oocyte numbers), oocyte quality, and deteriorated endocrine function. Yet, babies are being born to women who are post-menopausal, well beyond the age of 50. It appears that while the ovaries may become non-productive at menopause, the woman's uterus, given hormonal support, remains functionally capable of gestation beyond menopause, even into the fifth and sixth decades of life. It has not yet been unequivocally determined whether age affects endometrial receptivity and implantation. In 1999, 5,844 cycles of IVF using fresh, donated oocytes were performed on women above the age of 40. The live birth rate was 42.6% (Either 40+ or all- I need help verifying from article) compared to 9.7% for women above the age of 40 using conventional IVF treatment and their own eggs.

Although pregnancy may be successful in older women, it is associated with a higher incidence of complications that include pregnancy-induced hypertension, premature labor, membrane rupture, intrauterine growth restriction, and gestational diabetes (Tarlatzis and Zepiridis, 2003).

Arguments have been voiced suggesting such older women are inappropriate mothers, emphasizing that such technology will generate more orphaned children, controversial statements that evoke elder and gender bias. There are no restrictions against older men fathering children with younger wives, nor are there any restrictions for older women who desire to have children without medical intervention. Nonetheless, there is concern that older women may not be capable of coping emotionally, financially, or physically with stresses of raising a child from birth through teenage hood. This view is based on a cultural conception that defines the limits of the institution of 'motherhood.' Social norms appeared to have defined childbearing to within a certain age range, bounded at the upper limit by the onset of menopause which historically has been understood as the ultimate termination of fertility (Parks, 1999).

A contrary argument rebuts the idea of the incapability of older women by drawing similarities to other common familial relationships to refute negative views of elderly mothers. It is quite acceptable and necessary in many situations or cultures, for grandmothers to care for and raise their grandchildren. As society becomes more attentive towards alternative family structure, custodial grandparents is becoming more accepted and common. According to the US Census Bureau, in 2000, 6.5 million or 9 percent of children younger than 18 years old are living in a home that includes at least one grandparent (Lugaila, 2004). In this situation, the ages are similar to elderly mothers conceiving children. Norms are constantly being shaped and reformed. Now that our concept of 'fertility' has been challenged scientifically, our views on acceptable age of 'motherhood' may change with it (Parks, 2009).

Nonetheless, ethical discussions of post-menstrual motherhood must also include the doctor or health professional in the equation. And of this, there are two bioethical concerns. One concern relates to the ability for the older woman to be counted as a rational agent. It involves the dilemma of how health care professional should contribute by informing the patients of the health risks, as pregnancy in older women is often associated with a higher incidence of complications such as pregnancy-induced hypertension, premature labor or membrane rupture, intrauterine growth restriction, and gestational diabetes. Physicians also face a second ethical challenge regarding the judgment of allowing or performing these medical procedures to impregnate an older woman who is willing to take those medical risks for the sake of having a child.

Nadya Suleman was an unemployed single mother who had six other young children and on public assistance programs. Her doctor, Dr. Michael Kamrava, implanted six embryos via IVF and she gave birth to six children in January of 2009. There has been considerable bioethical debate whether the physician acted ethically in this case, raising many ethical issues when deciding how, or, if at all, IVF should be regulated.

Ethical Discussions Related to ART

Cryopreservation of oocytes and other ARTs is constantly being improved, raising the issue of how to appropriately educate those individuals who want to engage in these technologies. While informed consent is required, how will health care professional appropriately educate a vulnerable population of women desperately seeking to have children? How will health care professionals ensure that the patient really understands the risks and benefits?

All the information presented in the informed consent should be consistent with the specific nuances outlined in the classical ethical principles (described in Chapter 2-3) as they apply to ART.

- *Autonomy:* While individuals should have the right to make choices that could preserve their fertility when threatened by disease or in consideration of life-plans, risks and benefits need to be carefully weighed. Infertile couples must be aware that there is considerable variability in successful pregnancy rates associated with different clinics and centers. Not all infertility centers report an accurate success rates. They may inflate their success rates by screening couples and rejecting those whom they believe will not be successful in generating a child. Additionally, centers report different measures of success (e.g., successful pregnancy v. successful birth), making it difficult to compare safety and efficacy of the infertility centers. It is difficult to implement a universal standard to assess efficacy and safety of infertility centers in the USA. Perhaps, if it would be best to have the American Association for Reproductive Medicine, recognized nationally and internationally as the leading organization for multidisciplinary information, education, advocacy and standards in the field of reproductive medicine, should institute such standards.

- *Beneficence and maleficence:* The American Society for Reproductive Medicine (ASRM) reviews new technologies and publishes guidelines periodically that define minimum standards for ART programs. Because reproductive tissue storage is still in experimental stages, caution should be taken in the transition from research to treatment. Codes for minimum standards for practice and safety considerations should be set and implemented with the understanding that there is insufficient long term health assessment of ART methods.

Cryopreservation, for example, was initially legitimized for storing gametes or embryos of individuals at risk of losing their ability to reproduce due to disease. In 2009, there was over 700,000 new cases of cancer in women in the USA, and 8% of the cases occurred in women under 40, where many of them could potentially benefit from oocyte cryopreservation.[1] Given the nature of their illnesses, this cohort already assumes elevated chances of dying. This raises the question as to who is responsible for the fate of their cryostored reproductive material in the event that a woman, her partner, or both should perish. There is a highly apparent need for counseling services pertaining to cryopreserved material 'ownership' and the completion of an Advance Directive.

---

[1]http://www.cancer.org/acs/groups/content/@nho/documents/document/500809webpdf.pdf.

- *Justice - Cost Effectiveness and Insurance:* The high costs of these technologies raise several bioethical concerns related to providing equal access to new procedures. Two groups of individuals with vested interests in cryopreservation include patients diagnosed with cancer who may have a critical window available for preserving fertility, and women who are making lifestyle decisions to delay fertility due to social and economic constraints during their prime reproductive years. The basic difference between these two groups is that the former group has a medical necessity in preserving fertility, while the latter is influenced by convenience. Determination of medical necessity is the key in formulating cost-effectiveness and insurance coverage. In the United States ,where there is no universal healthcare and IVF resources are not scarce so long as an individual can pay out-of-pocket for an elective procedure, this determination is especially relevant (Parks, 1999).

There is a serious need to consider the economics of infertility treatment which currently involves costs that are often directly passed onto patients. This partially results into inequalities in access. The average cost of a successful delivery using ART ranges from $38,000-$85,000 (Henne and Bundorf, 2008) and depends on the number of cycles required to achieve a successful live birth. As of 2007, there is no national legislation addressing infertility (Van Voorhis and Syrop, 2000), and only fifteen states (Arkansas, California, Connecticut, Hawaii, Illinois, Louisiana, Maryland, Massachusetts, Montana, New Jersey, New York, Ohio, Rhode Island, Texas, and West Virginia) have mandated that insurance companies provide either limited or comprehensive coverage. Increased access and reduced financial burden to ART users in these states has increased utilization. One important consideration involves how many children produced via ART should be covered by health insurance?

Reproductive technologies are constantly improving and emerging and may dramatically reduce the costs of ART. Thus, individual decisions regarding personal reproductive choices have become increasingly complex. For every individual or couple, medical options must be assessed based on an overabundance of choices. In order to decide upon the best procedure for each individual couple, interdisciplinary counseling is crucial. Specialties should include pediatricians, psychologists, gynecologists, reproductive specialists, geneticists, etc.

In response to the high costs of IVF in the U.S., an increasing number of couples are choosing to travel abroad to countries such as India or Thailand where the cost is only $5,000-$20,000 (including airfare and accommodations). Private hospitals in Thailand that perform ART use highly qualified US-trained physicians and claim success rates equal to those reported by the best clinics in the US.

Egg and Embryo Donation- Defining Parenthood

Debates focusing on egg donation involve complex medical and bioethical issues such as establishing potential risks of developing cancer, infertility, donation motivations and payment, tissue commodification, and the importance of research in reproductive medicine. One issue often overlooked includes the simple challenges of concepts in societal establishments such as 'motherhood.' In this era of advanced reproduction, any offspring can have multiple mothers including genetic, gestational, donor, surrogate, social, adopted, and acting mothers. From a genetics perspective, DNA can be transmitted to the child from either nuclear DNA or mitochondrial DNA. Thus, a child can have nuclear DNA from a "father," "mother," or from mitochondria donated by another female individual. The use of mitochondrial DNA has been important in helping treat women who have genetic mutations in their mitochondrial DNA (see Chapter 4).

Moreover, new technological developments in stem cell science open the door to having two women donate their DNA to a child and even having two men donate their DNA. It is theoretically possible, then for a child to be born from a man and woman, two women, or two men. How will these technologies influence the social understanding of parenthood. To further complicate matters, non-human primates were created from six genetic parents. Roku and Hex are the world's first chimeric monkeys – created with genetic material from six 'parents' (Tachibana et al., 2012).[2]

In the wake of the fast moving reproductive advances, the term 'mother' has evolved and broadened to include women who are past reproductive prime, post-menopausal, oocyte donors, and surrogates. On one hand, assisted reproductive technologies can provide completely infertile women with the opportunity to birth their own child. On the other, those with the financial means to do so can completely evade pregnancy and delivery by paying a surrogate mother, ultimately having a genetically related child by indirectly exploiting economically vulnerable women.

---

[2] http://www.dailymail.co.uk/sciencetech/article-2082834/Miracle-chimeric-monkeys-cells-animals-spark-protests.html#ixzz2EDDYRrAe

To ensure the safety of a procedure while also promoting fairness, bioethicists consider and identify groups of vulnerable individuals. The primary aims of the regulation in reproductive and research donation should be to balance known and unknown harms, the rights of women and reproductive societal norms, and to minimize risks to individuals and groups when assuming the benefits of advancing technologies.

Ethics related to oocyte and embryo donation

The consent process for donating fresh oocytes to infertile couples is rigorous with respect to the critical medical information that is described. However, other issues should be included in the informed consent document, such as: 1) whether a family member or stranger should serve as either the gamete donor or gestational, 2) should the child be informed of how he or she was conceived and gestated, and 3) whether (and at what time) the donor would be willing to have the child contact or have a relationship with the donor. At this point, it is important that the procedures differentiate between autonomous, able agents, in comparison to those who may be operating under implicit and undisclosed pressures.

Since ART is not strictly regulated by government, there is a critical bioethical challenge related to the question of whether the infertility health care professional has the responsibility to ensure proper ethical compliance. Does the health care professional have the obligation or right to refuse treatment in a situation where there are questions as to whether the donor was coerced?

Privacy and Family in Egg Donation: Egg Donation process is a process which leads to the surfacing of complicated issues about the notion of family. Supplementary consent and the need for privacy are issues that arise when donors donate eggs to infertility treatment centers. This is a result of the added complexities stemming from a possible breach of confidentiality resulting in identity disclosure of the child or recipient to the other (Svanberg et al., 2003). Most countries support anonymous donation; in Sweden, however, when the offspring reach adult age, they have the legal right to obtain information about their donor's identity. Informed consent in Sweden would explicitly address the possibility of contact and identification by the child (Svanberg et al., 2003).

Anonymous donors raise more ethical questions outside of the issue of the right to information of the child. As of now, research done on the health risks of younger women donating eggs is scarce, given that many egg donors are anonymous. Consequently, there is little follow-up over the years to determine if any developments such as cancer or infertility result from their donations. Some anecdotal cases of donors developing cancer have led to an effort to establish a national registry to track their future medical history. There are numerous barriers to setting up a registry including cost, preference of donors to remain anonymous, and lack of motivation by physicians and clinics to establish a registry. This lack of framework raises ethical questions on the decision to adopt such medical procedures when and if proper future support and research architecture may be lacking. Given the same lack of framework, it is also very difficult decrease the risk of the kind of interbreeding between siblings.

Like organ donation, fresh oocyte donation to family members or friends is altruistically motivated, and may quell more qualms about privacy and family concerns. However, egg donation between relatives involves an additional level of complexity. The decision for couples to employ family members as fresh oocyte donors heightens the likelihood of the child identifying his or her genetic parents. Couples who foresee complications arising regarding family roles or relationships from this type of involvement with individuals outside the family might choose intra-family donation instead (Yee et al., 2007).

In a study of known donors, intra-family donors were self-initiated whereas friend-donors were mostly approached by recipients. Close-relation oocyte donation is based on several decision making factors: awareness of recipient's infertility and failed infertility treatment (the most influential reason), partner involvement, and information session availability. Recipients reportedly prefer knowing the donor because with anonymous donors, they feared passing on unknown and undesirable genetic traits to the child. (Yee et al., 2007).

Use of Frozen Eggs: After successful fertility treatments, patients often leave behind surplus frozen embryos or oocytes. In most cases, a representative of the fertility clinic contacts former patients about donation of this unused tissue. When the fertility doctor is primarily involved in the contact, there is concern that the doctor could influence decisions concerning donation due to the gratitude patients usually feel after successful treatment (Heng, 2006). In profit-driven private clinics in particular, doctors are likely to prefer donation for infertility treatment rather than for research. This way surplus tissue can be reused for infertility treatment in future patients, bypassing the hassle of recruiting and reimbursing more donors. Therefore, it has been suggested that third party liaisons or agencies contact couples regarding the fate of their spare embryos. The prohibition of medical professionals and health care institutions from directly contacting former patients may promote freer choice and informed decision making by former infertility patients. In order to avoid unnecessary risks to women donating fresh oocytes and the associated medical costs of the hormone treatment, a new oocyte-sharing strategy is available to mitigate the waste of such surplus frozen oocytes generated from ARTs. For example, successful IVF and intra cytoplasmic sperm injection (ICSI) usually generate oocytes in excess of clinical need that can then be frozen. These surplus oocytes can be donated or 'shared' with infertile women to achieve fertility and pregnancy rates comparable to fresh oocyte donation (Li et al., 2005). The fate of unused or excess frozen embryos generated through ARTs remains in a political grey area. Should these frozen embryos be restricted only to produce children or can they be donated for stem cell research? Bioethicists have proposed strategies such as 'egg sharing,' standardizing mandatory written directives for excess oocytes from ART, and other options to donate the excess embryos for research purposes.

Many factors influence couples' decisions to donate reproductive material, a choice often based on how a couple defines the status of an embryo which may be either as a potential child or as a basis for future scientific development. In addition, another influential factor may be whether donation should be treated as adoption or medical tissue donation by the couple (de Lacey, 2007). Between 48-54% of couples prefer to donate embryos for research rather than donate to an infertile couple (Nachtigall et al., 2005). Those preferring not to donate to another couple reportedly were disturbed psychologically by the possibility of creating legitimate and biological offspring who would be unknown to them. The 18% who preferred to donate their embryos to other couples based their decision on their belief that embryos are "living entities" (Nachtigall et al., 2005).

Religion and culture also play an important role in couples' attitude towards the spare embryos and whether the child produced has a right to know his or her genetic parents. Hindus practice sperm donation with a restriction that the sperm donor has to be a close relative of the husband.

In a study done, it was found that those who considered themselves religious were more concerned about the fate of frozen or unused **embryo**s, the future of those embryos, and the type of future research they would consent to using these embryos (Mohler-Kuo et al., 2009).

Donating eggs for research: When reproductive tissue donors are recruited for the purposes of research, they are technically referred to as "research donors" and are distinct from patients and research subjects. This distinction must be made because after these oocytes are obtained, U.S. regulations no longer recognize the donor as a research subject. As a result, donors usually end up exempt from critical follow-up treatment, psychological counseling, or placement in a long term registry where future health conditions can be tracked. The establishment of the term "research donor" is necessary for regulatory agencies to recognize reproductive tissue donors and establish much needed structured policies and guidelines regarding donation that are currently lacking (Magnus and Cho, 2005).

Research donation of fresh oocytes and embryos for both altruistic and familial reasons should require rigorous screening. Individuals who donate for the purpose of research advancement often cite altruistic reasons. However, sometimes clinics and researchers can uncover economic instability as an actual reason for donation while screening these individuals. Other times they discover an individual who has a family member with rare or incurable disease that scientific research using stem cells or embryos has the potential to cure. These individuals may have been coerced into this risky procedure by this family situation. In this case, researchers must effectively dispel unrealistic expectations surrounding therapeutic use (Levens and DeCherney, 2008). As many oocyte donors have been recruited from families of diseased or disabled patients, they must be informed that effective therapy may be decades away and that direct downstream benefit from stem cell research is highly unlikely. Those accepting donation for research should clearly state the nature of the experiments that will be employed when known and whether or not there are commercial outcomes expected from these experiments in which the tissue donor will not share (Greely, 2006).

The possibility of institutional bias and pressure projected onto prospective donors is an additional consideration. The ethical question is whether medical professionals and healthcare institutions are allowed to exercise undue influence on the informed decision of their former patients regarding donation of surplus frozen embryos for stem cell research or fertility treatment.

Legal Issues related to egg and embryo donations: Tissue ownership of embryos and cell line property are causes of profound legal, ethical, and political challenges. Furthermore, inconsistent international legislation regarding reproductive tissues can result in unique disputes. Embryos are the source of many legal disputes due to their shared possession of two individual's genetic material. Only a few states in the U.S. have explicit legislation concerning the ownership of embryos. As IVF and other reproductive technologies have become established treatments in medicine, many ethicists and researchers are calling for the establishment of a basic legal consent form and advance directive regarding the issue of ownership.

California, for example, enacted a statute effective in 2004 that engages couples in discussion regarding supernumerary embryos following fertility treatment. Detailed advance directives include:

- time limits on embryo storage following the death of a participant, both participants, divorce, or the decision to abandon the embryos.
- subsequent donation or transferring the ownership of unused embryos for research, to a living partner, or to another couple.

Informed and written consent is required by the California statute and is a proposed model for federal legislation (Langley and Blackston, 2006).

Ethics of donor financial compensation: Five models of compensation are used when financial incentives are offered to obtain fresh oocytes either for research or fertility: (1) free market, (2) pure gift, (3) fixed compensation, (4) minimum wage, and (5) reimbursement for expenses. As there is no worldwide consensus regarding the appropriate amount of compensation, free market principles prevail with a high rate of recruitment in response to high demand (Knoppers et al., 2007). An important consideration when evaluating financial concerns is whether there is a difference between donating oocytes for stem cell research or in order to generate a child.

Free or pure gift, on the other hand, is quite rare with respect to egg donation. Researchers are cautioned about performing this type of harvest because these women would be undergoing procedures that involve significant risks with no medical benefit. Fixed compensation is set irrespective of the donor's costs, time, or inconvenience. Minimum wage documents the number of hours involved in donating, and the women are compensated accordingly. While most anonymous donors are motivated by financial incentives, some unpaid donors find donation intrinsically rewarding, believing that it reinforces their feminine solidarity. The typical profile of an anonymous altruistic donor is a married mother in her late twenties. Discrepancies in financial compensation across countries can lead to "tissue medical tourism" where impoverished and vulnerable women are recruited to donate their oocytes or even to serve a surrogate mothers (Check 2006).

Indeed, compensation for egg donation is thought by some to promote the coercion and exploitation of economically vulnerable women into selling their eggs. Compensation can also promote commoditization of children or the commercialization of reproductive tissues, creating a market that might value this tissue over the well-being of women. In doing so, it may ultimately expose women to unidentified medical risks.

Lenient and inconsistent regulation and licensing of donor agencies can lead to excessive payments for eggs from so called "desirable" donors. Agencies can easily manipulate the truth regarding the genetic makeup of the donor when couples are willing to pay extravagant sums of money for eggs advertised to come from tall, blond, blue-eyed, Ivy League students, for example, while in actuality there is no method of guaranteeing intelligence or other phenotypes (Orenstein July 15, 2007).

California law bans the purchasing or selling of "donated cells" or reproductive tissue, and institutions are restricted to reimbursement only for specific expenses that fall within statutory exceptions. Regulations such as these are not standard in all states (Greely, 2006).

The ethics committee of the American Society for Reproductive Medicine (ASRM) issued a position paper in 2006 on compensation for reproductive tissues. It was decided that $5,000 dollars is an appropriate, reasonable and non-coercive sum for reimbursement for donation of oocytes. Sums over $10,000 were considered "not appropriate" [http://www.asrm.org/]. In a May 2007 survey of US egg donors, the national average for payment was about $4,200. On the high end of the spectrum are Jewish, Asian, and Ivy League donors who gain upwards of $15,000 (Covington and Gibbons, 2007; Orenstein, July 15, 2007). The development of a private online auction for eight model's eggs at one point created moral outrage. Beginning bids started at $15,000 and went as high as $150,000 depending on the model (Levine, 2010).

The United States has the highest pool of reproductive tissue donors due to its lucrative compensation practices. Despite this, the practice of donation is treated quite differently across nations. The 2004 Assisted Human Reproduction Act (AHR Act), passed in Canada regulates ARTs to protect and promote human health and safety in light of social, ethical, medical, and legal dilemmas. This legislation has prohibited monetary payments for gamete donation and only allows reasonable reimbursement for expenditures (Yee et al., 2007). Japan prohibits donation altogether due to the complications associated with both known and unknown risks. China does not address the issue, while most European countries that accept egg donation only allow reimbursement for direct expenses such as travel and time.

There are those who believe that it remains unclear whether financial compensation will provide enough incentive to meet the needs of infertile women. Despite this, there is a general consensus that it would be improper to offer enormous sums of money to egg donors that could sway their judgment." (Steinbrook, 2006).

Renting a Womb: The Gestational Surrogate

"Earlier this year in Gujarat, India, I came across a most unusual kind of outsourcing: womb-rental... An embryo that has been created in vitro by the American parents is implanted in the Indian woman's uterus and she goes through the pregnancy and delivers the baby -- and then hands it over to the Americans."

- Nicholas D. Kristof; The New York Times 2007

One cannot conclude a section on egg and embryo donation without reflecting on an increasingly common use of assisted reproductive technology – gestational surrogacy.   While surrogacy has ancient traditions (consider the biblical story of Sarah and Abraham and the servant Hagar who served as surrogate), the concept still raises eyebrows. Increased use of this birth method is due to improved technology: surrogacy is likely to result in a live birth with some fertility clinics claiming a 70-90 percent success rate (Lorraine 2008).

Additionally, with decreasing social stigma, more women are welcoming the idea of being a surrogate for altruistic and financial reasons. Surrogacy allows parenthood for gay couples as well as infertile couples. Interestingly, the US has become a popular site of "reproductive tourism" as many European countries ban surrogacy whereas an increasing number of states in the US are passing laws to legalize and regulate surrogate pregnancies. These laws ensure that the gestational carrier will give up rights to the child(ren) she bears, eliminating the heart-wrenching legal battles of the past when the surrogate refused to hand over the baby to the intended parents. While egg donors are almost always under 30, surrogates can be as old as 40 years of age. Compensation for the gestational carrier is not always known but typical payment agreements range from $20,000 to $25,000 in the US. Many are now turning to India, where the cost is outsourced at a tenth of the price (Lorraine, 2008).

Additionally, ethical and legal challenges include the use of surrogate mothers from poor third world nations who are vulnerable to economic pressures, and therefore, prone to many kinds of exploitation. Indeed, many ethicists have raised concerns about the possible exploitation and coercion of commercial egg donors and surrogates from a feminist and women's rights perspective (Widdows, 2009).

Regulation of Menses

Women's decisions to reduce the number of menstrual periods by extending the cycles of menstruation are motivated by lifestyle, economic, and medical reasons. Our modern and fast-paced society values efficiency and convenience. Today, women occupy roles that have not previously available to them, enabling them to assume greater responsibilities and levels of prominence than ever before. Control of their lives and bodies and the enhanced ability to compete with men in society has propelled the development and quick social acceptance, of extended-cycle oral contraceptives by today's women. By postponing or eliminating menses, women can more effectively compete in demanding jobs and attend important events, while simultaneously coordinating the days of menstruation and its related symptoms/inconveniences around their schedules. A significant anticipation is whether social constructs regarding menstruation and its effects on a woman's ability to perform in society will become altogether irrelevant. However, this re-conceptualization of menstruation also raises concerns by certain ethicists (Stein, 2009).

With the undesirable symptoms of menopause, women have sought out for medical relief. Chapter 10 discussed the medical risks of hormonal therapy, which appeared to have nonbeneficial side-effects of cancers and other health risks that were discovered at an unfortunate lag time behind the use of such hormonal therapy. This provides another example of a situation where scientific progress and its promotion to the public should proceed on a more cautious pace, a concept repeated in many chapters of this book. This is also another example of social constructs of beliefs that are rooted in scientific progress without sufficient long-term research on health.

There is a need to develop medical alternatives for women suffering the symptoms of menopause. Women in higher income brackets can pay for bio-identical hormones, marketed as 'natural remedies,' which are available in commercial hormone products. These natural remedies are less likely to be covered by insurance. Consequently, women who are economically disadvantaged do not have this option to purchase products that can bring them relief. As a result, it may be considered that such natural remedies provide a platform for exacerbated social inequality.

Ethics related to menopause: The historical and long-standing description of menopause as a 'deficiency', both psychologically and physically, has placed women in a vulnerable position. In the early 1980s, menopause had been identified and constructed to be an 'endocrine deficiency disease,' a stage at which preventative measures could be taken to counter diseases of aging such as osteoporosis and cardiovascular disease. It was also seen as a period critical for addressing femininity. Hormone therapy became popular at this time and defined femininity, whereas menopause was synonymous with the loss of femininity.

Some ethicists are concerned that society will exert the ability to "re-conceptualize menstruation as a disease in need of treatment" (Stein, 2009). Historically, debates around women's menstrual cycles have been cyclic-asserting in the 1870's and 1880's that women were unfit for mental labor in higher education due to menstruation, to the1942 war-effort propaganda films claiming that menstruation "is no excuse for absenteeism and self-coddling"(Houppert, July 17, 2007). The question then raises the debate of whether menstrual suppression techniques elevate the status of women in society by allowing them to rise above the inconvenience of menstruation, or whether this scientific ability introduced to society will now re-affirm and consolidate the notion that such natural process is a "disease" which deserves to be treated, leaving women with no excuses not to pursue such options, and suffer the unaccommodating and unfitting consequences of social perception. According to polls, 59 percent of women would be interested in not menstruating every month and one third would choose never to have a period. In the poll, only 7% would believe it is physically necessary to have monthly menstruation whilst 44% believed suppression is good.[3] In light of such statistics, ethicists must rigorously discuss how the regulation of menses will influence the life-style of professional, non-professional, and non-working women.

Since the 1990's, medical attention has been diverted to risk prevention and health promotion for women during menopause. Medicine and public health have aimed to empower the individual woman and to stress her informed consent in making decisions regarding risk. Social constructs concerning menopause have moved away from loss of femininity and now consider this a period of ageing and susceptibility to disease. Now that medical language employs choice

---

[3] http://www.sciencedirect.com/science?_ob=ArticleURL&_udi=B6T5P-4DMWYTV-5&_user=18704&_coverDate=11%2F01%2F2004&_rdoc=1&_fmt=high&_orig=search&_sort=d&_docanchor=&view=c&_acct=C000002018&_version=1&_urlVersion=0&_userid=18704&md5=c4a747d08c40d59e77c0c992c90e1f09

and autonomy in decision-making, individuals are considered responsible for their own health risk decisions and behaviors. However, power constructs and disparities continue to hinder individual freedom of choice. When women opt out of hormonal therapy either by choice or through inaccessibility, they are increasingly made to feel responsible for putting themselves at risk. This pressurized environment and medical rhetoric, which emphasizes moral expectations and individual risk assessment, may also lead to the further exploitation of women (Murtagh and Hepworth, 2003).

Conclusions

"Biology is now creating concepts of birth and parenthood faster than the standard English vocabulary can define them".

-Time Magazine in 1984 (Friedrich, Constable and Samghabadi).

Given the rate of scientific progress, bioethicists and scientists must also take into account social, legal and ethical concerns of their practices as well as their research on health and medical risks. Epidemiological studies including prospective, case-controlled, and longitudinal study designs are urgently needed to provide the data necessary to ensure the safety of future generations of women and their offspring. This recurring theme of gathering unobtainable data on long-term medical effects of assisted reproductive technologies is a critical piece in a majority of complex bioethical debates. Given the current lack of data and social pressure that promotes fast-paced discoveries, researchers, clinics, and regulatory bodies should proceed with caution as they continue to address medical, ethical, and legal issues of reproductive medicine. In addition, classical definitions of motherhood, fatherhood, and parenthood will need to be re-examined as new technologies emerge allowing scientists to create children using non-traditional methods.

References

Ameratunga, D., et al. "In vitro fertilisation (IVF) with donor eggs in post-menopausal women: are there differences in pregnancy outcomes in women with premature ovarian failure (POF) compared with women with physiological age-related menopause?" J Assist Reprod Genet, **26**(9-10):511-514, 2009.
Borini, A. and Coticchio, G., "The efficacy and safety of human oocyte cryopreservation by slow cooling." Semin Reprod Med, **27**(6):443-449, 2009.

Bredkjaer, H. E. and Grudzinskas, J. G., "Cryobiology in human assisted reproductive technology. Would Hippocrates approve?" Early Pregnancy, **5**(3):211-213, 2001.

Cappon, C., World's Oldest New Mom Dying After IVF Pregnancy at Age 72 Fox News. New York, Fox, 2010.

Check, E., "Ethicists and biologists ponder the price of eggs." Nature, **442**(7103):606-607, 2006.

Covington, S. N. and Gibbons, W. E., "What is happening to the price of eggs?" Fertil Steril, **87**(5):1001-1004, 2007.

Cutas, D., "Postmenopausal motherhood: immoral, illegal? A case study." Bioethics **21**(8):458-463, 2007.

de Lacey, S., "Decisions for the fate of frozen embryos: fresh insights into patients' thinking and their rationales for donating or discarding embryos." Hum Reprod, **22**(6):1751-1758, 2007.

Greely, H. T., "Moving human embryonic stem cells from legislature to lab: remaining legal and ethical questions." PLoS Med, **3**(5):e143, 2006.

Heng, B. C., "Donation of surplus frozen embryos for stem cell research or fertility treatment-should medical professionals and healthcare institutions be allowed to exercise undue influence on the informed decision of their former patients?" J Assist Reprod Genet, **23**(9-10):381-382, 2006.

Henne, M. B. and Bundorf, M. K., "Insurance mandates and trends in infertility treatments." Fertil Steril, **89**(1):66-73, 2008.

Hirth, R., et al., "Microtubal reanastomosis: success rates as compared to in vitro fertilization." J Reprod Med **55**(3-4):161-165, 2010.

Houppert, K., Final Period. The New York Times, (July 17, 2007).

Knoppers, B. M., et al., "Oocyte donation for stem cell research." Science, **316**(5823): 368-370; author reply 368-370, 2007.

Kort, D.H., et al. "Pregnancy after age 50: defining risks for mother and child." American Journal of Perinatology, 29:245-250, 2012.

Langley, L. S. and Blackston, J.W., "Sperm, egg, and a petri dish. Unveiling the underlying property issues surrounding cryopreserved embryos." J Leg Med, **27**(2):167-206, 2006.

Leslie, M., "Melting opposition to frozen eggs." Science, **316**(5823): 388-389, 2007.

Levens, E. D. and DeCherney, A.H., "Human oocyte research: the ethics of donation and donor protection." JAMA, **300**(18):2174-2176, 2008.

Levine, A. D., "Self-regulation, compensation, and the ethical recruitment of oocyte donors." Hastings Cent Rep, **40**(2): 25-36, 2010.

Li, X.-H., et al., "Cryopreserved oocytes of infertile couples undergoing assisted reproductive technology could be an important source of oocyte donation: a clinical report of successful pregnancies.", Human Reprod, **20**:3390-3394, 2005.

Loike, J. D., et al., "Jewish views on the beginnings of human life and the use of medical intervention to produce children." Am J Bioeth, **9**(11):45-47, 2009.

Loike, J. D., Tendler, M.D., "Halachic Challenges Emerging From Stem Cell Research." Jewish Political Studies Review, **21**:3-4, 2010.

Lorraine, A. K., The Curious Lives of Surrogates. Newsweek, 2008.

Lugaila, T., and Overturf, J., "Children and the households they live in: 2000." Census 2000 Special Reports, CENSR-14, U.S. Census Bureau, 2004.

Magnus, D. and Cho, M.K., "Ethics. Issues in oocyte donation for stem cell research." Science, **308**(5729):1747-1748, 2005.

Marten, R., "Souls On Ice: America's Embryo Glut and the Wasted Promise of Stem Cell Research." Mother Jones **July/August,** 2006.

Mohler-Kuo, M., et al., "Attitudes of couples towards the destination of surplus embryos: results among couples with cryopreserved embryos in Switzerland." Hum Reprod, **24**(8):1930-1938, 2009.

Mundy, L., Souls On Ice: America's Embryo Glut and the Wasted Promise of Stem Cell Research. Mother Jones. **July/August 2006 Issue,** 2009.

Murtagh, M. J. and Hepworth, J., "Menopause as a long-term risk to health: implications of general practitioner accounts of prevention for women's choice and decision-making." Sociol Health Illn, **25**(2):185-207, 2003.

Nachtigall, R. D., et al., "Parents' conceptualization of their frozen embryos complicates the disposition decision." Fertil Steril, **84**(2):431-434, 2005.

Orenstein, P., "Your Gamete, Myself." The New York Times. (July 15, 2007)

Parks, J., "Rethinking radical politics in the context of assisted reproductive technology." Bioethics, **23**(1):20-27, 2009.

Parks, J. A., "On the use of IVF by post-menopausal women." Hypatia **14**(1):77-100, 1999.

Serour, G. I., "Islamic perspectives in human reproduction." Reprod Biomed Online, **17 Suppl 3**:34-38, 2008.

Spar, D., "The egg trade--making sense of the market for human oocytes." N Engl J Med, **356**(13):1289-1291, 2007.

Stein, E., and Kim, S., The Cultural Story of Menstruation. New York, St. Martin's Press, 2009.

Steinbrook, R., "Egg donation and human embryonic stem-cell research." N Engl J Med **354**(4):324-326, 2006.

Svanberg, A. S., et al., "Characterization of potential oocyte donors in Sweden." Hum Reprod, **18**(10):2205-2215, 2003.

Tachibana, M., et al., "Generation of chimeric rhesus monkeys." Cell, **148**:285-295 2012.

Tucker, M., et al., "Human oocyte cryopreservation: a valid alternative to embryo cryopreservation?" European Journal of Obstetrics & Gynecology and Reproductive Biology, **113**(Supplement 1):S24-S27, 2004.

Van Voorhis, B. J. and Syrop, C.H., "Cost-effective treatment for the couple with infertility." Clin Obstet Gynecol, **43**(4): 958-973, 2000.

Walker, A. J., "His, hers or ours? - who has the right to determine the disposition of frozen embryos after separation or divorce?" Buffalo Women's Law Journal, **XVI** 39-64, 2008.

Widdows, H., "Border Disputes Across Bodies: Exploitation in Trafficking for Prostitution and Egg Sale for Stem Cell Research " International Journal of Feminist Approaches to Bioethics, **2**: 5-24, 3009.

Yee, S., et al., "A follow-up study of women who donated oocytes to known recipient couples for altruistic reasons." Hum Reprod, **22**(7):2040-2050, 2007.

Figure 1. Spectral karyotyping (SKY) which is a laboratory technique that allows scientists to visualize all of the human chromosomes at one time by "painting" each pair of chromosomes in a different fluorescent color   (Obtained from NIH.gov).

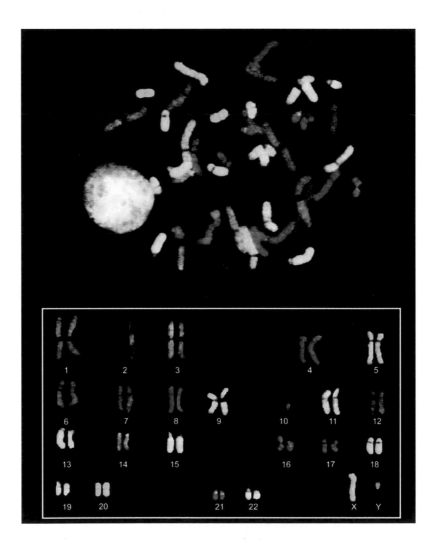

Chapter Thirteen

Ethical Challenges in Biodefense

Introduction

On Tuesday, September 18, 2001, one week after the 9/11 attack on the World Trade Center towers in New York City, letters containing anthrax bacteria were mailed to several news media offices and two U.S. Senators, ultimately killing five people and infecting 17 others. Bob Stevens was the first documented victim in the US killed by this bioterrorist attack. While a great deal of anxiety was generated as well as sadness for the five people who died from this anthrax attack, it appeared that the various governmental agencies involved handled this situation well. The perpetrator was never found and brought to justice (Bush and Perez, 2012).

According to the Centers for Disease Control a bioterrorism attack is "the deliberate release of viruses, bacteria, toxins, or other harmful agents used to cause illness or death in people, animals, or plants. Biological agents can be spread through the air, water, or in food".[1] Like a nuclear bomb, a biological weapon has the potential to cause massive loss of human lives and evoke fear and panic across any country. Bioweapons are extremely difficult to detect as they usually do not cause immediate recognizable symptoms of illness for several days.

History of Biological Weapons

Biological weapons are as old as war itself. The ancient Hittites marched victims of plague into the cities of their enemies; Herodotus described archers' firing arrows tipped with manure. By the 20th century, nearly every major nation developed, produced, and even used in battle a panoply of biological weapons including anthrax, plague, and typhoid (Anderson and Bokor, 2012].

It is difficult to predict when, or even if the United States will be attacked by a bioweapon. In 2010, Congress established the Commission on the Prevention of Weapons of Mass Destruction, Proliferation, and Terrorism, that

---

[1] American Medical Association, (2001). "Declaration of professional responsibility: Medicine's social contract with humanity." URL: http://www. ama-assn. org/ama/upload/mm/369/decofprofessional. pdf (accessed 2012).

predicted that the chances were better than 50-50 that a weapon of mass destruction would be used in a terrorist attack somewhere in the world by 2013.[2] Moreover, according to the members of this commission, the weapon of mass destruction is more likely to be biological than nuclear.

In order to prepare for a bioweapon attack, various simulations have been conducted. The "Dark Winter Exercise", for example, was coordinated by the Center for Strategic and International Studies and the Johns Hopkins Center for Civilian Biodefense Studies to simulate a bioterror attack using smallpox as the biological agent (Armstrong, 2012). Based on the results of this simulation, the organizers predicted that as many as a million people in the United States would be killed if such an attack actually occurred. Some experts, such as Milton Leitenberg[3] disagreed with the results of the "Dark Winter Exercise" and argued that this simulation relied on faulty premises designed to increase the death toll and assure a disastrous outcome. Based on Dr. Leitenberg's perspective, the death toll from the exercise would be in the tens of thousands, smaller than one million but astounding nonetheless (Galamas, 2011).

It is no surprise that governments around the globe are preparing for a potential bioterrorist event. Determining how a biological attack might unfold depends on a number of variables including which biological agent is used, the extent of its weaponization, the quantity and infectivity of the agent released, and the method of delivery. Some biological agents like the smallpox virus, are rapidly contagious and could spread widely from person to person with just a small number of particles released. Others, like the plague and tularemia bacteria, are not typically contagious but are relatively easy to make and disperse through water contamination.

Protecting the United States from Bioterrorism

The 9/11 attack triggered tremendous efforts to prepare bioterrorism countermeasures (Unlu et al., 2012). Even before 9/11, the White House and Congress had created a new division of the Centers for Disease Control, known as the National Pharmaceutical Stockpile that was designed to store medicines and vaccines for times of crisis. Since 2001, the federal government has invested more than $60 billion both to protect our country from a bioterrorist attack and to have in place a strategic response to a bioterrorist event. The government has

---

[2] http://www.forbes.com/sites/jamesglassman/2012/04/04/were-letting-our-bioterrorism-defenses-down/.
[3] Dr. Leitenberg is currently a Senior Research Scholar at the Center for International and Security Studies at the University of Maryland.

invested in (1) the development and distribution of air sensors, (2) in educating health providers about the symptoms of bioterror pathogens, and (3) in distributing medical supplies for biodefense to selected hospitals around the country. These responses have been based on government assessment of specific biological agents known as "material threats". Material threats are the most virulent pathogens to defend against and include smallpox, anthrax, ebola, plague, and a handful of lesser-known organisms.

In addition, Project BioShield was initiated in 2004 by the Department of Health and Human Services (DHHS) to oversee a program to develop and stockpile vaccines and treatments that are known collectively as "medical countermeasures" (Cohen, 2011). These countermeasures are designed to address the fact that bioterrorists can infect a variety of targets including human beings, water, food, environment, crops, or animals. In fact, argoterrorism is considered by some experts as the easiest bioweapon to employ.

As a countermeasure to bioterrorism attacks, the Bioterrorism Act of 2002 and the Food Safety Modernization Act of 2010 focused on pathogens that affect the food supply (Grundmann, 2011). Under this act, the U.S. Department of Health and Human Services (DHHS) has been authorized to ensure that all food facilities that manufacture, process, pack, distribute, receive, or hold food for consumption by humans or animals in the U.S be registered with the Food and Drug Administration (FDA). The FDA has the authority to administratively detain food if the agency has credible evidence or information that the food presents a threat of serious adverse health consequences or death to humans or animals (Danzig, 2011).

General Considerations in Biodefense

Much has been published on the potential threats and methods by which society can protect itself, as well as respond to the health crisis associated with a bioterrorist attack. There are several important questions, beyond the scope of this chapter, which should be fully addressed and resolved by government agencies in their preparations for a bioweapon attack.

- First, can our government successfully predict the risks and extent of a bioterrorist attack?
- Second, will our governmental countermeasures work efficiently and effectively to either thwart an attack or to respond appropriately?

- Third, has our government learned the vital lessons from our (non) responses to natural disasters such as Katrina, oil spills in the Gulf of Mexico, or Sandy, the perfect storm of 2012?
- Fourth, what are the best political and communication channels for countries to promote international cooperation to counter and to respond to bioterrorism?
- Finally, there is a need to develop specialized ethical guidelines for biodefense?

Ethical Challenges in Biodefense

There are a panoply of diverse ethical considerations and challenges that must be discussed or debated that relate to biodefense.[4] In this chapter, seven vital ethical issues related to bioterrorism are reviewed and specific recommendations that relate to bioterrorism are proposed. These seven ethical issues are:

1. Allocation of resources and personnel,
2. Triage assessment,
3. Clinical testing of potential therapies or vaccines in young children,
4. Preventing unauthorized individuals from entering research laboratories,
5. Dual use – publication of papers containing useful information that also could be used to create bioweapons,
6. Dual use – curtailing the development of harmful technologies while promoting beneficial applications of these technologies by scientists,
7. Allocation of *Educational Resources.*

Allocation of resources and personnel: One critical ethical issue related to allocation of personnel is what risks must health care providers take to save other lives?   There are several views concerning this issue. Some ethicists espouse the autonomous rights of health care providers to balance the health risk with their right of self-preservation in entering and remaining at bioterrorist response sites. Other bioethicists follow the recommendation of the American Medical Association's Council on Ethical and Judicial Affairs. This Council issued

---

[4] As of November 2012, Pub Med search revealed that there were almost 200 review articles related to "health care and bioterrorism", 480 review articles on "health and bioterrorism" and only 20 review articles related to "ethics and bioterrorism".

a "Declaration of Responsibility," requiring physicians to apply their time, knowledge, and skills when needed, even though doing so may put them at risk.[5] Their recommendations parallel the ethics of mandating that all members of the National Guard or Armed Services risk their lives to save others. On a practical note, there should be more discussion on ways to encourage health care providers to engage and respond to a bioterrorist event. Specifically:

1. Nursing staff and other non-MD support staff can play key roles in providing health care in these emergency situations but many of them are not educationally prepared to recognize a bioterror event or know how to best respond.
2. Many health care providers are parents who do not have child care resources to cover the continuous and prolonged time that a response requires.
3. Health care providers may want to place their family safety ahead of their duties to respond to the victims of the bioterrorist attack.
4. Health care providers have been known to avoid or leave their duties because of fear for their own safety.

Several suggestions have been proposed to ameliorate the problems just mentioned (Posid, 2011). First, the government should institute educational programs and training drills to all health care providers who will be first and second responders to a bioterror attack or pandemic. Second, the government should institute child care programs to all health providers (nurses, physicians, etc.) during these emergencies.[6] With respect to issues #3 and #4, there is a need for opportunities to openly explore and resolve the dilemma of whether to put self and family safety issues before the obligations to care for bioterror victims. One controversial suggestion is that the government ensures that in a time of emergency, certain groups such as government officials, health care professionals and their families, and even undertakers as described by Camus in his classic work, *The Plague,* receive priority access to limited health care resources and treatments [15]. Whatever policies are recommended and implemented must be clearly outlined, transparent, publicized, and acceptable to the public.

With respect to allocation of equipment and medications, there are many unanswered practical questions such as how much money should be allocated to provide the necessary equipment and medication in times of crisis? While the US

---

[5] Ibid, footnote #1.
[6] Where to set up these child care centers is another debatable issue.

government has millions of vials of smallpox vaccine stockpiled, there are not enough ventilators to meet the demand of an anthrax attack. Many published articles on distributive justice related to the areas of natural and man-made disasters are available that can serve as background lessons for proper allocation of resources in bioterrorism (Geale, 2012). Among the many states that have disaster plans, New York State's plan for allocating ventilators during a pandemic offers a viable model for just guidelines. [7] *Triage assessment:* Publications are available that discuss the ethical virtues of treating patients either on a "first come, first treat basis" or triage in order to save "the greatest number of lives" (Szalados, 2012). Related to this sentinel issue is the ethical challenge of how health care providers should be instructed to triage those individuals who will receive comfort care rather than aggressive care because they are not expected to survive. In other words, should treating those most likely to survive trump treating those who require more extensive care because of their critical condition? This issue arose in Katrina and has been debated in the literature and in the courts without any clear consensus (Geale, 2012). Likewise, there is no consensus on other ethical issues such as whether health care providers should administer high doses of opiates that may shorten lives but minimize the suffering of those whose chances of survival are slim. This point also raises the ethical issue of whether to free up scarce hospital beds by discharging patients earlier than necessary to make room for new sicker arrivals.

The World Medical Association (WMA) offers several ethical recommendations related to triage in the event of a natural disaster.[8] The WMA recommends that "the physician must act according to the needs of patients and the resources available. He/she should attempt to set an order of priorities for treatment that will save the greatest number of lives and restrict morbidity to a minimum". This is one ethical view that has guided medical response to natural disasters and may be applicable to bioterrorism. Priority should be given to treat patients with life-threatening conditions in the best possible manner to ensure that resources and health care personnel are used wisely so they are available to treat the maximum number of victims in need.

Additionally, there are divergent approaches regarding how and where to establish health care facilities at the onset of a disaster (Cruz et al., 2006). Several European countries favor the use of specific non-hospital facilities as health care centers to avoid the bio-contamination of patients or health care providers already in the hospital. Obviously, when a disaster strikes, setting up

---

[7] http://www.health.ny.gov/diseases/communicable/influenza/pandemic/plan/.
[8] http://www.wma.net/en/30publications/10policies/d7/index.html

separate centers of response will be more costly and require great thought and planning on how to rapidly populate those centers with the necessary equipment and personnel.

From an ethical or philosophical perspective, issues of allocation and triage can be viewed from at least two alternate theoretical perspectives (Iserson and Moskop, 2007). Some bioethicists consider applying a utilitarian approach where the medical needs and resources should be provided to ensure the greatest number of survivors. These bioethicists view an "extended moral horizon" to examine not just the policy effects on individual human victims, but also to apply their policies on humanity as a whole. In contrast, other bioethicists consider a Kantian or non-consequentialist model that focuses on imperatives, such as "first come, first treat" or triage to save the most salvageable. Whatever model is adopted for bioterror situations, it is important to train triage officers to properly and ethically manage these disasters in a consistent and just manner (Hick et al, 2012). These officers should have the capacity to manage and control both victims and health care providers under situations where panic could cause absolute disruption of an appropriate and well-coordinated bioterror response.

Clinical testing of potential therapies or vaccines in young children: Good empirical evidence is available documenting that clinical testing of potential medications on adults or military personnel may not be valid predictors in assessing the therapeutic responses of infants and children (Couzin-Frankel, 2011). Hence, the ethical question is should there be clinical trials of these untried medications with potentially harmful side effects in young children in preparation for a terrorist attack? The model of the Biomedical Advanced Research and Development Authority (BARDA) used for adults is that non-approved FDA medications can be stockpiled and used in a crisis situation provided that there are good data for phase 2 trials. Thus, small clinical trials should be conducted involving children to assess the efficacy of life-saving procedures and medications because it is well known that children should not be treated as small adults and their responses cannot always be extrapolated from adult responses (Couzin-Frankel, 2011).

Preventing unauthorized individuals from entering our research laboratories: There are multiple measures in place to ensure biosafety within most US research institutions. Yet, there is still concern that unauthorized individuals could gain access to secure laboratories. Even more frightening is the possibility that individuals employed by a biosafety laboratory could use their access to pathogens to set up bioterrorist activities. While it is difficult to completely protect a facility, it is helpful when all members of the facility remain vigilant and ready to provide information to the head of the laboratory if they observe questionable activities. Serving as a whistleblower is not always an easy activity as there may be retaliation or legal and other repercussions if their information is not accurate; yet, without their vigilance, a threat may not be averted.

Raising awareness of those involved in research can be extended to the entire population at large. New York City commuters constantly hear on their subways and bridges that everyone should keep an eye out for potential dangers such as suspicious packages. The public should be instructed on the proper way to inform authorities of questionable activities that may suggest a potential bioterrorist attack.

Dual-use – Publication of manuscripts containing information that could be used to create bioterror weapons:

Our scientific enterprise is characterized by a commitment to information sharing as a means to accumulate and disseminate knowledge through a collaborative and collective effort. The chief justification of openness is that it contributes to both generation and acquisition of scientific knowledge.

Figure 1. N1H1 Virus (from NIH image gallery)

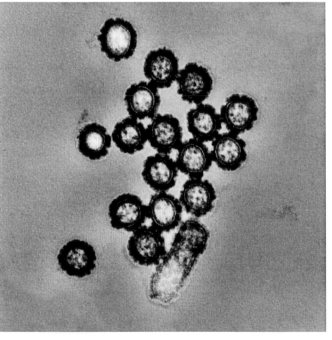

Dual-use in biology relates to the knowledge and skills developed for legitimate scientific and commercial purposes that also have the potential to be misused by those with hostile intent. How can society preserve the openness of scientific research while still preventing information from research papers to be used for terror by non-state organizations or individuals? This is a major ethical concern for ethicists. A second ethical concern is whether publishing in professional journals creates a real danger in dissemination of biodefense information to terrorists.

During the end of 2011 and through June of 2012, the potential publication of genetic modifications of the H5N1 influenza flu virus triggered a significant series of bioethical debates on the issues of *dual-use* that awakened the press about the importance of bioethics (Osterholm and Relman, 2012). The National Science Advisory Board for Biosecurity's (NSABB) recommendation on 20 December 2011 not to publish the two H5N1 papers in full detail was unprecedented and delayed their publication. This delay in publishing methods for genetically bioengineered H5N1 avian influenza highlights the current status of the dual-use issue and has brought ethical considerations related to bioterrorism into the forefront. With respect to dual-use, one underlying bioethical challenge is how best to balance scientific openness (autonomy to publish and freedom of the press) with censorship and homeland security issues. This dilemma of dual-use is not unique to bioweapons but has historical origins in nuclear physics and bacterial genetics.

As a case in point, it remains unclear whether deliberately publishing false methodologies in nuclear physics during the 1940s and 1950s delayed the Russians and Chinese from developing their own nuclear bombs (Finney, 2012). In contrast, it appears that scientist-based self-regulation adopted at the Asilomar Conferences in the 1970s successfully prevented the release of genetically modified bacteria containing human oncogenes into the environment (Falkow, 2012). The dual-use issue at the Asilomar Conferences involved transfecting a recombinant DNA molecule made in the laboratory with genes from the tumor virus, SV40, into a strain of the human commensal bacterium, Escherichia coli. It is interesting that during the Asilomar Conferences, the issue of publishing or refraining from publishing the methodology was not a major issue.

There are several outcomes that have emerged from our debates and experience regarding the issue of whether to publish critical methods for genetically modifying the H5N1 virus. First, was vital information revealed to terrorists in these H5N1 debates? These debates, for example, established that setting up a highly sophisticated laboratory to genetically modify this strain of influenza virus is time-consuming and costly. Second, terrorists may realize from these debates that our capacity to develop effective vaccines against influenza virus renders this pathogen as a less desirable candidate for a bioweapon than anthrax. Finally, any global outbreak of H5N1 would more likely have a higher mortality rate in an underdeveloped country where terrorists reside than in western countries. There are certainly many scientists who believe that the open debates may be more informative to the terrorists than simply publishing the methodologies. In the end, the decision to publish was based on the assessment that these methods would be more beneficial in creating better vaccines and therapies than to be used to create more potent bioweapons. One should keep in mind that there is little evidence that suggests that human beings are better equipped using genetic engineering than 'nature', using natural selection to create a lethal pathogen.

Even if a society accepts the concept that certain biotechnological methods should be restricted for publication, who should make those decisions? Should regulations be promulgated by a standing governmental panel, such as NSABB's, that is composed of scientists, journal editors, and government officials? Perhaps an ad hoc committee should be created only when an issue arises such as H5N1.

Dual use – curtailing the development of harmful technologies while promoting beneficial applications of these technologies by scientists: History has revealed that it is quite difficult to limit or restrict technological development and the dissemination of scientific information that may be harmful. Yet, scientist-based self-regulations have been shown to be an effective measure to regulate technological development and progress.

The Asilomar Conferences first planned in the 1970s will go down in history as a unique example of scientist-based self-regulation. As mentioned earlier, the basic issue that generated these conferences was whether it was safe to clone certain eukaryotic genes, such as insulin or oncogenes, into the common bacteria, E. coli. These conferences concluded with a scientist-based self-imposed moratorium which stated that only bacteria that could **not** survive outside of a laboratory could be used for these types of experiments.

Other lessons emerged from these conferences. First, the people who sounded the alarm about genetically engineering bacteria with oncogenes were not politicians, religious groups, or journalists: they were scientists. Second, participants assigned a risk estimate to different types of experiments they envisioned and they implored that everyone should join in choosing in what facilities the experiments would be conducted. Third, and most important, these conferences demonstrated that scientists can effectively self-regulate scientific research. Since its inception, and with the exception of the anthrax events of 2001, there has been no documented release of harmful genetically engineered bacteria outside of any laboratory. Finally, the inclusion of nonscientists in forming these policy decisions strengthened and legitimized the efforts and led to an increased public awareness of this research and a more general willingness to accept biological research using DNA technologies. The entire process was open to reporters and journalists to keep the public updated with the decisions that would potentially guide both the creation of new organisms and the protection the environment.

Allocation of Educational Resources

Educating researchers and health care providers regarding the principles and practices of the responsible conduct of research may be another means to protect society from bioterrorist threats. First, it is critical to convey the concept that moral responsibility must be placed on the individual investigator. Scientists serve on the front line of discovery and should accept the ethical responsibility to avoid contributing to the advancement of biowarfare and bioterrorism (Faden and Karron, 2012: Somerville and Atlas, 2005). It is important to instruct a generation of young scientists in what constitutes research that may have unintended social consequences. Second, society functions much better when there is cooperation, communication, and concern for others. Individuals should feel comfortable revealing to authorities information about potential health and bioterrorist threats.

How should this educational process be put into place? Middle schools and high schools should incorporate some of these principles into a course on moral development and the responsible conduct of research.

Conclusions

The H5N1 debate triggered passionate dialog among biomedical scientists, publishers, and ethicists about biosafety, biosecurity, and bioterrorism, not to mention the social responsibility of scientists to ethical challenges of biodefense. These debates concerning the publication of ways to genetically alter virus transmissibility is an essential focus of contemporary research, not just for H5N1, but for all infectious agents. Hopefully, the publication of the H5N1 papers will serve as the scientific foundation for effective new vaccines and the development of other preventive measures and therapies.

This chapter briefly touched on several ethical challenges regarding biodefense. While there is no consensus on how to resolve many of these issues, the following recommendations to assist in developing sound policies and just guidelines should be considered:

- It is crucial to prepare in advance of a bioterrorist attack a set of ethical guidelines gleaned from lessons learned from effective or ineffective responses to natural disasters.

- In science, as in other professions, financial gain can be an incentive to recruit individuals who might engage in unethical practices. Society may not be able to prevent this type of recruitment but it is vital to educate our youth about responsible moral conduct as it relates to science and thus to infuse them with the bioethical mantra that it is not what can be done but rather what should be done.

- Primary physicians, nurses, and other health care providers should be educated about the ethical response to bioterrorism as well as the medical aspects of bioterrorism detection, surveillance, and management. Likewise, a cadre of triage managers should be educated who will be called upon to supervise disaster

- The public needs to be informed about the threats of bioterrorism and how government agencies are prepared to respond to a bioterrorist attack. The public must understand the principles of triage and their ethical obligations in times of disaster.

In conclusion, there is a need to develop a working consensus of bioethicists, scientists, government officials, and the public regarding management and implementation of ethical guidelines in time of crisis. The resolution that led to the publication of the H5N1 papers demonstrates that scholars have the capacity to resolve complex ethical issues.

References

Anderson, P. D. and Bokor G., "Bioterrorism: Pathogens as Weapons." Journal of Pharmacy Practice, 25(5):521-529, 2012.

Armstrong, M., "Rehearsing for the Plague: Citizens, Security, and Simulation." Canadian Review of American Studies, 42(1):105-120, 2012.

Bush, L. M., and Perez, M. T,. "The anthrax attacks 10 years later.", Ann Intern Med, 156:41, 2012.

Cohen, J., "Reinventing Project BioShield." Science, 333(6047):1216-1218, 2011.

Couzin-Frankel, J.,"Panel Endorses Anthrax Vaccine Study in Children." Science, 334(6056): 577-577, 2011.

Cruz, A. M., et al., "Emerging issues for natech disaster risk management in Europe." Journal of Risk Research, 9(5):483-501, 2006.

Danzig, R., "A Decade of Countering Bioterrorism: Incremental Progress, Fundamental Failings." Biosecurity and Bioterrorism: Biodefense Strategy, Practice, and Science, 10(1):49-54, 2011.

Faden, R. R., and Karron, R. A., "The obligation to prevent the next dual-use controversy." Science, 335(6070): 802-804, 2012.

Falkow, S., "The Lessons of Asilomar and the H5N1 Affair." mBio 3:5-8, 2012.

Finney, J. L., "Dual Use: Can We Learn from the Physicists' Experience? A Personal View." In A Web of Prevention:" Biological Weapons, Life Sciences and the Governance of Research, (edited by Caitriona Mcleish, Brian Rappert) pg: 67-76, 2012.

Galamas, F., "Profiling bioterrorism: present and potential threats." Comparative Strategy 30(1):79-93, 2011.

Geale, S. K., "The ethics of disaster management." Disaster Prevention and Management, 21(4):445-462, 2012.

Grundmann, O., "Recent Advances in the Prevention of Bioterrorism Attacks." Journal of Bioterrorism & Biodefense, 2:1, 2011.

Hick, J. L., et al., "Allocating scarce resources in disasters: emergency department principles." Annals of Emergency Medicine, 59(3):177-187, 2012.

Iserson, K. V. and Moskop J. C., "Triage in medicine, part I: concept, history, and types." Annals of Emergency Medicine, 49(3):275-281, 2007.

Osterholm, M. T. and Relman D. A., "Creating a mammalian-transmissible A/H5N1 influenza virus: Social contracts, prudence, and alternative perspectives." Journal of Infectious Diseases, 205(11):1636-1638, 2012.

Posid, J. M., et al., "Centers for Disease Control and Prevention's Bioterrorism Preparedness Program." Encyclopedia of Bioterrorism Defense. Wiley Online Library, 2011. [http://onlinelibrary.wiley.com/doi/10.1002/0471686786.ebd0021.pub2/abstract?systemMessage=Wiley+Online+Library+will+be+disrupted+on+15+December+from+10%3A00-12%3A00+GMT+%2805%3A00-07%3A00+EST%29+for+essential+maintenance&userIsAuthenticated=false&

Somerville, M. A. and Atlas, R. M., "Ethics: a weapon to counter bioterrorism." Science, 307(5717): 1881-1882, 2005.deniedAccessCustomisedMessage=].

Szalados, J. E., "Triaging the fittest: Practical wisdom versus logical calculus?*." Critical care medicine, 40(2):697, 2012.

Unlu, A., et al., "The Impact of 9/11 on Information Policy in the United States: A Current Perspective on Homeland Security and Emergency Management." Journal of Applied Security Research, 7(3):320-340, 2012.

Figure 2: **Methicillin-resistant Staphylococcus aureus**. A bacteria that causes infections and is one that is resistant to many antibiotics (obtained from NIH.gov).

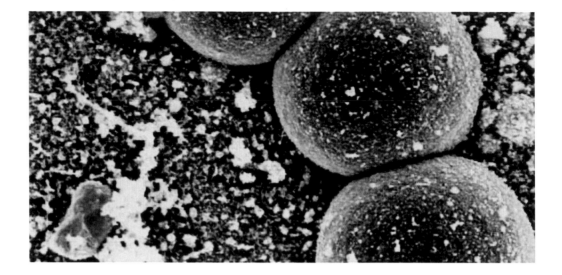

Chapter Fourteen

Supplementary Materials

Supplement A - Writing a science-based op ed piece

One important element in science is presenting bioethical information and opinions to colleagues and to the public is a cogent and interesting manner. In this chapter, we briefly review essential guidelines in writing an op ed piece for either a newspaper or for a scientific journal. We then present two sample-op ed pieces that were published in 2013.

There are six basic guidelines that need to be addressed before writing an op ed piece.

1. Identify a bioethical topic that is timely, interesting, and controversial. Often the reporting of a new biotechnology that is receiving international publicity is an opportune time to write a bioethical op ed piece.
2. Identify the audience that you want to address and educate. Then select several appropriate publications that you believe would be willing to publish the article. If you want to target the general public, newspapers such as the New York Times, Wall Street Journal, and Washington Post are some of the most prestigious. It is important to recognize that publishing in these papers is quite difficult. If you want to target scientific colleagues than Journals such as Science and Nature are the most difficult and prestigious. However, there are other excellent scientific magazines, such as "The Scientist" or "The New Scientist" that would consider your work. Sometimes if the target audience is even more selective then there are a variety of scientific journals that accept opinion pieces. Always check the impact factor for each journal via a Google search.
3. Write an article with an interesting and engaging introduction to draw in the reader. This can be done by providing a clever title or by describing an interesting story or case study.
4. Structure the article as follows:
   a) Include in your introduction what dilemma you will present and what is your opinion to resolve this dilemma.
   b) Focus the middle of the article on information that supports your opinion and approach. Go easy on the "I" word, and banish the phrase

"I think" altogether. Throw in humor whenever possible. Don't hesitate to include verifiable statistical information and quotes from experts that validate your position.

c) Conclude the article with a brief summary and the ramifications of your views. Try to include a quotable sentence that can be highlighted.

5. Once you write this first draft of your article, select the target publication and read the authors instructions carefully, paying attention to word count. Read some of op ed pieces that that publication has printed to assess whether your article is appropriate for that specific publication. Let your classmates review the article before submitting the article. Generally post the article within the email and not as an attachment.

6. Write an engaging cover letter explaining why your article is timely and interesting. Remember, many op ed pieces are written by invited experts or written by "professionals". You can, however, include in the cover letter that as a student from a major Ivy League University, you believe your voice should be heard.

Sample Op Ed #1– Published in "The Scientist" October, 2013

Three-Way Parenthood: Dealing with the logistics of embryos created by three-parent IVF technologies that avoid the transmission of mitochondrial disease

By John D. Loike, Michio Hirano, and Yehezkel Margalit

When first used in humans in the 1970s, in-vitro fertilization (IVF) raised significant ethical, legal, and philosophical concerns. The ability to manipulate human reproduction was viewed in many circles as an attack on the traditional family and an odious attempt to assert human dominion over nature. Terms such as "designer babies" and "playing God" were commonly applied to IVF. Nevertheless, much of the scientific community touted the potential benefits of these technologies, viewing them as the start of a new era of medicine. Indeed, despite those dire predictions four decades ago, IVF is now widely accepted and has enabled infertile couples to conceive more than five million healthy babies.

Fourteen years ago, my Columbia University colleagues and I (JL) examined the mitochondrial origins of Dolly, the cloned sheep, and proposed the concept of a "three-parent" fertility procedure to treat mitochondrial disorders (Evans, Gurer et al. 1999). The unique genetic information within mitochondria enables these organelles to function as the biochemical engines of the cell. However, sometimes deleterious mutations occur in mitochondrial DNA (mtDNA) that cause myriad human pathologies—such as heart problems, liver failure, brain disorders, blindness, hearing loss, myopathy, and in the most extreme cases, death. These mitochondrial disorders are incurable and are passed down maternally from generation to generation. One in 6,500 children worldwide is affected with mtDNA defects. (See "Power Failure," May 2011.)

To prevent defective mtDNA from being passed from mother to child, scientists in the U.K. are planning to offer a "three-parent" fertility procedure. Based in part on protocols developed by scientists at the New York Stem Cell Foundation and at Columbia University Medical Center (Pfeffer, Horvath et al. 2013), this procedure modifies standard IVF technology to create an embryo from the eggs of two women and sperm obtained from one man. Specifically, nuclear DNA from the egg of a woman carrying mitochondrial defects is transferred into the enucleated cytoplasm of a donor egg that harbors nonmutated mtDNA. This genetically reconstituted egg is then fertilized in vitro by sperm from a male partner, and the resulting embryo is implanted into the uterus of the woman with the mitochondrial disorder. This embryo will contain genetic material from three donors, but will not express any symptoms of the mitochondrial disorder.

The potential for creating children from multiple parents is not limited to producing offspring that might have a mitochondrial disorder. In May 2013, Shoukhrat Mitalipov and his colleagues at the Oregon Health and Science University published a milestone article describing the use of IVF technology to transfer genetic material from any nonsperm cell into a human egg, therebygenerating a pre-implantation embryo from which human embryonic stem cells can be readily isolated and maintained in the laboratory (Tachibana, Amato et al. 2013). One of many potential outcomes of this research is the ability to create a human embryo without any male genetic contribution—by transferring the nucleus from one woman into an enucleated egg of another woman—or to create an embryo from even more than three genetic parents—by merging multiple embryos into a single chimeric infant, as has already been achieved in rhesus monkeys (*Cell*, 148:285-95, 2012).

All of these genetic engineering procedures raise both legal and ethical concerns. Legal issues include: Who are the legal parents of a child generated from genetic material obtained from multiple donors? Would such a child have the right to know the identity of all his gene donors? In an article to be published in the *Harvard Journal of Law and Gender* (in press), we propose a legal solution to address some of these issues (Margalit, Levy et al. 2014 - in press). We propose that intentional parents—i.e., individuals who will assume responsibility of child care and agree to act as parents to the child—should be recognized as the legal parents of the child. We also propose that it is necessary to legally validate and define the parental intent and responsibilities of all parties involved in a pre-authorized contractual agreement. These proposed definitions of parenthood should supplement and expand biological and genetic considerations resulting from advances in molecular biology.

One of many ethical concerns raised by such technologies is whether these advances in reproductive medicine could lead to the creation of "designer babies," in which parents select the genetic composition of their children for enhancement or for health reasons. The fear in creating designer babies is that it may herald a new era of "consumer eugenics" with potentially unknown consequences for humankind. From an ethical perspective, any procedure involving genetic engineering should require that all genetic donors submit a medical history (and perhaps their complete genome sequences as well) to provide an early warning of future health risks for the child. We also believe that as children reach legal maturity, they have the right to know their genetic origins. We recognize that as with any new technology, there is always the fear of abuse. But we argue that the potential reproductive benefits of these technologies will trump those ethical fears.

That the road from scientific innovation to societal acceptance is often rocky is a given, and is emblematic of scientific innovation. As these genetic engineering technologies develop and become safer and less expensive, the potential to enable people with genetic defects to conceive a healthy child is a dream that should be vigorously pursued.

Evans, M. J., C. Gurer, J. D. Loike, I. Wilmut, A. E. Schnieke and E. A. Schon (1999). "Mitochondrial DNA genotypes in nuclear transfer-derived cloned sheep." Nat Genet **23**(1): 90-93.

Margalit, Y., O. A. Levy and J. D. Loike (2014 - in press). "The New Frontier of Advanced Reproductive Technology: Reevaluating Modern Legal Parenthood." Harvard Journal of Law and Gender.

Pfeffer, G., R. Horvath, T. Klopstock, V. K. Mootha, A. Suomalainen, S. Koene, M. Hirano, M. Zeviani, L. A. Bindoff, P. Yu-Wai-Man, M. Hanna, V. Carelli, R. McFarland, K. Majamaa, D. M. Turnbull, J. Smeitink and P. F. Chinnery (2013). "New treatments for mitochondrial disease-no time to drop our standards." Nat Rev Neurol.

Tachibana, M., P. Amato, M. Sparman, N. M. Gutierrez, R. Tippner-Hedges, H. Ma, E. Kang, A. Fulati, H. S. Lee, H. Sritanaudomchai, K. Masterson, J. Larson, D. Eaton, K. Sadler-Fredd, D. Battaglia, D. Lee, D. Wu, J. Jensen, P. Patton, S. Gokhale, R. L. Stouffer, D. Wolf and S. Mitalipov (2013). "Human embryonic stem cells derived by somatic cell nuclear transfer." Cell **153**(6): 1228-1238.

Sample Op Ed #2 is both a review and opinion article– Published in "Journal of In Vitro Fertilization" October 2013.

Gestational Surrogacy: *Medical and bioethical implications of bidirectional maternal-fetal cell exchange and epigenetics*

John D. Loike, Ph.D., Tovah Z. Moss, Ruth L. Fischbach, Ph.D., M.P.E.
Center for Bioethics, Columbia University College of Physicians and Surgeons,

Abstract: While increasing numbers of women engage in gestational surrogacy, medical, bioethical, legal, social, and financial issues linked to surrogacy continue to be a source of contentious debate. From a medical perspective, we review recent scientific evidence to show how maternal-fetal cell exchange and epigenetic processes affect the future health of both the surrogate and fetus. Maternal-fetal cell exchange and epigenetics establish an intimate biological and genetic connection between the surrogate and the child she is gestating. In light of these discoveries, the ethical complexities of surrogacy, related to its laws, informed consent, and contractual agreements between the various parties need to be careful re-examined. We propose that: a) all parties involved undergo a comprehensive medical history, genetic screening and genetic counseling, b) informed consent documents should be modified to include the disclosure, in general terms, of the potential medical risks associated with maternal-fetal cell exchange and epigenetics that the surrogate or child may experience in the future, c) legal contractual documents include the option of a disclaimer that indemnifies parties involved from future medical costs incurred (beyond the birth of the child) that are a result of maternal- fetal cell exchange or epigenetics, and d) a national registry be established where all health and genetic information about the gamete donors, gestational surrogate, and the progeny be available to all parties who wish anonymity in surrogacy.

Introduction

Surrogacy is an arrangement in which a woman carries and delivers a child for another couple or person. There are two basic forms of surrogacy. Traditional surrogacy refers to situations in which the gestational carrier provides the oocyte and gestates her genetically-related embryo. Before IVF, traditional surrogates were artificially inseminated with donor sperm from the husband of an infertile couple. IVF paved the way for Gestational surrogacy (Brinsden 2003) referring to a pregnancy in which the genetic mother and gestational birth mother are not the same individual. In this paper we focus on gestational surrogacy where a woman gestates an implanted embryo generated from the sperm and egg obtained, via IVF, from individual(s) or a couple who intends to be the legal, rearing parent(s) of the child.

The first successful pregnancy following gestational surrogacy was reported in 1984 (Utian, Sheean et al. 1985), only six years after the first test tube baby was born.

In this case, a woman's uterus had been previously removed without oophorectomy, leaving her incapable of gestating an embryo but retaining her capacity to naturally ovulate. The woman and her husband provided their eggs and sperm for IVF and one *in vitro* generated embryo was implanted into a host uterus of a third party for gestation and ultimate delivery of a healthy child. In this particular case, the surrogate relinquished any legal parental responsibilities after the birth of the baby.

Up until 1994, surrogacy was generally used by couples where the woman did not have a functional uterus (about 1 in 100,000 women) and could not gestate or give birth to a child (Burry 2007; Dermout, van de Wiel et al. 2010; Erickson 2010). Since 1994, gestational surrogacy has become an increasingly popular and viable option for other couples such as gay/lesbian couples (Norton et al., 2013) or for fertile women who do not want to become pregnant for non-medical reasons. Public awareness of surrogacy has increased in part because of its publicized medical and non-medical use by actors and actresses. Celebrities such as Sarah Jessica Parker, Nicole Kidman, Keith Urban, Elton John and David Furnish, have commissioned surrogate women to bear their children. In fact, recent statistics show that the number of infants born to gestational surrogates almost doubled from 2004 to 2008, from 738 babies to almost 1,400 (Gugucheva 2010). According to the Centers for Disease Control and Prevention, gestational carriers were involved in 915 cycles, or 1%, of assisted reproductive technology (ART) cycles using fresh non-donor embryos in the United States in 2008 (Centers for Disease Control and Prevention 2013). While there are no official records, several surrogate agencies and surrogacy support-group-Web sites confirm the ascending use of surrogacy.

Who volunteers for surrogacy? Currently, many surrogates are recruited through a commercial agency in the United States and then matched to the intended parents. Interestingly, military wives have been cited as being popular sources as surrogates, [leading surromomsonline.com], and comprise 12 to 19 percent of their surrogate pool (Nosheen and Schellmann August 10, 2011). However, there have been virtually no significant studies on the characteristics of typical surrogates in the last decade (Greenfield, 2012). Studies reported over 10 years ago describe surrogates to be married, aged in the mid-20s, have several children, and have attended college (see Reames, et al, 1999). The surrogacy industry in the United States was reported in 2006 to generate revenues of more than $38 million with a 6-8% a year growth rate (Spar 2006; Boston Women's Health Book Collective. 2011).

A critical factor that couples considering surrogacy discuss with their physicians and prospective surrogates relates to the health of the surrogate, both before and during pregnancy. Yet, we believe that couples wishing to engage gestational surrogates often over-simplify health consequences of surrogacy by focusing only on aspects of the life-style of the surrogate that usually is limited during pregnancy. Recent scientific nuances associated with surrogacy, however, suggest that a more comprehensive analysis should take place to better understand that subtle, as well as potentially serious, medical and health issues that may occur to the surrogate during pregnancy and beyond, as well as during the life time of the child.

In this article, we present some emergent scientific discoveries in maternal-fetal cell exchange (microchimerism) and epigenetic processes that may profoundly influence the medical condition of the surrogate and the fetus she gestated. In light of these findings, we propose that a comprehensive medical history and genetic screening of the surrogate candidate and biological parents be provided to all parties involved in surrogacy (including the child when he/she reaches adulthood) in the informed consent document before surrogacy is initiated. In addition, we advocate genetic counseling to all parties to ensure that they understand the information stated in the informed consent document. The sharing of medical information of the gestational surrogate, the biological parents and the child does not end at birth. As future health issues develop in the either the surrogate or child, it is important to make that information available. Yet, some surrogates may not want to reveal their identity. Thus, we propose that a national registry be established to allow the input of anonymous information concerning the health issues and genetics about the gamete donors, surrogate, and progeny. Such information could serve to be invaluable medical considerations if any of the parties involved in surrogacy develops health issues later in life. Finally, financial considerations must be re-assessed in light of epigenetics and maternal-fetal cell exchange as these process may illicit future medical problems and costs years or decades after the child is born from the surrogate. The legal question concerns the issue of who is financially responsible to cover the medical costs of future medical problems in the surrogate that arise from the millions of fetal cells permanently implanted in her organs or from maternal cells that are transferred to the child. Similarly, who will cover medical costs arising from the surrogate-based epigenetics that contribute or cause health problems in the child? In response to this legal quandary, we propose that an option for a disclaimer be considered in the legal contract between the surrogate and biologikal parents. This disclaimer would indemnify all parties from financial compensations regarding future medical issues (e.g., two years after birth of the child) that arise in either the surrogate or child.

Maternal-Fetal Cell Transfer

Maternal-fetal cell exchange (microchimerism) is a well-documented biological process that occurs in normal pregnancy. Research has shown, for example, that stem cells[1] from the fetus cross the placental barrier and implant into various tissues (such as the brain and muscle) of the mother (Klonisch and Drouin 2009). These cells continue to proliferate and remain within the mother's body for her entire life (Klonisch and Drouin 2009; Williams, Zepf et al. 2009). There is also evidence that stem cells from the mother cross the placental barrier and implant into tissues within the fetus (Klonisch and Drouin

---

[1] There is some controversy whether stem cells or other bone marrow progenitor cells actually cross the placenta. Other cells includes T and B cells, NK cells and granulocytes as well as myocytes, hepatocytes etc; (see Nelson 2012).

2009). This bidirectional cell exchange, demonstrated in normal pregnancy between the mother and the fetus, underscores that the mother and fetus are intimately connected, biologically, beyond the defined time that the fetus remains in the womb.

The transfer of fetal cells into the pregnant woman may explain an unresolved question of why a pregnant woman does not reject the implanted embryo as a foreign tissue. Theoretically, a woman carrying an embryo should immunologically reject it since it is not a perfect genetic match to her body (Ay, Buzas et al. 2012). Current evidence reported by Leber and colleagues, however, suggests that the maternal immune system becomes aware of the presence of the embryo-derived cells as foreign tissue and actively tolerates them (Dutta and Burlingham 2011; Leber, Zenclussen et al. 2011). Furthermore, they suggest the embryo or fetus itself contributes to its own tolerance (Leber, Zenclussen et al. 2011) to prevent any rejection process to take place. In addition to maternal-cell microchimerism, hormonal changes in the pregnant woman also suppress her immune system to allow her to gestate a foreign embryo. These proposed mechanisms may help clinicians understand why neither the pregnant woman nor the fetus rejects the transplanted cells that result from microchimerism. Equally important, is the fact that these processes may offer a new insight and methodology to apply in organ transplantation. Recipients of allogenic organs could theoretically be immunologically primed to receive a specific organ receiving transplanted stem cells from the donor in a defined tolerization protocol similar to that given to a person with defined food allergies. Moreover, alterations of the hormonal balance of a female organ recipient may further enhance immunological tolerance in advance of an organ transplant. In this way, one could envision the reduction or elimination of immune-suppressants after organ transplantation.

Health Consequences of Fetal-maternal Cell Exchange in Surrogacy

There are also no known biological reasons why maternal-fetal microchimerism should not occur in surrogacy as in normal pregnancy. Yet, there are only a few reports that substantiate this process in gestational surrogacy. Several studies in animals (Mitchell and James 1999) and humans (Williams, Zepf, et al. 2009) indicating that this process occurs in surrogacy as well. In the human study (Williams, Zepf, et al., 2009), allogeneic male fetal cells were shown to persist for up to 9 years in the circulation of healthy post-partum women who conceived using egg donors and delivered male infants.

There is now a need to further explore and examine the physiological effects of fetal to maternal cell exchange in surrogacy pregnancy. At this point in time, most studies assess maternal-fetal cell exchange by identifying the presence and number of cells containing the Y chromosome in women who have had children. The presence of these Y chromosome cells are most likely to originate from male fetal cells that migrated into her body during pregnancy. In this manner scientists can assess whether there is an association between microchimerism and specific disease states.

One disease commonly examined is cancer. Current evidence indicates that several forms of cancer may arise and develop from specific stem cells present in the human body. Recently, "cancer stem cell models" have been proposed to explain the origins and heterogeneity of tumors (Vries, Huch et al. 2010). Substantial scientific data suggest that several hematological and solid tumors originate from stem cell-like cells that are uniquely capable of propagating a tumor.

Several studies that have examined the association of male fetal cells in women who have had children [see (Kallenbach, Johnson et al. 2011) for a review], investigators showed that cervical cancer, thyroid cancer, melanoma, colon, and lung cancer is linked with an increased presence of male fetal cells within the host woman. Interestingly, other studies have shown that the presence of male fetal cells in women was strongly associated with a life-long **reduced** risk of developing breast cancer (Kallenbach, Johnson et al. 2011; Kamper-Jorgensen 2012). However, these are only preliminary reports and more research is required to validate and understand how the presence of fetal male cells in women decrease or increase the onset of cancers. With respect to maternal cells transferred to the fetus, there are almost twenty cases of babies born containing rare tumors whose genetic fingerprinting match that of the mother suggesting that the tumor were cause by her cells that turned malignant (Alexander et al., 2003; Isoda et al., 2009).

Fetal-maternal cell transfer may also be critical in the observed increased risk of other diseases such as the onset of various autoimmune diseases (Fugazzola, Cirello et al. 2011; Nijagal and MacKenzie, 2013). One unanswered question is whether diseases that the host mother contracts later in life are due, in part, to maternally implanted fetal cells that contain genes linked to these diseases. Some researchers, for example, have reported that many fetal cells implant into areas of the woman's central nervous system (Klonisch and Drouin 2009). If the fetal genome contains genetic mutations that cause, for example, the onset of Alzheimer's disease, Parkinson's disease, spinal muscular atrophy (Finkel type), or amyotrophic lateral sclerosis (ALS), the implanted fetal cells in the surrogate could theoretically increase her chances of developing these neurodegenerative diseases.

Epigenetics

Traditionally, changes in the sequence of base pairs, gene number, or gene copies are the most studied mechanisms to understand the genetics of human disease. However, the study of epigenetics is elucidating new mechanisms by which environment impacts heredity. Epigenetics is the study of the mechanism by which heritable changes in a phenotype occur in the absence of any alterations in the DNA sequence. The underlying mechanism in epigenetics is mediated by methylation or acetylation of specific base pairs in the genome or DNA associated proteins (such as histones) (Shufaro and Laufer, 2013). In this manner, epigenetics regulates the expression of a large variety of genes and establishes specific gene expression patterns in daughter cells to ensure the faithful inheritance of the chromatin architecture. Epigenetics is an important process in pregnancy, where the woman's life style and indeed her environment influence the health and genetics of the fetus she is carrying.

There are many human studies reporting that health risks to an infant are mediated by underlying epigenetic mechanisms resulting from the life-style of a non-surrogate pregnant woman. Prenatal nutrition, for example, influences offspring schizophrenia via epigenetic processes (Kirkbride, Susser et al. 2012) and the child's cognitive capacity as a young adult (Boeke et al. 2013). The nutrition of a woman during her childhood also has been shown to be associated decades later with her child's risk for cardiovascular disease, diabetes mellitus, and hypertension (Martyn, Barker, Osmond, 1996). Equally important is that the birth weight of a grandchild is associated with the diet of the grandmother during pregnancy (Lumey and Stein 1997). Recent evidence also suggests that epigenetic regulation may explain how exposure of pregnant women to environmental toxicants may induce asthma-related immune responses in their offspring (Milne, Greenop et al. 2012). Other studies have shown that in autism environmental factors seem to play an even greater role than genetic factors (Hallmayer, Cleveland et al. 2011). Even behavior during pregnancy may have epigenetic effects on the offspring (Charney 2013). Cigarette smoking during pregnancy, is another life-style that is strongly associated with reduced birth weight, poor developmental and psychological outcomes, and increased risk for diseases and behavioral disorders later in life. Recent evidence suggest that these effects are epigenetically mediated (Knopik et al., 2012).

As stated above, evidence is rapidly accumulating that environmental factors and experiences of the pregnant woman become embedded in the genome of the fetus (Martin-Subero and Esteller 2011). While studies have not focused on surrogacy, the cellular and hormonal environment of the surrogate, as well as her diet, lifestyle, and psychological state are thus likely to influence the personality and health of the fetus. As of September 2013, there are no concrete studies that demonstrate the effects of epigenetics in artificial reproductive technologies or in surrogacy. However, animal studies indicate differences in the methylation patterns of various genes are observed as a consequence of ART process (Horsthemke and Ludwig, 2005) In another study, superovulation and in vitro culture of oocytes were shown to effect the epigenome of the derived embryos/offspring (Grace and Sinclair 2009), and alterations in epigenetics of sperm was shown to be associated with impaired male subfertility (Houshdaran et al., 2007). Several human studies present data that epigenetic mechanisms may operate in understanding how the life-style of pregnant women influences the health of their children. We propose that based on these studies, epigenetic factors and the life-style of the surrogate should be considered in surrogacy as they may affect the future health of the fetus and its future progeny.

Bioethical issues emerging from microchimerism and epigenetics

One critical outcome from bi-directional cell exchange between a pregnant woman and her fetus is the fact that the mother and fetus are intimately and biologically connected beyond the defined time that the fetus is gestating in the womb. Traditionally, a surrogate has been viewed as merely a woman loaning or renting her uterus, and indeed her entire body for the nine months of pregnancy. Incorporating the fetal-maternal cell exchange and epigenetic paradigms raise significant medically-related issues that have previously not been addressed, such as serious future medical concerns that potentially could arise in the fetus, surrogate, or both.

Maternal-fetal cell exchange and epigenetics also generates significant bioethical conundrums. The autonomy of the surrogate, for example, may be trumped in favor of protecting the health of the fetus. Pregnant women found to be drinking alcohol or taking in harmful substances (e.g., cocaine) have been incarcerated against their will (Flavin 2009). The genetic privacy of both the surrogate and gamete donors may also be trumped in the future in favor of full disclosure of the genetic family histories or the results of genetic screening of all parties involved in the surrogacy arrangement. Additionally, women signing informed consent forms may not be given adequate details about potential negative outcomes to their health as they are lured into the surrogacy process (Davies 1985). The risks, harms, discomforts, and potential deprivations that surrogates may endure during pregnancy and beyond, are often not presented in sufficient detail in the informed consent process (Relph and Amanda 2010).

A precedent in providing an extensive genetic history is found in infertility clinics where the genetic history of the gamete donor(s) given to the prospective couple is often a critical determinant in choosing the appropriate donor (Solomon, Jack et al. 2008). Clearly, the couple seeking the "perfect healthy baby" should carefully study the genetic family history of the gamete donor(s) if known and available. Who decides whether to abort a fetus that will be born with Down's syndrome or cystic fibrosis? What happens if the baby is born with a serious birth defect and the biological parents choose to reject the baby? In each circumstance, who is contractually obligated to keep the baby? Many of these issues have been previously discussed (see Ber 2000; Brinsden 2003) regarding gestional surrogacy.

In 2001, some of these issues were brought to life in a case where a couple backed out of their surrogacy arrangement after being informed that the surrogate was carrying twins. After costly litigation, it was determined that the surrogate mother was the legal parent and therefore had the right to give the babies up for adoption (Osagie 2010).

In response to the role of maternal-fetal cell exchange and epigenetics in the health of the surrogate and child that she gestated is the need to obtain the most accurate medical history from the surrogate and the biological parents. Moreover, genetic screening of all parties will enhance our understanding of the potential medical risks that the child or surrogate may encounter in the future that arise from epigenetics and/or microchimerism. We advocate that the medical information obtained from the medical history and genetic screening must be presented to the biological parents and surrogate candidate, via a genetic counselor and in an informed consent document, before surrogacy is initiated. The informed consent should reveal that for nine months, the fetus should be viewed as an implanted integral functioning organ that shares and exchanges numerous physiological and epigenetic processes. In addition, the informed consent document should state in general but clear terms that maternal-fetal cell exchange and epigenetics means that medical and psychiatric health issues may arise in the surrogate or child well beyond the delivery of the child.

Related to this bioethical concern is the legal/bioethical issue of who should cover medical costs of the surrogate or child that result from microchimerism and/or epigenetics. Traditionally, efforts have been made to ensure that surrogacy arrangements are not transformed into commercial transactions. Legal agreements have stated that the prospective parents compensate the surrogate mother fairly and appropriately for her expenses, e.g., costs of IVF, pregnancy, delivery (if not covered by health insurance), adoption procedure, insurance, and legal fees. Post-partum financial considerations related to post-partum depression or other psychological or medical sequelae resulting from pregnancy or delivery have also been included in legal agreements.

Maternal-fetal cell exchange and epigenetics will complicate the financial coverage of health issues going forward since many of the health risks (such as the onset of cancer) may not develop for decades after the surrogate gives birth to the child. Theoretically, all parties involved in surrogacy must agree on who covers future medical costs incurred by the surrogate or child. However, this may present a legal or financial conundrum that may be difficult to resolve before initiating surrogacy. One option would be for insurance companies to offer policies that would cover these costs at an affordable premium. Another option is for all parties to sign a disclaimer that indemnifies them from future medical costs (e.g., greater than two years post-partum).

Regulation of surrogacy lacking in the United States. Israel is the first country in the world to legalize state-supervised surrogacy, has very strict regulations on surrogacy that mandate, for example, psychological testing for women engaging in surrogacy (Lee 2009). It is the only country to legislate granting government control of surrogacy agreements. According to its Surrogacy Law, all persons involved, including both the surrogate mother and the potential parents, must be thoroughly informed of the medical, psychological, and legal aspects of surrogacy and must sign a legal contract that is approved by a special government committee (Shalev and Lemish 2011).

Establishing a National Registry for Artificial Reproductive Technologies

From an ethical, legal, and medical perspective, surrogacy *should not* be modeled in the same fashion as a kidney, liver, lung, or heart transplant. These organ donations, and even blood transfusions, usually take place within the context of life-threatening medical situations. In contrast, surrogacy is an elective procedure. In addition, genetic pre-disposition to diseases have not been shown to be a major concern to the organ recipient. Many recipients of kidneys or hearts are elderly and are not worried that in twenty or thirty years they may develop some form of cancer or genetically-associated dementia (Dossetor 1995). These patients recognize that without an immediate kidney or heart donation, their life expectancy can be viewed in months, not in decades.

The fetus is not merely a temporary organ implant but will attain personhood as a privileged entity in its own right. It seems obvious that surrogacy raises complex medical and ethical issues and should be viewed more seriously than the mere borrowing of a woman's uterus for nine months. The future of both the fetus and surrogate are entangled to a great extent: the well-being of the fetus is dependent on the surrogate, and the surrogate's entire body is affected by the process of gestation.

Currently, there is growing momentum that allows people to provide gametes anonymously. In some instances, surrogates may want evoke their autonomous bioethical right not to reveal their identity to the child they gestated. This may create another bioethical dilemma since future medical developments may prove to be useful medical information to either to the surrogate or to the child. The creation of a national computer-driven registry might be a viable approach to maintain anonymity while generating potentially important medical information to the appropriate party. Such registries are being established in other countries such as Israel (Blyth, 2012) and Great Britain (Egras, 2012). These registries contain necessary health and family information that would be available to those involved in the surrogacy cooperative health partnership.

Conclusions

Professionals involved in surrogacy from infertility specialists to genetic counselors should consider the implications of the significant advances in maternal-fetal cell exchange and epigenetics that are transforming our understanding of pregnancy. The informed consent document should state that gestational surrogacy, is a form of assisted reproductive technology, and should be viewed as a complex form of a cooperative health partnership in which intimate biological bonds are formed between the surrogate and the child she gestates. The consent form should also discuss the medical concerns that may arise in the future from epigenetic factors or maternal-fetal cell exchange to both the surrogate and the child.

As with any medical process, we must be careful neither to glorify the benefits nor over-simplify the risks and ethical concerns at stake. Though surrogacy offers a somewhat miraculous option for those who may have trouble conceiving a genetic child, it is rife with medical, legal, and profound ethical dilemmas. By providing a thorough medical information disclosure that includes genetic screening, all parties involved in surrogacy will have a better understanding of the risks and humanitarian rewards of gestational surrogacy.

References

Alexander, A., Samlowski, W.E., et al. (2003) Metastatic melanoma in pregnancy: risk of transplacental metastases in the infant. J Clin Oncol 21: 2179-2186.

Ay, E., K. Buzas, et al. (2012). "Recent Results on the Development of Fetal Immune System: Self, Epigenetic Regulation, Fetal Immune Responses." In Maternal Fetal Transmission of Human Viruses and their Influence on Tumorigenesis (Gyo¨rgy Berencsi III, Editor; Springer Publishing-Dordrecht, Heidelberg, New York, & London). Pg:51-82.

Ber, R. (2000). "Ethical issues in gestational surrogacy." Theoretical Medicine & Bioethics, 21(2):153-69. Review.

Blyth, E. (2012). "Access to genetic and birth origins information for people conceived following third party assisted conception in the United Kingdom." The International Journal of Children's Rights. 20: 300-318.

Boeke, C.E., Gillman, M.W., et al., (2013). "Choline intake during pregnancy and child cognition at age 7 years." American Journal of Epidemiology, 177(12):1338-47. doi: 10.1093/aje/kws395.

Boston Women's Health Book Collective. (2011). Our bodies, ourselves : Informing and Inspiring Women Across Generations. New York, Touchstone Publisher.

Brinsden, P. R. (2003). "Gestational surrogacy." Humun Reproduction Update 9(5): 483-491.

Burry, K. A. (2007). "Reproductive medicine: where we have been, where we are, where are we going? An ethical perspective." American Journal of Obstetrics and Gynecology 196(6): 578-580.

Centers for Disease Control and Prevention. (2013). Section 2: ART cycles using fresh, nondonor eggs or embryos (part C) Available at: http://www.cdc.gov/ART/ART2008/section2c.htm. Accessed February 4,

Charney, E. (2013). "Behavior genetics and postgenomics." Behavioral Brain Science, 35(5):331-58. doi: 10.1017/S0140525X11002226.

Davies, I. (1985). "Contracts to bear children." Journal of Medical Ethics 11(2): 61-65.

Dermout, S., H. van de Wiel, et al. (2010). "Non-commercial surrogacy: an account of patient management in the first Dutch Centre for IVF Surrogacy, from 1997 to 2004." Human Reproduction 25(2): 443-449.

Dossetor, J. B. (1995). "Economic, social, racial and age-related considerations in dialysis and transplantation." Current Opinion in Nephrology and Hypertension 4(6): 498-501.

Drabiak, K., C. Wegner, et al. (2007). "Ethics, law, and commercial surrogacy: a call for uniformity." The Journal of Law, Medicine & Ethics 35(2): 300-309.

Dutta, P. and W. J. Burlingham (2011). "Microchimerism: tolerance vs. sensitization." Current Opinion in Organ Transplantation 16(4): 359-365.

Ergas, Y. (2012). "The Transnationalization of Everyday Life: Cross-border Reproductive Surrogacy, Human Rights and the Re-visioning of International Law." Human Rights and the Re-Visioning of International Law (February 26, 2012).

Erickson, T. (2010). Surrogacy and Embryo, Sperm, & Egg Donation: What Were You Thinking?: Considering IVF & Third-Party Reproduction. Bloomington, IN, iUniverse.

Flavin, J. (2009). Our bodies, our crimes: the policing of women's reproduction in America, NYU Press.

Fugazzola, L., V. Cirello, et al. (2011). "Fetal microchimerism as an explanation of disease." Nature Review Endocrinology 7(2): 89-97.

Greedfield, D.A. (2012). "The evolving world of ART: who are the intended parents and how are their children doing?" Minerva Ginecol, 64(6):455-60.

Gugucheva, M. (2010). "Surrogacy in America". Council for Responsible Genetics,

Http://www.councilforresponsiblegenetics.org/pageDocuments/KAEVEJ0A1M.

Hallmayer, J., S. Cleveland, et al. (2011). "Genetic Heritability and Shared Environmental Factors Among Twin Pairs With Autism." Archives of General Psychiatry, 68(11):1095-1102.

Horsthemke B, Ludwig M. (2005) "Assisted reproduction: the epigenetic perspective." Human Reproduction Update, 11:473–82.

Isoda, T., Ford, A.M., et al. (2009) "Immunologically silent cancer clone transmission from mother to offspring." Proceedings of the National Academy of Sciences U S A 106: 17882-17885.

Kallenbach, L. R., K. L. Johnson, et al. (2011). "Fetal cell microchimerism and cancer: a nexus of reproduction, immunology, and tumor biology." Cancer Research, 71(1): 8-12.

Kamper-Jorgensen, M. (2012). "Microchimerism and survival after breast and colon cancer diagnosis." Chimerism, 3(3): 72-73.

Kaplan, B.J., Leung, B.M., et al. (2013) "Increasing the quality of life from womb to grave: the importance of pregnancy and birth cohorts." Applied Physiology Nutrition and Metabolism, 38(1):85-9. doi: 10.1139/apnm-2012-0080.

Kirkbride, J. B., E. Susser, et al. (2012). "Prenatal nutrition, epigenetics and schizophrenia risk: can we test causal effects?" Epigenomics 4(3): 303-315.

Klonisch, T. and R. Drouin (2009). "Fetal-maternal exchange of multipotent stem/progenitor cells: microchimerism in diagnosis and disease." Trends in molecular medicine, 15(11): 510-518.

Knopik, V.S., Maccani, M.A., et al., (2012) "The epigenetics of maternal cigarette smoking during pregnancy and effects on child development." Development & Psychopathology, 24(4):1377-90. doi: 10.1017/S0954579412000776.

Leber, A., M. L. Zenclussen, et al. (2011). "Pregnancy: tolerance and suppression of immune responses." Methods in Molecular Biology, 677: 397-417.

Lee, R. L. (2009). "New trends in global outsourcing of commercial surrogacy: A call for regulation." Hastings Women's Law Journal, 20: 275-300.

Lumey, L.H. and Stein A.D. (1997). "Offspring birth weights after maternal intrauterine undernutrition: a comparison within sibships." American Journal of Epidemiology, 146:810–819.

Markens, S. (2007). Surrogate motherhood and the politics of reproduction, University of California Press.

Martin-Subero, J. I. and M. Esteller (2011). "Profiling epigenetic alterations in disease." Advances in Experimental Medicine and Biology 711: 162-177.

Martyn, C.N., Barker, D.J., and Osmond, C. (1996). "Mothers' pelvic size, fetal growth, and death from stroke and coronary heart disease in men in the UK." Lancet, 348:1264–1268.

Milne, E., K. R. Greenop, et al. (2012). "Maternal use of Folic Acid and Other Supplements and Risk of Childhood Brain Tumors." Cancer Epidemiology, Biomarkers & Prevention: a publication of the American Association for Cancer Research, cosponsored by the American Society of Preventive Oncology.

Munyon, J. H. (2003). "Protectionism and freedom of contract: the erosion of female autonomy in surrogacy decisions." Suffolk University Law Review 36(3): 717-744.

Nijagal, A. and MacKenzie, T.C. (2013). "Clinical implications of maternal-fetal cellular trafficking." Seminars in Pediatric Surgery, 22(1):62-5. doi: 10.1053/j.sempedsurg.2012.10.011.

Norton W, Hudson N, Culley L. (2013). "Gay men seeking surrogacy to achieve parenthood." Reproductive Biomedicine Online, 2013 Apr 6. pii: S1472-6483(13)00180-6. doi: 10.1016/j.rbmo.2013.03.016.

Nosheen, H. and H. Schellmann (August 10, 2011). "The Most Wanted Surrogates in the World." The Investigative Fund.
http://www.theinvestigativefund.org/investigations/gender/1413/the_most_wanted _surrogates_in_the_world.

Osagie, E. K. (2010). "Surrogacy: Whose child is it?" Journal of Medicine and Medical Sciences 1(11): 505-509.

Pande, A. (2011). Commercial surrogacy in India: Nine months of labor?, Thesis: University of Massachusetts Amherst.

Relph, A. S. (2010). "Contract Pregnancy: Exploitation in Action?" Online Journal of Health Ethics 6:1-7.

Shalev, S., Lemish, D. (2011) "Women as Consumers of Reproductive Technology: Media Representation versus Reality," Journal of Interdisciplinary Feminist Thought, 5:1-23, (Article 2).
http://digitalcommons.salve.edu/jift/vol5/iss1/2

Smerdon, U. R. (2008). "Crossing bodies, crossing borders: International surrogacy between the United States and India." Cumberland Law Review, 39: 15-84.

Solomon, B. D., B. W. Jack, et al. (2008). "The clinical content of preconception care: genetics and genomics." American Journal of Obstetrics and Gynecology, 199(6 Suppl 2): S340-344.

Spar, D. L. (2006). The baby business: How money, science, and politics drive the commerce of conception, Harvard Business Press.

Utian, W. H., L. Sheean, et al. (1985). "Successful pregnancy after in vitro fertilization and embryo transfer from an infertile woman to a surrogate." The New England Journal of Medicine, 313(21): 1351-1352.

Vries, R. G., M. Huch, et al. (2010). "Stem cells and cancer of the stomach and intestine." Molecular Oncology, 4(5): 373-384.

Wells, S., J. A. Pinkerton, et al. (2009). Our Bodies, Ourselves: Reading the Written Female Body, The University,[The Claude Moore Health Sciences Library, Historical Collections and Services].

Williams, Z., D. Zepf, et al. (2009). "Foreign fetal cells persist in the maternal circulation." Fertility and Sterility, 91(6): 2593-2595.

Supplement B. Informative or controversial web sites and videos

Bioethics:

- http://stemcellbioethics.wikischolars.columbia.edu/Module+2+-+Intro+to+Stem+Cell+Bioethics
- http://stemcellbioethics.wikischolars.columbia.edu/Understanding+Research+Ethics+and+Clinical+Trials
- http://bioethics.od.nih.gov/
- http://www.bioethics.gov/

Cloning:

- http://www.humancloning.org/
- http://www.ornl.gov/sci/techresources/Human_Genome/elsi/cloning.shtml
- http://www.un.org/law/cloning/
- **Video-** http://www.youtube.com/watch?v=dV2OxSGhwjY- **cloning animals**
- **Video-** http://www.youtube.com/watch?v=jLy-tYq8qV0

Stem Cell Science:

- http://stemcellbioethics.wikischolars.columbia.edu/Module+1+-+The+Biology+of+Stem+Cells
- http://stemcellbioethics.wikischolars.columbia.edu/Module+4+-+Somatic+Cell+Nuclear+Transfer
- http://stemcellbioethics.wikischolars.columbia.edu/Module+5+-+Induced+Pluripotent+Stem+Cells
- http://stemcells.nih.gov/info/basics/
- http://stemcells.nih.gov/info/resources.asp
- **Video-** http://www.youtube.com/watch?v=3orSvpgj1sc
- **Video-** http://www.youtube.com/watch?v=J_U3YLgGZ4k

Human-animal Chimeras

- http://stemcellbioethics.wikischolars.columbia.edu/Module+7+-+Human-Animal+Chimeras
- http://www.scientificamerican.com/article.cfm?id=human-animal-chimeras
- http://www.bbc.co.uk/ethics/animals/using/hybridembryos_1.shtml

Human Genetics

- http://ghr.nlm.nih.gov/
- http://www.ashg.org/
- http://www.ornl.gov/sci/techresources/Human_Genome/medicine/assist.shtml
- **Video -** http://www.youtube.com/watch?v=_xmZAJ0TVxo

Reproductive Medicine

- http://stemcellbioethics.wikischolars.columbia.edu/Ethical+Considerations+of+Egg+Donation
- http://www.britannica.com/EBchecked/topic/498625/human-reproductive-system
- http://www.centerforhumanreprod.com/
- http://www.figo.org/about/comms/ethical_aspects
- **Video- egg donation-** http://www.youtube.com/watch?v=1uyaDi-3He8
- **Video- egg donation-** http://www.youtube.com/watch?v=maukoE5r7Sg
- **Video- egg donation-** http://www.youtube.com/watch?v=qcYWxVdqR8Y

Supplement C. Acknowledgements:

This textbook has been in the works for several years. Throughout this period various students in "Crossroads in Bioethics" and "Bioethics for Biomedical Engineers" have made valuable contributions and suggestions. We cannot begin to cite all of these individuals but we thank all of our students, TAs, and colleagues for their thoughts, suggestions, and comments. Specifically, the authors would like to thank the Dr. Deborah B. Mowshowitz, Chair of the Undergraduate Committee and Director of Undergraduate Programs and Laboratories, the Department of Biology at Columbia College, Dr. Andrew Laine, Department Chair and Professor of Biomedical Engineering and of Radiology (Health Sciences), and the Department of Biomedical Engineering for the opportunity to teach these courses.